Ancient Aliens
and the Age of Giants

Through the Wormhole : 2

www.larsbergen.com
www.sharondelarose.com

Non-Fiction — Extraterrestrial

Nordic Aliens and the Fairies of Ireland
Nordic Aliens and the Greek Gods
Nordic Aliens and the Legend of the Four Cities
Nordic Aliens and the Amazon Queens
Nordic Aliens and the Lost Kingdoms of the Americas
Nordic Aliens and the Star People of the Americas
Nordic Aliens and the Moon-Eyed People
Nordic Aliens and the Forbidden Islands of the Gods
Nordic Aliens and the Greek Gods of Africa

Ancient Aliens and the Lost Islands
Ancient Aliens and the Age of Giants

Alien Nightmares: Screen Memories of UFO Alien Abductions

Speculative Science Fiction

Fomorian Earth: Star Borne: 1
Shades of Moloch: Star Borne: 2
Renegade Genius: Star Borne: 3

Are You Thinking What I'm Thinking Blog
www.alliemars.com

Travel Blog
www.gipsyking.com

Other Books by Sharon Delarose

Themes include Coffee Table Nature Books,
Dogs, Kids Books,
and other assorted sundry
www.sharondelarose.com

Ancient Aliens
and the Age of Giants

Through the Wormhole
Look at the evidence, and judge for yourself.

by Lars Bergen and Sharon Delarose

GITYASOME BOOKS - A DIVISION OF GYPSY KING SOFTWARE

No part of this book may be reproduced, scanned, distributed, or transmitted in any electronic or printed form, including photocopying, recording, and all other information storage and retrieval systems, without written permission from the author, except in the case of brief quotations embodied in articles written as book reviews.
Thank you!

While the author has made every effort to provide accurate internet addresses, neither the publisher nor the author assume any responsibility for errors, or for changes that occur to internet websites. Further, the publisher and author do not have any control over, and do not assume any responsibility for third-party internet websites or their content.
The web is ever-changing.

Copyright © 2014, 2019 by Sharon Delarose
All rights reserved.

Published by Gityasome Books
a division of Gypsy King Software, Inc.
www.sharondelarose.com

Printed in the United States of America
First Edition

ISBN: 1500345563
EAN-13: 978-1500345563

Dedicated to
everyone who believes
that extraterrestrial life exists
on the other side of a wormhole,
and that ancient alien astronauts
visited us in the past.

Rediscover the lost age of giants.

We are not alone.
We have never been alone.

Contents

Who Were the Giants? 9
    The Grigori of the Bible 9
    The Book of Giants 23
    Nephilim 24
    Fomorians..28
    Norse Mythology 32
    Native American Giants...40
    Mesoamerican Giants 51
    Mound Builders 71
    Titans, Daityas, and Sumerian Giants 76
    Gutians 77
    Ipsolini and Spali...78
    The Giants of Basque 78
    King of Turan 80
    Macrobians..80
Giant Skeletons 83
    Goliath...83
    Fomorian Bones 84
    Mummies in the United States...87
    Calaveras Skull of California 100
    Mound Builders of Georgia..102
    Swamp Giants and Cannibals...104
    Giant Skulls That Fit Over Your Head............................110
    The Wild West 120
    Lost Cities...125
    Around the World 126
Engraved Stone Tablets 133
Where Are the Bones?...145
    Crumbled to Dust 146

TABLE OF CONTENTS

    Skeptics in Charge..147
    Make Room for Daddy 153
    The Bone Collectors 156
    Human Relics...161
    Destruction of Bones in the Bible......................................169
    Destroyed to Prevent Resurrection....................................170
    Superstition 173
    Casualties of War..180
    War Trophies...182
    Shrunken Heads..186
    Ground into Flour and Baked into Bread.........................187
    Corpse Medicine...188
    Bone China 190
    Grave Robbers 191
    Pirate Treasure 195
    Witches, Giants, and the Fires of Fear...............................196
    Cremation 199
    Battle of the Bones...201
19th Century Stone Age Giants...207
Epilogue 233
Book Excerpt: Ancient Aliens and the Lost Islands..................239
Book Excerpt: Alien Nightmares 259
    Flying Saucer in My Back Yard..261
Glossary of Biblical Giants 267

WHO WERE THE GIANTS?

How big were the giants? Who were they, and why should we care beyond idle curiosity? Because according to Norse tradition, they will be back, and this time with a vengeance.

Are you thinking it sounds like a tall tale of the whopper that got away? Of course it does, which is what somebody wants us to believe. Exposing the truth about giants would be more devastating than exposing the truth about extraterrestrials, because they WERE extraterrestrials, and they left behind proof which the government grabbed as quickly as any crashed UFO.

Legends of giants exist in every corner of the world, and many cultures believe that an entire race of giants predated humans. Giants existed before us, and alongside us for awhile, but we rose up against them, and went after them with everything we had, until we wiped them out.

From the Grigori and Nephilim of the *Bible*, to the giants of the Norse, Aztecs, Native Americans, Mesoamericans, Celts, Greeks, Hindus, Persians, Mound Builders, and others, we can study these ancient giants from several vantage points.

The Grigori of the Bible

The Grigori were giants who came down from the stars — the original, extraterrestrial giants who mated with humans and produced most of the other giants on Earth. In the *Book of Enoch*, they were called the Grigori, Egregori, or Watchers. Enoch was a biblical prophet, and the grandfather of Noah. The controversial *Book of Enoch* was embraced as scripture by some of the earliest Church Fathers, but it is excluded from most bibles that exist today. It does, however, appear in *The Apocrypha and Pseudepigrapha* of the *Old Testament*, and in bibles of some of the Oriental Orthodox religions.

You don't think of the *Bible* as having multiple versions, each one different from its brethren. Translations vary, sometimes radically, and entire books (chapters) are included or excluded.

Giants are one of the reasons that the *Book of Enoch* got banned, as Enoch didn't mince words about this race of beings. He didn't gloss over their existence, or leave us with a vague phrase that could be misrepresented. Enoch went into detail about a class of angels known as the Grigori who traveled back and forth between the 5th heaven, and Mount Hermon on Earth. The angels were presented as solid flesh-and-blood entities — not mystical, invisible, ghost-like apparitions — and Mount Hermon on Earth was one of their landing zones.

Mount Hermon, though singular, actually denotes a cluster of mountains with three distinct peaks known as "the Hermonites." These mountains straddle the border between Syria and Lebanon, approximately 40 miles from the Sea of Galilee where Jesus spent much of his time teaching. Moses battled the residents of Mount Hermon, and the Lord himself appeared in the vicinity at various times.

The Grigori were supposed to watch over humans, but not get intimate with us, or become our friends and teachers. Those who did their jobs as instructed were accepted as holy angels, but a handful of Grigori had other ideas, and these became the fallen angels. They fell in love with us, and wanted to take human women as wives. They also wanted to teach us forbidden knowledge. Both acts were taboo and got them in a lot of trouble.

WHO WERE THE GIANTS?

They lusted after the daughters of men, which is where we get biblical references to "the sons of God with the daughters of men." Whether they were his sons physically, or just figuratively, is one of those topics that sets off heated arguments, and is not relevant to the existence of giants as a species.

The Grigori were described as "countless soldiers of human appearance" and their size was larger than that of the great giants — which were their hybrid children, the biblical Nephilim. The *Book of Enoch* stated that 200 came down to Mount Hermon with the intention of taking wives and begetting children, and these would have been the original, full-blooded giants. Their Nephilim offspring were half-human, so when calculating a size for their fathers, we must factor that in.

We know several Grigori by name, including 20 who were led by Semjaza. They were called the "chiefs of tens" which suggests leadership of troops. There were also "chiefs of fifties" and "chiefs of hundreds" who took part in the intermingling.

Semjaza may have led the 20, but he wasn't at the top of the rebellion — five others held the top spots: Jequn, Asbeel, Gadreel, Penemu, and Kasdeja — with Jequn being the mastermind of the entire rebellion against the rules that prohibited them from mingling with us.

These five ringleaders led many Grigori astray by convincing the 20, all of which were then named and formed a pact. If these 20 were "chiefs of tens," that may be where we get 200 as the number of Grigori who got involved with their human charges, as 20 x 10 = 200.

So what was this forbidden knowledge? What got the Grigori in so much trouble, besides sex? Science, mostly.

Penemu, which is an interesting name as we use "pen" to denote a writing instrument, taught us how to use ink and paper, how to read and write, and he "cured stupidity in humans." That was his great sin — teaching us to read and write, as this education was forbidden to us.

Kasdeja taught us about death from snake bites, abortion, heat stroke, and other deadly "strikes" of demons and spirits. Gadreel taught us warfare. Semjaza taught enchantments and root-cutting, while Armaros sinned by teaching the resolving of enchantments. Various interpretations for enchantments include spells and incantations to bind men, or snake charmers. Some texts use "conjuring" instead of enchantments.

Shamsiel taught us the signs of the sun. Araqiel got in trouble for teaching us divination by geography, communicating with the dead, reading signs in the fire, and in the motion of the water, weather conditions, palmistry, and oracle bones.

Baraqel taught us astrology. Baraqel is named as the 9th of the 20 Watchers who led the rebellion. Ezeqeel taught us meteorology, or knowledge of the clouds. Kakabel taught us all about the constellations, and he was the 4th of 20. Asradel taught us the phases of the moon.

Azazel, who was the 10th of 20 in the Ethiopic version of the *Book of Enoch,* may have caused the most trouble with his teachings, which included weaponry and cosmetics. He taught men how to make swords, knives, shields, and coats of mail. He taught women the art of deception through cosmetics and jewelry — how to ornament the body, dye the hair, paint the face and eyebrows, beautify the eyelids, and use antimony as an eyeliner and mascara. He taught women about various coloring tinctures, and gemstones. He taught humans how to work metals into bracelets and ornaments.

What Azazel taught women became one of the fundamental evils in the Salem witch trials which took place thousands of years later. Witchcraft wasn't just about casting spells and causing bad luck, it was about deceiving men into believing that you were more beautiful than you actually were. Yes, this was a punishable sin.

The 1600s brought an era of strange laws to England, not the least of which involved witchcraft and sorcery. An Act of Parliament was passed in 1670 prohibiting the use of beauty aids to lure a man into marriage. *The Albany Law Journal, Volume LVII*, published in 1898, quoted the law as such:

> "That all women... whether virgins, maids or widows... impose upon and betray into matrimony any of his majesty's male subjects, by scents, paints, cosmetics, washes, artificial teeth, false hair, Spanish wool, iron stays, hoops, high-heeled shoes or bolstered hips, shall incur the penalty of the laws now in force against witchcraft, sorcery and such like misdemeanors, and that the marriage, upon conviction, shall stand null and void."

A History of Witchcraft in England from 1558 to 1718 by Wallace Notestein in 1909, assures us that witches were actively being put to death in the 1600s. Though many were acquitted after the law was passed, some were still convicted and put to death, including Ann Tilling and Judith Witchell, who were hanged in 1672. Ann Foster was hanged for witchcraft in 1674. Temperance Lloyd, Mary Trembles, and Susanna Edwards were executed for witchcraft in 1682. While they were not put to death for luring a husband, it demonstrates that a woman could have been put to death on such a charge.

Where did our ancestors get the idea to punish the use of beauty aids to land a husband? And to put such a deadly penalty on it? Did this go all the way back to Azazel and the other Grigori teaching us forbidden knowledge?

It's too bad that the punishment went to the women instead of the men, because it was Azazel's teaching men about weaponry that caused us so much heartache in those early days, and even still today. We quickly fell into lawlessness and bloodshed when we discovered the power of weapons.

Azazel is named in *some* versions of the *Bible* in the *Book of Leviticus*. His name was omitted from the *King James Bible* which was printed 59 years before the beauty aid law was passed. In fact, his name was removed from all but a handful of bibles being replaced with "scapegoat." In one translation which includes his name, Azazel is labeled a demon. Translations of Leviticus 16:8 as it appears in various bibles:

- KJ21: "And Aaron shall cast lots upon the two goats — one lot for the Lord and the other lot for the scapegoat."
- ASV: "And Aaron shall cast lots upon the two goats; one lot for Jehovah, and the other lot for Azazel."
- CEV: "where I will show you which goat will be sacrificed to me and which one will be sent into the desert to the demon Azazel."

It's almost as if we're erasing the history of the giants by rewriting their story, word by word. You will not find a list of named Grigori rebels in the *Bible*, or a detailed account of their sins in teaching us. You have to look in books that were banned from most bibles, such as the *Book of Enoch* and the *Book of Giants*. Azazel is named in the *Book of Giants*, and both books were found among the Dead Sea scrolls, whose dates range from 408 B.C. to 318 A.D., though the *Book of Enoch* already existed as part of the *Ethiopic Bible* and a handful of others when the scrolls were found. Much of what we know about the Grigori and their offspring, the Nephilim, comes from the *Book of Enoch* and the *Book of Giants*.

Remember how *scapegoat* was substituted for Azazel in most bibles? Enoch 10:7-9 expands on the fallout to the Grigori, and how Azazel became the scapegoat.

"…and that not all the sons of men shall be destroyed through the mystery of all the things which the Watchers have spoken, and have taught their sons. And the whole Earth was defiled through the example of the deeds of Azazel; to him ascribe all the sins."

And God said to Gabriel: "Go against the bastards, and those cast off, and against the children of fornication, and destroy the children of fornication, and the children of the Watchers from among men; lead them out, and let them loose that they may destroy each other by murder; for their days shall not be long…"

WHO WERE THE GIANTS?

This comes from the *Book of Enoch* as published in 1882, translated from the Ethiopic by Reverend George H. Schodde. *Fornication* refers to sexual intercourse between the Watchers (Grigori) and humans. It names Azazel, and denounces all of the Grigori who took women. Their punishment was to watch their Nephilim children destroy one another, after which they themselves would be imprisoned for the rest of their lives.

These passages answer one of the big questions relating to the destruction and mayhem that the second generation giants caused. Where were their Grigori parents? Why didn't the first generation intervene, and stop their children from wreaking havoc if they truly loved humanity? Why didn't they teach their children to live among humans responsibly?

Because they *couldn't*. They were *prevented* from becoming a buffer, or teaching their giant children. They were whisked away in punishment. Humans wouldn't have been able to control a child whose father was a giant. We didn't have the physical strength, and we were as children ourselves, still being taught by the Grigori. Perhaps the lesson of watching the destruction was meant to demonstrate the sheer folly of it. If you love humans as much as you claim, do you *really* want to subject them to *this*?

Another unanswered question is how it was possible to have sexual relations in the first place. These giants were huge as you'll see, and unless humans in those days were much bigger than today, how would sex have even been possible without killing us? How does a woman of 5 or 6 feet tall, mate with a giant of 10 or 15 feet tall? Stand in the middle of a room, look up at the ceiling, and imagine a person who stands twice or even three times your height, who is forced to stoop over because they stand taller than your ceiling — maybe your eyes are level with their belly button. Then imagine having sex with them.

If we survived the act itself, how could the women survive childbirth? Unless they were using advanced medical technology to make it work, it seems inconceivable that multitudes of women didn't just split wide open long before the baby popped out. Perhaps that's why the Grigori taught us the secrets of abortion. Whatever the answers, Enoch personally witnessed the misery of the first generation Grigori up in their 5th heaven prison.

Enoch had a fascinating history. Like the Grigori, he traveled back and forth between Earth and the heavens. Enoch traveled to the 4th heaven where the sun and the moon exist, according to *The Early History of Heaven* by J. Edward Wright, and *The Book of the Secrets of Enoch*. He saw the Grigori on his visit to the 5th heaven, and he described them as troops and soldiers of human appearance but whose size was greater than the great giants (e.g. their hybrid children, the Nephilim.) Their faces were withered and melancholy, as they'd been punished for getting involved with humans. Enoch also mentioned the 8th and 9th heavens as being where the signs of the zodiac reside.

This reference to numbered heavens is interesting, as the Grigori came down from the 5th heaven, and they were flesh-and-blood humanoids. When you compare the Grigori and their numbered heavens to the legends of the Norse gods and their nine worlds, a pattern of extraterrestrial visitation starts to materialize. Not only did the Norse gods include a race of giants — one of their worlds, called Asgard, was also referred to as *heaven*. In addition, another of their worlds had a region, not the entire world but a region of it — called *Hel* with one "L". Is it possible that at least some of these heavens were actually planets?

There is a book known as the *Qabbalah* which many believe pre-dates the world religions in its origins. In *Qabbalah — The Philosophical Writings of Solomon Ben Yehudah Ibn Gebirol*, by Isaac Myer in 1888, we get a glimpse into an ancient system of thought where gods such as Nebo were associated with seven planets or seven heavens. Nebo is mentioned in the *Bible* as a false god, as well as being a god of the Babylonians. *Bible* dictionaries list *Bel* as another spelling for Baal, and they list Nebo as a well-known deity of ancient Babylon, Mesopotamia and Sumer.

WHO WERE THE GIANTS?

> NLV: Isaiah 46:1 — "The false gods, Bel and Nebo..."
> NLT: Isaiah 46:1 — "Bel and Nebo, the gods of Babylon..."

Nebo's ziggurat, which was his Temple at Borsippa, was referred to as "the house of the seven bonds (planets) of heaven and Earth." *Planets* in parenthesis is part of the *Qabbalah* text.

The tower of the seven planets, or stations, was attached to his house and comprised of seven stages. Each stage was the astrological color of the planet to which it was devoted. Towers devoted to planets were common, such as the Temple of Babylon with its "house of the seven spheres of heaven and Earth."

Also in the *Qabbalah* is the concept of "heavens" being identified with planets, or heavenly bodies, from which angels travel to and from Earth. The universe and zodiac as seen by ancient people included seven orbiting planets in a zone called *the seven bell-wethers* which were "sheep, wanderers, and watchers."

We already know that the Watchers (Grigori) came down from the 5th heaven, and now we have the "seven planets of heaven" — is this a definition of the seven heavens?

A *wether* is a sheep that leads the flock, and he is wearing a bell around his neck. A bell-wether is a ringleader, someone who leads a mob or mutiny, starts a trend, or becomes a leader of men, much like the Grigori who *mutinied* because they didn't like the rules that separated them from us.

The *Qabbalah* has an image that depicts the Tree of Life with its orbits of planets, and this image is nearly identical to the nine worlds of Norse mythology, except that in Norse mythology, the planet Earth (Midgard) is in the center, whereas the sun is in the center of the Tree of Life. In addition, the planet names are different, with the *Qabbalah* labeling them as planets in our solar system, versus planets such as Asgard and Múspelheim in Norse cosmology which may or may not represent our solar system.

Along with nine worlds, Norse mythology brings us a race of giants. *Ancient Aliens and the Lost Islands: Through the Wormhole* by Lars Bergen and Sharon Delarose explores the Norse worlds and their giants — worlds which were once connected to Earth by what sounds suspiciously like portals or wormholes. The Norse giants had access to Earth, just like the Grigori giants had access to Earth, and both wreaked havoc. The Norse giants are currently *forbidden* to visit us again until the end of our world, which explains why they aren't among the UFO visitors. They've been prevented from coming here by the Aesir gods who live on the planet Asgard, aka heaven, which is ruled by Odin.

Is there any connection between the Norse giants who were banned from Earth for their destructiveness, and the Grigori giants who were banned from Earth for the same? Is this a case of one religion being overwritten by, or merged with the beliefs of another? Or is this an independent source to further prove the existence of the giants who came down to Earth?

As with the Grigori, some of the Norse giants were friends of man, while others were our nemesis. Odin was our friend, as their end-of-the-world prophecy has Odin coming back to fight alongside humans against the destructive giants. He was descended from giants at least in part, and he will die fighting for us, as will his son Thor.

So we take the *Book of Enoch*, the *Book of Giants*, the *Bible*, Norse mythology, and the *Qabbalah*, and from these we can extrapolate that the rebel Grigori were extraterrestrial, interplanetary giants, who were not supposed to get involved with humans for whatever reason, or teach us, but did anyway.

Should we perceive the Grigori as angels, or demons, for teaching us astrology, meteorology, writing, warfare, divination, and such? There are multiple schools of thought, and many ancient astronaut theorists are attempting to demonstrate that what the rebel Grigori did was GOOD for us, and thus, they were not the evil beings that we've been led to believe; but there is a darker possibility as well — a much darker possibility.

In his book *The Wars of Gods and Men*, ancient astronaut theorist Zecharia Sitchin depicted the biblical *Book of Genesis* as being an edited version of a more detailed, and much older text. The expanded *Book of Genesis* suggests that extraterrestrials came to Earth, and being astronauts, they didn't want to personally perform heavy labor. Their solution? Interject their DNA into the existing humanoids of Earth, in order to create a more intelligent species of humanoid that they could use as workers. This is presented as the Missing Link.

Now if you were holding down a species into slavery, the last thing you'd want is for them to have knowledge. You'd want to keep them ignorant. By adding Zecharia Sitchin's theory, you come up with a reason for WHY the Grigori blunder was so bad — the sin of giving knowledge to slaves.

However, there are explanations that don't involve slavery or DNA diddling. What if the rebel Grigori simply got bored with just watching over us, and wanted to use us for their personal entertainment? Think about what they taught us: cosmetics, divination, and warfare.

What if they wanted our women, and provided cosmetics specifically to doll us up for their own pleasure? We never hear about how *we* wanted *them*, only how *they* wanted *us*. Given their great size, which was enormous as you'll see in later chapters, it's hard to believe that our human women were willing participants in this love nest.

As for weapons and warfare, what if it wasn't about hunting or war? What if this involved building coliseums for gladiator games? We know that in ancient times, humans were often forcibly pitted against one another in death arenas. We were pitted against animals as well, such as lions, tigers, panthers, boars, rhinos, and bears. Even today, humans go up against bulls in bullfighting rings, as an echo of eons past. Given only a brief description of what the Grigori taught us, you can interpret it to support multiple theories.

As for divination, our ancestors were skilled in the arts of reading earth signs, tracking, determining the weather by studying the water and sky, and diagnosing health issues by studying signs on the body, including the palms of the hand and soles of the feet. This sounds like a positive.

Thus the Grigori were either our teachers and mentors, who wanted to lift the yoke of slavery from our necks; or they were bored, horny, bloodthirsty astronauts who wanted to manipulate us for their own use or amusement.

There is another interpretation if you think about how we might act in a similar circumstance, and it makes sense. Earth today is teeming with people, cities, high-rise buildings, trains, planes, pollution, noise, and only a few humans are still living in the pristine wilderness of our ancestors.

The Grigori were physical beings — and if their planet is advanced enough to build interstellar spaceships, then they probably don't have much left as far as wide open spaces, sparkling blue lakes, and the peaceful sounds of nature. In the same manner that we covet the olden days, and some of us move off to a remote mountain to rekindle a life in harmony with nature, maybe the Grigori coveted that as well.

Consider what we know about their downfall. It wasn't *immediate*. They didn't come down, intermingle, and start a war with their brethren all in one month. They stayed down here long enough to teach us, and produce no less than two generations of offspring. There were entire cities and colonies of giants by the time this war broke out with their fellow Grigori.

It takes a human about 15 years to reach adulthood, so two generations would denote a minimum of 30 years, and that's being conservative. Nor does it factor in the generations to the Great Flood which they allegedly triggered.

We can't even begin to fathom how they think, or how they'd react to astronaut soldiers committing desertion, and thumbing their noses at the chain of command, which in essence is what happened. We have no idea how they run their society. If it was a case of military desertion, that would be far-reaching in a space program. You cannot spend decades training an astronaut, only to have him bail the minute he sets foot on a desirable planet. You have to maintain discipline, and our own military has strict rules about soldiers deserting. The Grigori were described as "countless soldiers of human appearance..." so they were not only astronauts, but soldiers, and a full *two hundred* of them broke ranks and deserted.

Once the mutineers made their stand, it's possible that their superiors said, "Okay, have at it, let's see how this plays out. We'll be more than happy to say 'I told you so' when all hell breaks loose because our kind cannot live in harmony with a smaller humanoid species. There are logical reasons that we don't intermingle, but go ahead, and find out for yourselves the hard way. We'll stay up here safe and sound, and we'll watch. Don't ask for our help when it gets ugly, though, because *we will not help you*. Understood?"

This is a logical extrapolation from the facts, which are scarce. We aren't privy to the detailed discussions that took place — all that came down to us are the headlines. Allowing them to play it out would have been a logical way to demonstrate that intermingling is disastrous, and that is a lesson that would carry forward in their history, in their travels to other humanoid planets, and in their relations with us moving forward.

When it got ugly, it was humans who begged for help, because our lives were no longer of love and peace and plenty — we'd become slaves to feeding and caring for the giant offspring of the Grigori, and the mutineers themselves apparently didn't get the lives they were anticipating either. From the *Book of Enoch* as translated from the Ethiopian, by Richard Laurence in 1838, Archbishop of Cashel, Late Professor of Hebrew at the University of Oxford:

> "Then they took wives, each choosing for himself... and the women conceiving brought forth giants... These devoured all which the labour of men produced, until it

> became impossible to feed them. When they turned against men, in order to devour them, and began to injure birds, beasts, reptiles, and fishes, to eat their flesh one after another, and to drink their blood… and men being destroyed, cried out; and their voice reached to heaven.
>
> "Then [the angels] looked down from heaven, and saw the quantity of blood which was shed on Earth, and all the iniquity that was done upon it…"

The point where the Grigori start to teach us how to make weapons and armor, and the art of warfare, comes right after the segment where the giant Nephilim are eating everything in sight, including humans. The Grigori, unintentionally, had created a nightmare on Earth, and were desperately trying to fix it. The result was even more bloodshed.

We cried out for help, to be rescued from these cannibalistic giants who devoured everything in their path, and in answer came the Great Flood to wipe most of them out. Even the *Book of Enoch* specifies that it was the *offspring* of the giants with humans that was causing us so much grief.

Yes, the original Grigori are the ones who set the wheels in motion for everything that took place, but they are *not* described as the giants who directly caused us so much heartache. In all likelihood, they suffered the consequences of their children right along with us, as giants were devouring one another and perhaps even their own parents. Then comes the judgement — the decision of how to deal with this ugly problem on Earth.

> "… destroy the children of fornication, the offspring of the Watchers, from among men; bring them forth, and excite them one against another. Let them perish by mutual slaughter… They shall all entreat thee, but their fathers shall not obtain their wishes respecting them…"

The Grigori mutineers were forced to watch this play out — to watch their children slaughter one another, while they were powerless to help. They were *prevented* from helping, as part of the sentence for their wrongdoing. Not only that, their children and grandchildren, who were the Nephilim and Elioud — as the various named clans of giants such as the Anakim, Rephaim, Amorites, and others — were egged on in some way to war against one another. They were *intentionally* agitated to kill one another. So when we read the many stories of ferocious, cannibalistic giants, in the centuries that follow, who did not perish in the flood or by the hands of their brethren, we must keep in mind that these are not the original giants who came to Earth. Thus, we cannot assume that extraterrestrial giants would force us to feed them, or face becoming their next meal should we not feed them enough. We cannot portray all giants as being of a monstrous race, in spite of the horrific stories that our ancestors have left for us to study. It was their offspring, such as the Nephilim, that held that distinctive honor. These later generations were cannibals; they considered humans to be a proper meal, and this included the Nephilim of the *Bible*, the Quinames of Mesoamerica, and others.

The Book of Giants

This brings us to the *Book of Giants*, which is mostly in fragments and easier to understand if you've first read the *Book of Watchers*, which is Enoch 1:1-36. There are multiple versions of the *Book of Giants*, including a Manichean version, and an Aramaic version, and this book did not paint a pretty picture of the giants. It agrees with the *Book of Enoch* that 200 descended to Earth, but it refers to the 200 as "demons." The *Book of Giants* described how they revealed forbidden knowledge to us, but then it got ugly.

Giants enslaved humans, and killed hundreds of thousands of us in battle. They forced human women into marriage (or perhaps just sexual relations.) They enslaved the nations of Earth. They wreaked havoc on humans, and on Earth itself. They argued with one another, stole each other's wives, and killed each other. These human-giant hybrids destroyed cattle, plants, sea animals, and ate humans for dinner.

There was a great war between the law-abiding Grigori who kept their distance from humans, the rebel Grigori who commingled with us, and their Nephilim children. At one point the rebels took their law-abiding brethren hostage, and were answered by being blasted with fire and brimstone after the hostages were rescued. This *Book of Giants* by W. B. Henning comes from the *Bulletin of the School of Oriental and African Studies, Volume XI, Part 1*, published in 1943:

> "And those two hundred demons fought a hard battle with the [four angels], until [the angels used] fire, naphtha, and brimstone…"

Is this a reference to the cities of Sodom and Gomorrah, the two cities blasted in the *Bible* by fire and brimstone for their wickedness? Even the Great Flood, which was supposed to wipe out the troublemakers, failed in its task as giants still existed after the flood. There are hundreds of flood stories told around the world, and they all differ in who survived. The Great Flood did not kill off every giant on Earth.

Nephilim

Three generations of giants are listed in the *Book of Giants*: the Grigori, or full-blooded giants who came down; the half-human Nephilim, which were the offspring of the Grigori with humans; and the Elioud, which were the children of the Nephilim. The Elioud (also called Eliud/Elyo/Eljo) would have been anywhere from 25% giant to 75% giant depending on whether the second parent was human, Nephilim, or Grigori.

What else do we know about these human-giant hybrids? There were several tribes: the Emims, or Emites, who were a tribe of Rephaim. They were *the dreaded ones*. The Rephaim were

WHO WERE THE GIANTS?

a race of giants in Iron Age Israel, which dates them at 1200-500 B.C. Dating them to the Iron Age is interesting because so many giants date back to the Bronze Age which precedes the Iron Age. This suggests that some of the giants who were labeled "Nephilim" may not have been second-generation, but came a generation or more later.

King Og was one of the last surviving Rephaim, and this is where we start to get data on their size. His bed was 9 cubits long. A biblical cubit is 18 inches, times 9 equals 162 inches, which means that his bed was 13.5 feet long. Elsewhere, either his bed or coffin was described as 6 feet wide.

King Og, who was listed as both Amorite and Rephaim, was killed by Moses, which further supports the case that he and the people who were killed along with him worshipped gods such as Molech and Baal. His height was the "height of cedars" and his strength, the "strength of oaks."

The giant race of Amorites were described as having the "height of cedars," which suggests that they were roughly 12 feet tall, if you take a foot and a half off of Og's bed length.

Compare that to a record holder from the *Guinness Book of World Records*. Robert Pershing Wadlow was just under 9 feet tall, which makes him at least 3 feet shorter than King Og who represented an entire race of giants. Wadlow's photos are widely available on the internet, so you can visualize how the biblical world of the Nephilim who towered over him might have looked.

Another clan of biblical giants was the Anakites, who were descended from Anak. These tribes may have all represented a single race, with their names determined by their fathers, like saying that you were a Robinson, or Collins, or Jones. They existed in the stories of Moses, and they may have been the same as the people of Anaq from Egyptian texts. Our ancestors did not have a defined spelling for every word, and names were often spelled phonetically, with each scribe spelling it differently. Thus Anak and Anaq, which sound the same, may have *been* the same.

ANCIENT ALIENS AND THE AGE OF GIANTS

We think of biblical history in terms of what's written in the *Bible*, without taking into account the many extra-biblical texts that provide a different view of the same stories. The Egyptian texts relating to the Anaq date from 2055-1650 B.C. These Anaq were expelled from Canaan, a region that was described as a *land of giants*, or a land of primeval giants, even after the Great Flood. Some giants found refuge in the cities of Gaza, Gath, and Ashdod. Coincidentally, Gath was home to the giant Goliath.

The Nephilim were savage giants who pillaged Earth, dominated and endangered humans, and they "feasted upon" humans. They even devoured one another. The Nephilim turned out to be troublesome beyond imagining. Everything God created on Earth, they destroyed. The Grigori who begot the Nephilim became ostracized fallen angels for creating this serious problem.

> Enoch II 6:1-8 — "And it came to pass, after the children of men had increased in those days, beautiful and comely daughters were born to them. And the angels, the sons of the heavens, saw and lusted after them, and said to one another: 'Behold, we will choose for ourselves wives from among the children of men, and will beget for ourselves children.'
>
> "And Semjaza, who was their leader, said to them: 'I fear that perhaps ye will not be willing to do this deed, and I alone shall suffer for this great sin.'
>
> "Then all answered him and said: 'We all will swear an oath, and bind ourselves mutually by a curse, that we will not give up this plan, but will make this plan a deed.' Then they all swore together, and bound themselves mutually by a curse; and together they were two hundred.
>
> "And they descended on Ardis, which is the summit of Mount Hermon; and they called it Mount Hermon, because they had sworn on it and bound themselves mutually by a curse.
>
> "And these are the names of their leaders: Semjaza, who was their leader… Asael [Azazel]… [and the naming goes on.] These are the leaders of the two hundred angels, and the others who were with them."

WHO WERE THE GIANTS?

Enoch II 7:1-6 — "And they took unto themselves wives*, and each chose for himself one, and they began to go in to them, and mixed with them, and taught them charms and conjurations, and made them acquainted with the cutting of roots and of woods.

"And they became pregnant and brought forth great giants whose stature was three thousand ells.** These devoured all the acquisitions of mankind till men were unable to sustain themselves.***

"And the giants turned themselves against mankind in order to devour them. And they began to sin against the birds and the beasts, and against the creeping things, and the fish, and devoured their flesh among themselves, and drank the blood thereof. Then the earth complained of the unjust ones."

Enoch II 8:1 — "And Azazel taught mankind to make swords and knives and shields and coats of mail..." ****

* In ancient times, *wife* denoted a woman, not just a married woman.
** Three thousand ells is probably a mistake on the part of the scribe or translator.
*** The giants ate all the food and livestock that humans had generated, which caused humans to starve, and left the giants without food as well. The result was that the giants became cannibals, and ate both humans and other giants.
**** Perhaps teaching us weapons and warfare was to protect ourselves against the giants-turned-cannibal. Taken in context, this makes more sense than the other theories.

On the one hand, the Grigori taught us valuable knowledge, which was good for us, but bad for them. On the other hand, their offspring, the Nephilim, wreaked havoc on Earth, which was very bad for everybody, and probably not their intention.

The flood was supposed to wipe out the giants, but giants still existed after the deluge, including King Og in the *Bible*, who was later slain by Moses. The demise of Sodom and Gomorrah came after the flood — two cities also linked to giants.

Fomorians

Now we depart from the biblical giants, to the giant legends in other ancient texts, which brings us to the Fomorians. This race of nasty giants ruled the high seas around what is now Ireland, England, Scotland, Norway, Sweden, Denmark, Finland, Germany, Poland, and the islands of the Hebrides, Orkneys, and Shetlands. For the most part they did not penetrate all the way inland, preferring to colonize the coastal areas to launch ships from. On islands such as Ireland, where you are never far from the ocean, they ruled from coast to coast.

According to legend, the earliest races to arrive in Ireland after the Great Flood encountered the Fomorians, who seemed to have always been there. This would set the Fomorian time frame at 4722 B.C. or earlier, based on the legend that they were in Ireland when Partholón arrived. One estimate put his arrival at 278 years after the deluge, which archeology dates at 5000 B.C. This was after Moses battled the biblical giants, some of which fled the region to take up residence elsewhere. The Fomorians worshipped the same gods as Moses' pagan enemies.

Other estimates put Partholón much later, at 2680 B.C., so you can see how ancient chronologies vary. As the Ceide Fields of Ireland are dated at 4000 B.C., and they are listed as the oldest fields in the world, a date of 4722 for Partholón is more viable, as someone had to create those fields.

The Fomorians remained in Ireland throughout the reign of Partholón and his successors Nemed, the Fir Bolg kings, and into the Tuatha dé Danann kings, who were the first with the ability to go nose-to-nose against the Fomorian giants and take them down a few pegs, eliminating their brutal grip over Ireland. The Tuatha dé Danann reigned during the Bronze Age, by various estimates arriving in either 1897 B.C. or 1477 B.C.

Fomorian in its various spellings denoted foreigners, foes of the sea, under sea, devils in human shape, seafaring, and even giants. The Famhairs of Scotch Gaelic were often represented as giants who fed on humans. This aspect of the giants is echoed around the world, so it is very likely accurate.

The Manx word for Fomorians denoted giants, gigantic, or huge, though it also referred to pirates, which was their lifestyle. Manx comes from the Isle of Man — a small island in between Ireland and Great Britain. In Ireland, the Fomorians were considered giants, and sea robbers of "superhuman size."

Proceedings of the Society of Antiquaries of Scotland, Volume 20, published in 1886, discussed the origin of the Fomorian race, whether they were from the countries Africa or Pomerania, or descended from Cham (Ham) the son of Noah. The very name Pomerania means "land at the sea" and it spanned the northern coast of what is now Germany and Poland along the Baltic Sea. Several cultures lived in Pomerania, some of which were associated with cannibalism, just like the giants.

Fomorian legends don't say much about ancestry, although at least one of them was blonde with fair skin, and their territory was nearly identical to that of the later Vikings, as was their lifestyle. They did not seem to share the gods of the Vikings, however. One Fomorian god was an evil god mentioned by name several times in the *Bible*, as a pagan god not to be worshipped. The god's name was Moloch, Molech, or Molekh, among other variations, and worshipping him, or sacrificing children to him, was punishable by death in the *Bible*, so his followers would surely flee to the farthest places they could find.

> CJB: Leviticus 20:2 — "Say to the people of Isra'el, 'If someone from the people of Isra'el or one of the foreigners living in Isra'el sacrifices one of his children to Molekh [Molech], he must be put to death; the people of the land are to stone him to death.'"
>
> AMP: 1 Kings 11:7 — "Then Solomon built a high place for Chemosh, the abominable idol of Moab, on the hill opposite Jerusalem; and for Molech, the abominable idol of the Ammonites."

Molech was a god of the giant Fomorians, which suggests a connection to the biblical giants. Remember the giants that were expelled from Canaan and fled to Gaza, Gath, and Ashdod? Gaza and Ashdod are on the coast of the Mediterranean Sea, and as the crow flies, 2516 miles from Dublin, Ireland, with many obstacles in between. The giants were hounded, and persecuted, in and around the Holy Land, so it makes sense that they'd look for a new home where they wouldn't be bothered. Ireland is an island, so nobody would be sneaking up on them overland.

There don't seem to be legends of Fomorians coming down from the stars or the heavens, so it is unlikely that they were first-generation giants. Is it possible to determine a timeline from the Grigori to the Fomorians? The best we can do is estimate, as scholars cannot pinpoint the biblical timeline with accuracy.

The *Book of Enoch* stated that the Grigori came down to Mount Hermon in the days of Jared, and that the flood was supposed to wipe out the offspring including the Nephilim and the Elioud. The Grigori were on Earth at the time of Adam and Eve as well. By most dating estimates, Adam and Eve existed in the Stone Age, when humans were using stones and bones as tools, and had been doing so for millions of years.

Famed underwater archeologist Robert Ballard discovered evidence that suggests that there was a major flood in 5000 B.C., and many are claiming that what he discovered is evidence of Noah's Great Flood. As always there are skeptics, but the date actually works. If you compare it to a timeline of archeological accomplishments, such as the building of the pyramids, Stonehenge, Newgrange, and North American Mound Builders, they all came after 5000 B.C., with the Mound Builders dating to 4500 B.C. This would date Adam and Eve to approximately 7000 B.C., and hence, the Grigori arrival.

If the Fomorians date back to 4722 B.C., that's over 2,000 years after the Grigori arrival, which puts the Fomorians pretty far down the chain of giants. They wouldn't have been first, second, or even third generation giants. If the Fomorians started with giants who survived the flood, it still puts 278 years between the Fomorians and their giant ancestors, although in those days lifespans measured in centuries rather than decades. An explanation for the change in lifespans is given in the book *Ancient Aliens and the Lost Islands* by Lars Bergen and Sharon Delarose.

Like the Nephilim, the Fomorians were a nasty race, who occasionally devoured humans. They also sacrificed people to the god Molech, and they cut off your nose for non-payment of taxes, which were called "tributes" in those days. The Fomorians were not the only race to institute this ugly nose tax; the Vikings who followed, and who lived in the same regions, also cut off your nose for non-payment.

Fomorians roared like bulls when they were angry, and being quick-tempered they were often angry. They were so stubborn that they spawned an old proverb about acting with "Fomorian obstinacy."

Fomorians lived by piracy, and the spoils of others. They were invaders, and marauders, who plundered, and slaughtered. They did not build — they destroyed. That sounds very much like the giants who were evicted from the land of Canaan, and who Moses battled. Fomorians were troublesome to the whole world (or at least, the world within their territory.) *Pre-Christian Ireland* by Ulick Joseph Bourke of the Royal University of Ireland, published in 1887, suggests that the Fomorians were actually the descendants of Canaan, son of Ham, grandson of Noah.

The Fomorians did commingle with others, and by one account, "the Irish intermarried with the cruel pirates in order to retrain their cruel recesses and render the pirates useful." As several heroes of ancient Ireland were begotten of giants, it must have worked.

All across Ireland are ancient stone monuments, with stones weighing upwards of 40 tons each, said to be the work of giants. One such giant was Parrahbough M'Shaggean, whose grave is 20 feet long by 5 feet wide. Human bones of "monstrous size" were found buried there.

The Fomorians may not have shared the Viking gods, but the similarity of their territories, and the love of being at sea for pirating and raiding, was uncanny. The homeland of the Vikings was nearly identical to that of the Fomorians, and their raiding routes were similar as well, though the Vikings may have traveled a lot farther.

The primary difference is that the Fomorians were giants themselves, where the Vikings worshipped gods who were giants, and by all of their myths, there's a strong possibility that their gods came down from the heavens, just like the Grigori. Perhaps the extraterrestrial Viking gods even assisted them, because one of the first-known Viking raids was on the island of Lindisfarne just off the coast of England, in 793 A.D.

According to *The Anglo-Saxon Chronicle* translated by E. E. C. Gomme in 1909, "there were excessive whirlwinds, and lightnings, and fiery dragons were seen flying in the air. To these tokens followed a great famine; and a little after that in the same year… the harrying of heathen men destroyed God's church at Lindisfarne by means of plunder and slaughter."

Fiery dragons could denote aircraft, and many giant legends are linked to fiery birds, flying boats, giant birds, dragons, and other airborne vehicles. So who were these giant Norse gods of the Vikings?

Norse Mythology

The Norse listed three races of giants, which may have been a single race that lived in three different regions, or worlds. The Jötnar, or singular Jötunn, lived on Jötunheim, which was one of the nine worlds in Norse mythology. Their very name is synonymous with both *giant* and *man-eater*.

The giants who lived on Jötunheim were Mountain Giants. The sons of Múspell were Fire Giants, from Múspelheim, and their legends promise death and destruction to humans in the Norse end-of-the-world prophecy known as Ragnarök.

The Frost Giants were from Niflheim which is a word similar to Nephilim. In those days words were written as they sounded, so cultures often spelled the same word differently, and the 1906 *Jewish Encyclopedia* includes "Nefilim" as a spelling for "Nephilim." Is it really a coincidence that Niflheim was the home of giants, and that the Nefilim *were* giants?

All three Norse worlds of giants are listed among the nine worlds of Norse mythology, along with another world called Asgard which they referred to as *heaven*. Asgard was the home of the Aesir gods, a race that was frequently at war with the giants.

The word *heaven* itself means different things including the atmosphere in which birds fly, and the space that holds the sun, moon, and stars. It's the realm where angels travel, and where the biblical God resides. The book *Ancient Aliens and the Lost Islands: Through the Wormhole* by Lars Bergen and Sharon Delarose goes deeper into the concept of extraterrestrial worlds, and ancient texts that give us clues, as well as the possibility of wormholes between our world and others.

Earth was one of the nine worlds and it was called Midgard. If our planet was one of the nine worlds, then what does that tell us about the other worlds? Were they planets as well, and if so, how did the Norse gods travel to Earth? Their legends told us that, too.

Asgard was connected to Earth via the bifröst bridge, which linked our two worlds, and the gods traveled across it every day. Descriptions of bifröst include: "for heaven's bridge burns all in flame." The bridge consisted of three colors, including red, and the red was "burning fire" which prevented the Frost Giants and Mountain Giants from using the bridge to get to Asgard, presumably from Earth. Yet the Aesir gods had no trouble crossing this fiery bridge. When our world ends, the Fire Giants will cross the bridge to come to Earth and wreak havoc.

We get another look at a potential wormhole in the legend of Eirek, a Norwegian prince who traveled to a place called *Deathless Acre*. Eirek was the son of King Thrand of Drontheim, Norway, as well as being the great-grandson of the Norse god Odin, so he would have known that places existed outside of our normal realm, and he would have been part-giant.

Eirek made a few stops before the big journey, including a visit to an emperor in Constantinople for advice on how to get to Deathless Acre. Directions in those days weren't as simple as saying "go north on the interstate." Maps were estimations drawn by hand, and they rarely included roads.

The emperor was a wiz at geography, and he told Eirek that the distance between heaven and Earth was 100,045 miles. To put this in perspective, that's less than halfway to the moon. Now why would this emperor even mention the distance to heaven, unless it was relevant in navigating to Deathless Acre? And by heaven, did he mean Asgard? If so, then Asgard would not have been a planet, but it *could have been* an orbiting starship.

Eirek's journey took him across a bridge and through what could only be described as a portal, because when he stepped into what he thought was a dragon's mouth, the dragon disappeared and Eirek found himself transported to Deathless Acre, nowhere near the bridge he'd just been standing on. He entered a world which seemed as bright as the sun, and he found a tower suspended in the air, without any support whatsoever. The only way in was to climb a slender ladder, which he did.

Deathless Acre is another name for Odainsakur in Gloesisvellir, which refers to a shining or glittering plain on Jötunheim. In other words, Eirek traveled to the world of the giants, which means that like the bifröst wormhole between Earth and Asgard, there must have been a similar wormhole between Earth and Jötunheim. In this light, the reference to the distance to heaven, or Asgard, makes a lot more sense. However, it does bring up another question: If Asgard was halfway the distance to the moon, then were these nine "worlds" actually orbiting starships? As he also described the land that he saw, which did not appear to be indoors, and because there was a time differential, it would suggest that he actually did travel to another world, and not just a starship.

The land was flat as far as the eye could see, and the grass was purple with the many flowers in bloom, which filled the air with the scent of blossoms. A gentle breeze was blowing and there wasn't a cloud in the sky. Joy and happiness prevailed in this paradise where night never fell, the world was as bright as the sun, and a half a year slipped by in just a few moments. This is what Eirek saw on Jötunheim — the world of giants.

While he did not describe the beings that he encountered, the entities who are most associated with Gloesisvellir are beautiful women sometimes called trolls. The king who rules over Odainsakur is a friendly giant.

Eirek's lineage makes him the great-grandson of Odin, who was one of the primary gods of Norse mythology. Odin was the ruler of Asgard, and his maternal grandfather was Jötnar, which means that he was at least partially descended from giants. If Odin carried giant's blood, then so did Eirek and his father King Thrand. The most likely candidate for King Thrand is Thrand, the son of Saeming who ruled the kingdom of Halogaland in what is now Norway. Saeming, or Saemingr, is also listed as a son of Odin.

Odin and his cronies possessed some pretty amazing technology besides the ability to travel between worlds. The Viking era began in 793 A.D., so this technology was described centuries before we actually developed it here on Earth. One legend relating to Odin sounds like he had access to a radio.

Several earthly kings honored Odin when he lived in Uppsala by making a gold-plated statue in his likeness. Odin was overjoyed by the notoriety that the statue represented, but his queen, Frigga, wanted the gold, so she ordered blacksmiths to strip the gold from the statue. Odin was angered at having his statue tampered with, and he had the blacksmiths killed. He then mounted the statue on a pedestal, and by the "marvelous skill of his art," Odin made the statue speak when a mortal touched it.

Coincidentally, the Fomorian giants also had oracles in the form of talking statues. One was called the Golden Stone, or Cermand Cestach for the god that spoke through it, or even Giant Ermand Kelstach. Like Odin's statue, it was covered in gold, and from it, the devil spoke to the druids.

The Fomorian oracle gave detailed advice, and one of its recipients was Conchobar mac Nessa before he became the king of Ulster, Ireland. The oracle told him to travel to the Isle of Man to have weapons made. That's a pretty detailed piece of advice.

Conchobar had family ties to the Fomorians. His half-sister was part-Fomorian, and she had a child by the half-Fomorian king of Ireland, whose name was Lugh. Unlike the nasty Fomorians, however, Lugh took after his father's people and brought benefit to the people of Ireland. He played a big part in the war that drove the Fomorians out of Ireland, and he killed his own Fomorian grandfather in the process.

Ireland had other talking oracles as well. There was a talking oracle in Killycluggin, and another called Lía Fáil in Tara — where the king lived.

Odin's statue spoke when you touched it. Today we have lamps that turn on and off with a touch, or a clap of the hands, and we have kid's toys that talk when touched or squeezed. We manufacture radios and speakers in all sorts of shapes including cars, boats, cows, dogs, rocks, beer cans, and even Elvis Presley. The only reason that Odin's talking statue was amazing is because humans had not yet invented the technology, but Odin, the Fomorians, and Native American giant Hiawatha all had radios, and Odin and Hiawatha had flying boats.

Odin's flying boat existed in the Norse legends of a ship called Skidbladnir. The attributes of Skidbladnir were so amazing that those who witnessed this marvel believed that incredible skill, cunning, and a "very great magic" had been used to build her.

Skidbladnir was a huge ship — big enough to carry an entire army across the ocean with all of their weapons and armament. As soon as her sails were set, no matter what the weather or wind, a "favorable breeze would arise and carry her to the place of destination." They never had to worry about the wind, the weather, or the waves — Skidbladnir went wherever they wanted her to go — because "she supplied her own breezes" much like a motorized boat of today.

In addition, she could sail through the air as easily as she could sail on water. That sounds similar to what we call an Unidentified Submersible Object or USO, which is a UFO that can travel underwater like a submarine, as well as fly through the air, and USOs are big enough to hold a fully equipped garrison. In addition, Odin had the ability to travel to faraway lands "in the twinkle of an eye."

We think of Odin as a fictional entity, a god who existed in mythology, but not only did he leave behind descendants, the ancient historians referred to him as a *man*, a flesh-and-blood man who'd taken on the airs of a god. A Danish historian who lived from 1150-1220 A.D. named Saxo Grammaticus wrote:

> "At this time there was one Odin, who was credited over all Europe with the honour, which was false, of godhead, but used more continually to sojourn at [the city of] Uppsala; and in this spot, either from the sloth of the inhabitants or from its own pleasantness, he vouchsafed to dwell with somewhat especial constancy."

Uppsala is a city in Sweden — which once had strong ties to the Aesir gods from Asgard. Saxo also mentioned several people who encountered Odin in person at various times, which indicates that his entire pantheon of gods and giants actually came to Earth from their other worlds, just as the Grigori came to Earth from the 5th heaven.

Norse mythology gives us a look at the end of our world, with giants coming to both help us, and harm us. This event is called Ragnarök, which begins with a giant named Eggther waking up the gods in the nine worlds to prepare for the final fight. Earth will shake and mountains will crumble, setting loose various creatures such as the Fire Giants, aka the sons of Múspell, who will come forth to do battle.

As with most end-of-the-world scenarios, things are going to get really ugly before the big battle begins. Earth will be plunged into three years of winter where it snows and snows with no sign of summer. The sun will turn black, and the moon and stars will seemingly disappear, which suggests that something will darken the sky such as volcanic ash. Earth will shake so violently that the very mountains topple over. Oceans will rise up to become devastating floods. Everywhere you look, you'll see flames and steam as high as the heavens, and Earth will become toxic. People will run for their lives, but there won't be anywhere safe to go. Humans will turn against one another other, and no man will have mercy for his neighbor.

Just when you think it can't get any worse, the sky splits in two and out come the sons of Múspell, riding across the bifröst bridge with their shining battle troops, and then the bridge breaks. These Fire Giants aren't here to save humanity — they're here to wage war on everyone and everything in sight, including the Aesir gods who are currently holed up safe in their homes in Asgard until the Big Day arrives.

The war will take place not only on Earth, but on some of the nine worlds as well, making this a galactic war. Odin will return, and Thor, and even Loki, to fight in this battle to end all battles. Thor will fight furiously on our behalf, but most of the old Norse gods will be killed. This signals the end of Earth as we know it, after which there will be a new heaven, a new Earth, and humans get divided up between several afterworlds or afterlives, depending on how we lived. There are beautiful places, and repugnant places. If there is a "new Earth" and we get divided up to live on "after-worlds," does that mean we are physically relocated to other planets? Or is this purely spiritual? We will not know the answer until that day arrives.

Ragnarök suggests that giants were of two factions, just like the Grigori legends. Another similarity to the Grigori is the concept of hell, which is spelled *Hel* in Norse mythology, and this Hel is an actual place. It is a kingdom on Niflheim encircled by a high wall, secured by strong gates.

Hel is associated with corpses, and the world of the dead, and it is ruled by a giant goddess of the same name — Hel. The goddess Hel "gives out lodging" to those who've died, and are sent to her. For all we know, the Norse Hel is nothing more than a physical graveyard for the beings of the nine worlds. Whatever it is, Hel is accessible to Earth, which suggests that Niflheim is accessible to Earth, just as Jötunheim and Asgard are.

Odin traveled to Hel on horseback, and he was not dead when he journeyed there. A Valkyrie named Brynhild visited Hel after her cremation, which suggests a burial. She was riding in a wagon covered with a rich cloth, along a road that bordered Hel. The wagon passed the house of a giantess.

The Norse Hel on Niflheim may have another connection with the biblical Nephilim. Remember the children of the giant Nephilim, who were called the Elioud, Eliud, or Eljo? Another strange coincidence is that on Niflheim, in Hel, there is a hall called Eljudnir or Éljúðnir, which means "sprayed with snowstorms" or "damp with sleet or rain." The similarity of words may just be a coincidence, but these coincidences just keep piling up with the giants, and the coincidences span the entire world from the Holy Land, to Europe, Scandinavia, Egypt, the Americas, and even the islands north of Australia.

As for the concept of giants on Earth who had access to radios and aircraft, another such giant was Native American Hiawatha, who had a flying canoe which played music.

Native American Giants

Hiawatha: This Native American peacemaker and giant was known by many names including Hiawatha, Manabozho, and Tarenyawagon. He was sent to Earth as a messenger of the Great Spirit, and he became a wise man, prophet, and leader.

He brought several warring tribes together to become the great nation of the Iroquois, uniting the Onondaga, Oneida, Seneca, Cayuga, and Mohawk nations into a single Iroquois confederacy. The earliest date for this is 1142 A.D., though we don't have definitive dates that historians agree on.

Two books take us into his world: *Legends, Traditions and Laws of the Iroquois, or Six Nations, and History of the Tuscarora Indians* by Elias Johnson, a Native Tuscarora Chief, published in 1881; and *The Myth of Hiawatha, and Other Oral Legends, Mythologic and Allegoric, of the North American Indians* by Henry Rowe Schoolcraft in 1856.

The legends begin with the Tuscarora creation story that there were two worlds, or regions of space: an upper world, and a lower world. The upper world was inhabited by beings who resembled humans, who were then transferred below, and the "lower sphere was about to be rendered fit for their residence." This lower sphere was Earth.

One of them prepared the surface of the continent for human habitation, by creating rivers, creeks, plains, etc. and populating it with plants and animals. Then a man and woman were created "out of the Earth" and given life. They were called Ongwahonwa, meaning "real people" aka humans. At some point, a company of humans was camped on the St. Lawrence River, and they were invaded by a nation of great giants called Ronongwaca whom they fought many wars against. After several disasters, including a blazing star that fell down and caused utter destruction, those who were left fought bitterly with one another, and almost destroyed themselves by reducing the population to where it couldn't fight the wild beasts.

WHO WERE THE GIANTS?

Then came Tarenyawagon (Holder of the Heavens) to unite the warring tribes, and he taught them how to fish, hunt and cook game. He provided them with seeds and grains, gave knowledge of bows and arrows, the art of war, agriculture, matrimony, worship, and he taught them how to expel monsters from the forest, including the Stonish Giants.

He took a human wife from the Onondagas, had a daughter by her, and they called him Hiawatha, which meant "wise man." Once his mission was fulfilled, he departed up into the sky:

> "'I have been allowed by the Great Spirit to communicate to you… The Great Creator of our bodies calls me to go. I have patiently awaited his summons. I am ready to go. Farewell.' As the voice of the wise man ceased, sweet strains of music from the air burst on the ears of the multitude. The whole sky appeared to be filled with melody, and while all eyes were directed to catch glimpses of the sights, and enjoy strains of the celestial music that filled the sky, Hiawatha was seen, seated in his snow-white canoe, amid the air, rising, rising, with every choral chant that burst out. As he rose, the sound of the music became more soft and faint, until he vanished amid the summer clouds, and the melody ceased."

Think about how this event unfolded. If the music was loud while Hiawatha's vehicle was on the ground, and then faded as it rose up toward the clouds, this suggests that the music came from the magic canoe itself, like a radio. Hearing music all around you without seeing who is making the music, in itself, was a wonder, and it's exactly what we hear when we turn a radio on.

His canoe was a "light and magic canoe, which shone with a supernatural luster, in which he performed so many of his extraordinary feats." In this vehicle:

> "He took his position, sometimes, on the top of high cliffs, springing, if needs be, over frightful chasms; and he flew, as it were, over great lakes in a wonderful canoe of immaculate whiteness and of magic power."

ANCIENT ALIENS AND THE AGE OF GIANTS

"He leaps over extensive regions of the country like an ignis fatuus. He appears suddenly like an avatar..."

Regarding the Stonish Giants, they were tall, hostile and fierce, of great strength, and they devoured men, women, and children. Their skin was so tough that arrows couldn't pierce it — arrows simply bounced off with a clatter. Some believe that this was a form of armor rather than their actual skin. Sometimes, instead of devouring their captives, they enslaved them and forced them to work. The slaves were doomed to dig, and carry, and endure pangs of hunger even when surrounded with food that they'd grown for their giant captors.

Another version of the giant cannibal that he battled, and the legend of his own birth, makes him a giant as well. His mother got pregnant with Hiawatha "by the west wind" or "the west" or someone who'd come out of the west — who did not ask for the consent of her parents, but simply took her. Three other sons were also born of this union, prior to Hiawatha, who was the youngest, and his mother died while giving birth to him.

As an adult, he wanted to find this father whom he'd never met, and his grandmother was unable to stop him, because "he had now attained manhood, possessed a giant's height, and was endowed by nature with a giant's strength and power." On a high mountain in the west he found his father, who put him on a mission to help "the people of this Earth, which is infested with large serpents, beasts, and monsters, who make great havoc among the inhabitants." The monsters were described in the footnote as "weendigo... commonly applied, at this time, by the Indians, to cannibals. Its ancient use appears, however, to have embraced giants and anomalous voracious beasts..."

In other words, not only was Hiawatha a giant, one of his missions was to help humans eradicate the giant cannibals who were plaguing them. He was a good ruler, who brought peace and prosperity, and he made the world a better place. He was a *good*, and *beneficial*, giant.

WHO WERE THE GIANTS?

Stop for just a moment, and think about this. He was a giant, with a flying canoe, who taught us everything from farming to weaponry. He also taught us how to protect ourselves from other giants. Doesn't this sound a lot like the Grigori history? Native American legends of evil, nasty tribes of giants were probably human-giant hybrids, like the Nephilim. Another such legend involved a cannibal-giant.

Si-Te-Cah: The Paiutes believed in a tribe of red-headed, cannibalistic giants that they called Si-Te-Cah, who lived hundreds of years prior to 1883. They were "beautiful giants" who lived between the Sierra Nevada and Rocky Mountains, but they were also barbarians who ate the Paiutes for dinner and kidnapped their women, so the two groups were at war.

Sarah Winnemucca Hopkins wrote about them in her book, *Life Among the Piutes: Their Wrongs and Claims*, published in 1883. She described how they dug holes in the trails at night, so that nighttime travelers would fall in and get trapped, and thus eaten.

Not only would the barbarians kidnap people to eat, they'd also eat their own dead, or dig up the dead of others who'd been properly buried and eat them as well. When at war, the barbarian women would carry off any who were killed, regardless of which side they fought on. Cannibalism was their way of life. In battle, they'd jump high into the air and catch arrows as they whizzed overhead, and then use those same arrows on their attackers.

The Paiutes adopted some of the giants into their own families, in the hopes of teaching them new ways that didn't involve eating others. They did everything they could to civilize the Si-Te-Cahs, but it didn't work. The Si-Te-Cahs could not be civilized. This is a common theme in the giant legends, as you'll see later with a much more savage race whose lifestyle, and skeletons, were like something out of the Stone Age.

After a lengthy war with many losses, the Paiutes finally drove the giants into a thicket. The giants numbered about 2,600 at that time, and the Paiutes set the thicket on fire. That drove the giants out of the thicket and onto Humboldt Lake, where they sailed off on bulrush, or tule boats. The Paiutes surrounded the lake to prevent the giants from landing, and they killed all who made an attempt. The giants were starving, and desperate.

One night they managed to land safely near a cave and they went into the cave. Once inside, they were trapped. The Paiutes guarded the cave entrance, and tried to talk to the Si-Te-Cahs. They promised to let the giants live if only the giants would promise to stop eating people. The giants refused. Exasperated, the Paiutes filled the cave entrance with wood, which the giants pulled into the cave, so the Paiutes just kept on adding wood until the cave filled up with it. Again, they offered a truce, if only the giants would stop being cannibals.

In the end, the Paiutes lit the wood on fire and left. Ten days later they went back to check on the cave, and a horrible stench emanated from inside — the rot of death.

Sarah's version stated that they were red-headed cannibals, but she did not use the word "giant" in the book — she used "barbarian." Other legends give them a giant stature, as does the controversial discovery of giant bones in Lovelock Cave, Nevada. The discovery was made by two miners in 1911, Samuel Pugh and James Hart, who'd been mining bat guano to be used as fertilizer, when they started finding artifacts and mummies.

An October 3, 1936, newspaper article in the *Nevada State Journal* posted an update on a mummy that had been found in a cave several years earlier. The mummy was dubbed the "Lovelock Giant" and its red-haired occupant was originally described as a whopping 11 feet tall. Apparently a mistake had been made in the earlier reports, the giant was a mere 9.5 feet tall, and it was in the possession of the Smithsonian Institute.

On August 3, 1952, the *Nevada State Journal* confirmed that the Lovelock mummy truly was a giant, based on a comparison of its woven, cone-shaped helmet, which matched the weaving of sandals that were all part of an extensive Prehistoric Nevada exhibit at the Nevada State Historical Society. One sandal was over 15 inches long, along with a jaw-bone that was "twice the size" of a modern man's. Other skeletons measuring up to 9 feet tall were also featured at the exhibit.

The article described how archeologist Llewellyn L. Loud from the University of California excavated 10,000 specimens of various types, which were divided between the University of California and the Nevada Historical Society. This would have included artifacts.

In 1924, a Dr. M. R. Harrington came on the scene, and collaborated with Loud. Harrington was the curator of the Museum of the American Indian in Los Angeles. Harrington's report confirmed that the Lovelock Cave legend regarding the incineration was indeed possible, as partially burned fire-arrow shafts were found in the cave.

So where was the original giant mummy of Lovelock? At the Smithsonian Institute, as originally reported? Or at the Nevada State Historical Society? And what happened to the display that included 9 feet tall skeletons?

On October 4, 1976, *The Portsmouth Times* published an article debunking not only the giant stature of the Lovelock mummy, but also the red hair and the cannibalism.

Unnamed scientists were claiming that there was no proof that the giants of legend were cannibals, and that any Indian remains found with red hair instead of black hair could be attributed to chemical staining.

Don Tuohy, the curator of anthropology at the University of Nevada, was confident that the "giant" myth was about to be debunked. Apparently, a bundle of "giant" bones were discovered tucked away and forgotten in a cabinet at the Nevada Historical Society in Reno. The bones were analyzed and the "giants" turned out to be only 6 feet tall. These new bones were thought to have come from Lovelock Cave, and the original story was repeated but this time, with a 6 feet 6 inch tall mummy. No mention was made of the Lovelock bones that were previously sent to the Smithsonian Institute in Washington, D.C.

The debunking article added that the first archeological dig was in 1912, with a second dig in 1924 which produced about 60 average-height mummies. Radio-carbon dating showed that the cave had been occupied from around 2000 B.C. through 900 A.D. Elsewhere radio-carbon dates were given as conservatively 1000 B.C. and 617 B.C. The differences probably come from the layers tested, as there were six distinct levels or layers.

The current status of the Lovelock Giant is that the story was successfully debunked, and that the original stature was exaggerated. Add to that Sarah's legend which doesn't mention giants, and the skeptics are satisfied.

Regarding whether the Paiutes considered the Si-Te-Cah to be giants, Sarah's book mentions stories of giants told to children, and when asked if the stories are true, parents answer, "Oh, it is only Coyote," which means that these are make-believe stories.

Coincidentally, *The Journal of American Folk-Lore, Volume XIV*, published in 1902, included giant legends from the Flathead Indians of Idaho — a state which borders Nevada. Lovelock Cave is in northern Nevada, so these legends could overlap. Several legends relate to how Coyote killed giants.

In one legend, a giant pleaded for his life. "Let me go free, Coyote," begged the giant. "I won't kill any more people. I'll be good friends with everybody if you'll let me go." Coyote was deaf to the plea and killed the giant.

Another legend tells of a giant who killed everyone that traveled through his valley. The people were starving because of the giant, so Coyote vowed that he would kill the giant. An old woman warned him that he might as well give up now, because he was "already in the giant's belly." Coyote succeeded in killing the giant.

In a 1979 report, The Bureau of Land Management linked the creation mythology of the Paiutes, Washos, and Diggers, including the belief in previous inhabitations of Earth, and cannibalistic giants.

Whether fairytale or truth, the Coyote legends, Sarah's Coyote disclaimer, and the BoLM confirm that the mythology once included giants. Perhaps, like the rest of the world, the Paiutes abandoned their belief in giants once the giants were eliminated, and rewrote their own history to better reflect "the truth." Most civilizations rewrite history, just like Azazel's name being replace with "scapegoat" in the *Bible*, and the burning of bibles whose content was undesirable, which we'll cover in-depth in the segment: *Where Are the Bones*.

As for the discrepancies in the Lovelock Giant skeleton, this is easily explained. A 1981 *Cultural Resource Series, No. 2* publication from the Bureau of Land Management, Nevada, had a segment on human skeletal remains from the Carson-Humboldt Sinks, which refers to the region around Lovelock. It confirms that the Smithsonian has several skeletons from Nevada, including at least one Paiute, though it doesn't specify Lovelock. It does, however, state that several specimens from this region have never been reported in the literature, and are presently stored in various university and museum collections.

Newspaper reports spanning decades state that over 60 mummies were pulled out of Lovelock Cave, ranging from 6 feet tall to over 9 feet tall, and at least one 9 footer went to the Smithsonian. Several 9 footers were on display in Nevada in 1952. Most of the 60 mummies were a puny 6 feet tall, however, and this explains how a set of 6 feet tall Lovelock bones was found forgotten in a cabinet, and later used to debunk the entire Lovelock Giant discovery.

Anáye: Another cannibalistic tribe was the fearsome Anáye, which means "alien gods." They were yellow-haired giants in the Navajo Origin Legend. They actively pursued, and devoured the Navajo, decimating the local population, and it was their own father Tsóhanoai who helped to slay them.

Apparently this father, or Sun God, lived somewhere off-world. He came to Earth and begot children without telling his otherworld wife. So far the legend reads like the Grigori downfall. Giants come down without permission, mate with humans, beget children who become cannibals, which causes trouble, and other giants are forced to come down and slay them.

Where the story diverges is that the human mother of the giants had no recollection of ever having laid eyes on the father. Was she implanted as with a test tube baby, or an alien abduction that results in pregnancy? Were these pregnancies kick-started in a laboratory, rather than a bedroom?

The human woman who begot the children, Estsánatlehi, claimed never to have seen the Sun God up close, and claimed that he never came down to Earth to visit her. In addition, he'd "visited" at least one other woman in the same way, as there were competing races of giants on Earth who were all his children.

Estsánatlehi's hybrid children were having trouble with a race of giants called the Anáye, who were also his children. Now we come to another similarity with the biblical Grigori — a great storm that wipes out the Anáye giants.

The Anáye were described as unnatural, or alien giants, and they were monsters born to virgins who had engaged in unnatural practices. This is in keeping with Estsánatlehi's claim not to know the extraterrestrial father. Allegedly, in the course of four days, these virgin-born children grew to the size of 12 year olds.

Estsánatlehi's sons and the other villagers were being terrorized, and eaten by the cannibal giants, so in desperation her sons found a way to journey to their father to ask for his help. The father responded by providing his hybrid sons with advanced armor and weaponry that did not exist on Earth.

In outfitting the afflicted sons for war, he dressed them in suits of metal armor. Each warrior was given a hat, shirt, leggings, and moccasins made of iron or knives. For weapons he gave them chain-lightning arrows, sheet-lightning arrows, sunbeam arrows, rainbow arrows, knives, and knife clubs. When they put on the armor, streaks of lightning shot out from every joint, and the lightning-arrow had the ability to blast a cleft into a mountain. Thus prepared, they set out to find their enemies.

Their father Tsóhanoai led them to the edge of the world, where Earth and sky come together. Sixteen wands or poles leaned from Earth up to the sky: four of white shell, four of turquoise, four of haliotis shell, and four of red stone. A deep stream flowed between the warriors and the wands, but when Tsóhanoai blew a great breath, he formed a bridge of rainbow that allowed them to cross over safely.

The red wands were for war, and the others were for peace. They climbed "up to the sky" on the red wands, until they reached the sky-hole. This hole was edged with smooth, shining cliffs that sloped deeply downwards — cliffs of the same material as the wands they'd climbed up.

Once at the top they could see Earth, but the view was similar to what we see from an airplane. Wooded mountains appeared like dark spots on the surface. Lakes gleamed like stars, and rivers like streaks of lightning.

Remember the bifröst bridge of Norse mythology that led from Earth to the world of giants? This was also known as a "rainbow-bridge" and red was the color that limited who could cross. Two different races, on opposite sides of the world, with radically different mythologies, and yet here we are with giants living somewhere up in the heavens, connected to Earth by a rainbow-bridge, with red as a color of significance.

How many different mythologies does it take before we realize that our ancestors around the world were telling us a story — the same story — of a race of giants who came down to Earth? Giants who we ended up at war with...

The Anáye legends also cross paths with the biblical Noah's Ark. These boys were successful in eliminating some of the giants, but there were just too many for them to handle, so their mother Estsánatlehi used technology that was sent down by their father to create a great storm.

This technology was in the form of magical hoops, and using these hoops, Estsánatlehi sent a terrible storm which destroyed all but four of the giants. The storm was so powerful that it reshaped the entire Earth.

She rolled hoops in each of the four directions, and then up into the sky. The sky-borne hoop rose up into the sky out of sight, and thunder was heard. Nothing happened for four days, but on the fourth day, the sky grew dark, except for a great white cloud that descended from above, amidst the sound of thundering.

Whirlwinds sprouted up all around, which uprooted trees and tossed boulders as if they were pebbles. For days the winds blew, and the hail and sharp stones pelted them, such as they'd never witnessed before. They remained safe because something special was done to protect their house, though the description of this is beyond understanding.

When the protective covering around their house was removed, and they were allowed to come out of the house, they marveled at the changes to the landscape. A great canyon had formed nearby, and the shape of the bluffs all around them was different. All of the giants were gone except four.

Their father came down and collected the bodies of the dead giants, along with the armor and weapons that he'd given his sons. At their mother's request, he provided her with a house that floated on top of the water, with plants and animals to take on the boat. He gave her elk, buffalo, deer, sheep, rabbits, and prairie dogs. She wanted this houseboat so that when the people increased, they would not bother her.

Not only does the story of the flood and houseboat resonate with Noah's Ark, but also with the red-haired Si-Te-Cah giants who lived on rafts to stay out of reach of their enemies. And remember, Estsánatlehi's own sons were hybrids — humans fathered by yellow-haired giants — floating on a raft in the lake.

WHO WERE THE GIANTS?

This legend of slaying the giants who were terrorizing Earth is connected with the Fourth World, or Fourth Age. The Third World was destroyed in a Great Flood, and those who survived the flood did so because they had a raft, or climbed to the top of a mountain where they ascended into the Fourth World through a hollow reed, which may have been like the rainbow wands that led up into the sky, allowing you to look down on Earth.

The Great Flood was heralded by animals running past. For three straight days, animals ran as if fleeing from some great danger. Deer, and turkeys, and antelopes, and squirrels — all trying to escape a great wall of water but the trouble was, the water came from every direction, so there was no place to run. By some legends we are now living in the Fourth World, and by others we're in the Fifth World, or Fifth Sun.

Every Native American nation has its own legends, and most have legends of giants and floods. The giants in Mesoamerica, however, left behind more physical, tangible evidence. Mesoamerica spanned from what is now Mexico down through Central America, and the Toltecs may have been a race of advanced giants who predated the Aztecs.

Mesoamerican Giants

The Toltec era began in 544 A.D. and continued until about 1052 A.D., although archeological evidence dates them much earlier, if it turns out that they were the builders of the great city of Teotihuacán. They predated the Aztecs, and much of what we know about the Toltecs comes from Aztec legends. The Aztecs dominated Mesoamerica from the 14th through the 16th centuries.

The Aztecs perceived the Toltecs as their intellectual and cultural predecessors, but scholars disagree on the location and breadth of the Toltec kingdom, as well as its connection to the Aztecs and Mayans. Some scholars place them in the Fourth Sun of the Aztecs, which is the cycle prior to our own — us being in the Fifth Sun.

Like the Navajo, the Aztecs believed that there have been five suns, or cycles of creation and destruction, and that we are in the fifth cycle. The cycle that was destroyed by a rain of fire from the sky was the Rain Sun. The cycle destroyed by hurricanes was the Wind Sun, and it was an era where humans were of normal size until we angered the gods and they turned us into monkeys. Water Sun was destroyed by a flood, and our cycle will be destroyed by earthquakes; thus, we live in the Earthquake Sun.

Giants ruled the world during the Jaguar Sun, and that world was destroyed by jaguars, which sounds farfetched until you see images of the Jaguar God and his brethren.

The Aztecs had a concept of thirteen heavens, and the ruler of the 8th heaven was Tlaloc, who is either depicted as wearing goggles and a face mask, or as an entity that looks like a military vehicle. The vehicle image carved in stone comes from the Temple of Quetzalcoatl in Teotihuacán, and archeologist Manuel Gamio equates the vehicle with Tlaloc. Scholars don't agree on whether Tlaloc was a Jaguar God or a Water God, and some believe that he represents both.

His association with water is based on Aztec mythology, but Teotihuacán predates the Aztecs, and while they may have drawn from earlier mythology, they also transformed it to their own purposes. Ethnologist Miguel Covarrubias suggested that all Mesoamerican rain- or water-god figures traced back to the Olmec were-jaguar, including Tlaloc. Archeologist Alfonso Caso also referred to the Olmec jaguar as "a god who is probably an ancestor to Tlaloc."

The connection between a water-god and a jaguar may seem improbable, but jaguars are big, jungle cats who make their home near water. They take baths, and even hunt in the water. They are expert fishermen, wiggling their tails in the water like bait to attract fish.

It was jaguars who destroyed the world of giants, and if Tlaloc is a Jaguar God, this is what he represents:

WHO WERE THE GIANTS?

JAGUAR GOD
2ND CENTURY

HUMAN VEHICLES
20TH CENTURY

The round openings were originally capped with jet-black obsidian glass that reflected the sun and caused the "eyes" to gleam, and this would have resembled shining headlights.

According to *The Population of the Valley of Teotihuacán* by Director of Anthropology Manuel Gamio in 1922:

> "...about the wonderful history of the people of Teotihuacán, the visitor will be greatly impressed on examining personally the gigantic pyramids, and wandering slowly through the majestic ruins bathed in golden sunlight under a deep blue sky... He will stand amazed before the multicolored mythological monsters raising their undulating plumage and inspiring a shuddering awe with the fixed and penetrating look of their black eyes of shining obsidian."

> "Inlaid obsidian chips represent the eyes of the mythological figures represented thereon in sculpture."

The ancient city of Teotihuacán where this image was found is near Mexico City. Teotihuacán was one of the most important cities of its era, and yet we don't know who built it, although the Toltecs are a top contender.

Most of the city was laid out in 150 B.C. The temple with its vehicle-like Jaguar God was completed by 200 A.D. The central part of the city, where the elite class spent most of their time, was destroyed by fire in 750 A.D.

The Oxford Companion to Archeology, edited by Brian M. Fagan and published in 1996, states that *Teotihuacán* means "Place of the Gods" and that the name was given by the Aztecs who came later, so the gods must have lived in this city.

200 A.D. — that's when the builders finished a stone temple decorated with images that looked like vehicles — in a city that was under construction even before Christ was born. In other words, the gods who are associated with the vehicle images are contemporary with the era of Jesus Christ. And... the vehicles were depicted over 1500 years before we invented automobiles!

WHO WERE THE GIANTS?

The Nahuan people define the word "Tolteca" to mean artist, artisan, or wise man, and they believed that the Toltecs were the originators of all civilization, even though other cultures such as the Olmecs existed before them. "Toltecness" meant art, culture, and civilization. If a ruler could assert Toltec ancestry, it strengthened his claim to power.

The Aztecs described Toltec buildings and palaces as being built of gold, jade, turquoise, and quetzal feathers. The Toltecs were skilled in the arts of jewelry, metallurgy, and pottery, so much so that their potters were said to have "taught the clay to lie." The artistry of their murals has been compared to the Renaissance painters of Florence, Italy.

The Toltecs produced abundant maize crops, and naturally colored cotton of red, yellow, green, orange, scarlet, violet, black, grey, white, and blue, according to several sources including *The Native Races of the Pacific States of North America, Volume III*, by Hubert Howe Bancroft in 1875. If you're thinking this is just some tall tale of our imaginative ancestors, the United States International Trade Commission mentioned it in their 1995 publication on the *Andean Trade Preference Act*:

> "A promising alternative is a variety of cotton, said to have been developed by the Incas, that naturally grows in tones of beige, brown, purple, red, green, and blue. The plant has been dubbed 'ecological cotton' because it makes artificial dyes unnecessary... It has been grown by 600 peasant farmers in a 2,500 hectare area of the central Huallaga region of Peru."

The Toltecs existed long before the Incas — did the Toltecs introduce this natural-colored cotton that the Incas are credited for? Inca legend claims that the Incas were originally cave-dwelling cannibals until the god Manco-Capac came and lifted them out of barbarity. He instructed the savage cave-dwellers, much like the Grigori instructed humans. In the chapter, *19th Century Stone Age Giants*, you'll meet a Stone Age tribe of giant cannibals that lived in 1500s and even into the 1800s, who apparently never got the memo.

The Toltecs built pyramids, manufactured obsidian blades and arrowheads, and they had workshops that were capable of mass production. They were also warlike, with powerful armies.

Archeologists are still trying to determine which region the Toltecs ruled, and where their cities were located. Evidence of their civilization extends all the way down through Central America and into South America, including Ecuador and Peru, where they may have influenced the Incas, according to *Mexico: Its Ancient and Modern Civilisation* by Charles Reginald Enoch in 1909. Is it possible that they were brethren of Manco-Capac?

As legend goes, the Sun sent his "children" down to help the savage humans who practiced cannibalism, and who sacrificed human victims to gods who were gross like themselves. The bearded Manco-Capac was his son and emissary, and a teacher of men. Manco's sister was sent down as well.

Quetzalcoatl, the primary god of the Toltecs, was described as "a white man of a foreign race, with noble features, long beard, and flowing garments." Quetzalcoatl forbade the sacrifice of both humans and animals. He lived among the people for awhile, and then he left, promising to return.

We get a deeper look at this enigmatic person in *The World's History, Volume I*, edited by Dr. Helmolt in 1901. Quetzalcoatl arrived in northern Mexico by boat, with a few companions. "To the naked savages… he was a marvelous apparition, a figure clothed in shining raiment, and wearing a beard, an appendage unusual among the natives."

Prior to his arrival, the natives were "wandering huntsmen" and he taught them agriculture, weaving, writing, worship, and the calendar. He abhorred human sacrifice, contrary to the many who engaged in such bloody worship in his name. If the Incas prior to Manco-Capac were practicing human sacrifice, is it possible that sacrifice was the norm prior to the arrival of

WHO WERE THE GIANTS?

Quetzalcoatl, and that it was just too ingrained to fully put an end to, as the legends suggest?

And who were these Toltecs that the Aztecs held in such awe? There were so many conflicting legends. The Aztecs believed that the Mayans were Toltec, and the Mayans believed that the Toltecs were Nahuatl. We believe that Toltecs built Teotihuacán, and we're certain that they built the city of Tula or Tollan which means "place of reeds."

If Teotihuacán was built by the Toltecs, it would move their origins back from 544 A.D. to 150 B.C., and it would tie in with the extraordinary legends that surround them. At its height, Teotihuacán was the sixth largest city in the world. Its name has also been interpreted as the "place where gods were born" or "place of those who have the road of the gods."

Teotihuacán had multi-family, multi-level, residential apartment complexes to accommodate the influx of people who migrated there, and each ethnic group had its own segment of the city. One estimate puts the population at 250,000 people in a city of just 12 square miles. To put this in perspective, Jersey City, New Jersey had a population of 247,597 and a size of just under 15 square miles of land in 2010.

We're still exploring the city of Teotihuacán and its pyramids. In 2005, a 330 foot long tunnel was discovered underneath a pyramid. Oddities were found in the tunnel which included hundreds of small, yellow spheres of unknown purpose. They were made of clay covered with jarosite, which would have originally shone with a brilliant luster. Jarosite is pyroelectric, which means that that it can generate electricity.

Teotihuacán boasted the Pyramid of the Sun, and Pyramid of the Moon. It offered separate areas for housing, temples, marketplaces, and a palace. Both the temple and palace were attributed to the god Quetzalcoatl.

We don't know what happened to the residents of this city. The buildings that were associated with the ruling class were sacked and burned, which suggests that the people rose up against the rulers. Another theory is that the city was invaded by enemies. Or perhaps the rulers just up and left, similar to what happened in the city of Mycenae, Greece, and the destruction that followed came from the people that were left behind.

If Teotihuacán was indeed built by an extraterrestrial race, maybe they went back to wherever they came from, leaving humans to our own devices. When the rulers of the Mycenaean civilization in Greece disappeared, in roughly 1100 B.C., Greece was plunged into the Dark Ages. Palaces were abandoned or destroyed; all vestiges of government vanished; and the culture went backward. Simple, barbaric pottery replaced the ornate pottery of the previous era. Did Teotihuacán suffer the same fate? Did the gods come down all around the world, pull us out of savagery, teach us what they could, and then leave us to carry on?

According to *Historical Data from Ancient Records and Ruins of Mexico and Central America* by Louis Edward Hills as published in 1919, Quetzalcoatl was a bearded, white man. Elsewhere, he was described as a bearded, white, holy man, who traveled the lands teaching a path of virtue and justness. His teachings were not well received, and he predicted that a great calamity would befall the people, but that he would someday return to a better reception.

Hills' book stated that the Pyramid of Cholula, which is within 100 miles of Teotihuacán, also existed before the Aztecs, and that it was built by a race of giants. The giants were descended from survivors of the Great Deluge, and one of them was named Xelhua.

Xelhua was one of seven giants in Aztec mythology who escaped the Great Deluge by climbing to the top of one of Tlaloc's mountain abodes, where the Quiname giants hid inside caverns. After the waters subsided, Xelhua built a pyramid in Cholula as a memorial to Tlaloc, but the gods did not want this pyramid built, and they hurled fire at the pyramid, killing scores of workmen. Work on the pyramid was discontinued.

WHO WERE THE GIANTS?

This event — the attack on giants who attempted to build a pyramid — took place right around the same time that a giant race known as the Quinames were being defeated. Think back to the biblical story of the Grigori city of giants being blasted from the skies with fire, naphtha, and brimstone. Halfway around the world, gods were also hurling fire at the Cholula pyramid to stop its construction... Coincidence?

Hills' book states in no uncertain terms that evidence of three distinct races had been found in the Valley of Mexico: Aztec, pre-Aztec, and primitive, and included bones that indicated a race of giants. He surmised that the giants were one in the same as those who'd built Tula, Cholula, Teotihuacán, and Mitla, and that these giants were the biblical giants who'd been ousted from their lands. He also equated them with the Toltecs, and Bochica, whose legends are in the *Stone Age* chapter.

The giant Xelhua had five brothers, each of whom founded nations. His brother Tenuch was the ancestor of the Aztecs — does that mean the Aztecs were descended from giants? Or did they just worship giants? Quetzalcoatl was Xelhua's half-brother.

The Quiname giants were a powerful race, who had enslaved the Olmecs long before Cholula or Teotihuacán were built. They were brutes. They ate the raw meat of animals and birds, which they hunted indiscriminately. They ate fruits and wild herbs, because they could not be bothered to cultivate any other food for themselves. They did, however, manufacture an alcoholic beverage known as pulque, which comes from the agave plant and looks like milk. This was a beverage allowed only to the gods, nobility, and priests, and as a very rare gift to a commoner.

The giants ran around naked, with their hair disheveled, and got drunk on pulque. They were a cruel, yet proud race, and they received the Olmecs cordially at first. Perhaps they were congenial out of fear, because they were vastly outnumbered.

The Olmecs were initially treated well, although they looked on the giants with terror. Once the giants realized how afraid the

Olmecs were, they took on the role of lord and master, granting a great favor by allowing the Olmecs to live there. In repayment, they expected the Olmecs to serve as slaves, and provide the giants with food. They relied on their new "servants" for subsistence.

The Quiname giants had another vice as well — sex. They refused to take Olmec women as wives because what they really wanted was to commit sodomy, according to *The Native Races of the Pacific States — Primitive History, Volume V,* by Hubert Howe Bancroft in 1882, though it wasn't clear whether they were sodomizing each other, or the Olmec men, though one might surmise the latter. The Olmecs went out of their way to offer up their daughters, *and their own wives*, to the giants, but the Quinames refused them. You don't go offering your wife unless it's an act of desperation.

I'm going to go out on a limb here, as this issue of sodomy has come up in several giant legends. The Grigori giants got in trouble for coveting women, and begetting children. The biblical city of Sodom was associated with giants, and it was destroyed. Is it possible that the giants switched to sodomy in order to circumvent the issue of producing offspring? To prevent women from dying in childbirth? Or in hopes that their brethren would allow them to live, instead of killing them off, but it didn't work?

The Olmecs decided to rid themselves of these oppressors, so they played a trick on the giants. They invited the giants to a sumptuous feast of food and alcohol. Due to their unrestrained appetites, the giants ate and drank until they were "stretched senseless like so many blocks of wood on the ground." Once laid out, the Olmecs killed them.

The demise of the Quinames is dated sometime between 107 and 299 A.D. This puts them in the same time frame as the Fomorian giants, and except for the sodomy, nakedness, and being disheveled, the description is much the same. They did not produce anything for themselves — they took from the labors of others, and even enslaved others to produce for them, just like the Nephilim giants, and the Fomorians giants.

WHO WERE THE GIANTS?

The historian Oviedo believed that the Quiname giants of Mexico were identical to the race of giants that lived near the southernmost tip of South America around the Strait of Magellan. Other historians equated them with a race of giants in Peru who were "destroyed by fire from heaven."

The Royal Commentaries of Peru by Garcilasso de la Vega in 1688, gives us one of the most chilling accounts of giants, because if it accurately reflects history, it answers many of the open questions from other giant legends. It also gives an alternate view on why the giants are extinct.

Garcilasso was the son of an Incan princess by a Spanish conquistador, and he was raised on the legends of the Incas. Garcilasso's version comes straight from the oral traditions of the Incas, which refers to Peru although it may include portions of Ecuador, as the divisions in those days did not match today's.

Several giants arrived on a ship and landed at the Cape of St. Helen near Puerto Viejo, in Peru. They were "men of an extraordinary size," with eyes as big as saucers peering out from big heads. Long hair hung down to their shoulders, and they may have had hairy bodies because some "were naked, and without other covering than long hair, which nature had given them." Others were clothed in animal skins. Whatever the hairiness, it did not extend to their faces because they were beardless.

They were giants of the biggest variety, with an ordinary man standing about knee high against them. As preposterous as this sounds, we know that legends and bones support giants of up to 15 feet tall. Compare this to the size of an average Peruvian. One report gives an average height of 5 feet 5 inches for Peruvian men, and just under 5 feet for Peruvian women, as of 2005. A person of 5 feet tall would stand just a little taller than the knees of a giant 15-footer.

After landing, the giants "consumed the whole country," eating up all the food until it became scarce. So far, this matches all of the other giant legends, including the Nephilim of the *Bible*.

Then the Peruvian story diverges to give details about the mating habits of the giants.

They brought no women with them on the ship, so they did not have access to women their own size. That left the native populace, which was a third their height, and they killed the local women in an attempt to have sex:

> "They lived with great abhorrence, and in ill correspondence with the people of the country, for their women, they could not use without killing them."

The giants were too big for the native Peruvians to fight, and they despised the giants for eating up all the food and killing their women. Then the giants took it to a whole new level, and this was just too much for the men to handle. The giants began to sodomize one another in public, for all the world to see:

> "Some years being passed, since these giants resided in those parts, and having no women fit for them, with whom to couple for propagation of their race, their numbers began to diminish. And [being denied] the natural use of women… they burned in lust one towards the other, and used sodomy publicly in the face of God, and the Sun, without shame or respect one to the other…"

That became their downfall. Without women, they couldn't spit out baby giants, and they started dying out as a race. Apparently they weren't dying out fast enough, because the locals were pleading with God to rescue them from these giant tyrants and their yoke of oppression. You can imagine the scene — all the food gone, your women brutally killed, giant men having sex with one another in public, and you thinking that you're next up in this act that will kill you.

God heard the cries of the frantic men and came to the rescue, in a scene reminiscent of the destruction of the biblical cities of Sodom and Gomorrah:

WHO WERE THE GIANTS?

> "...there issued a dreadful fire from Heaven, with great noise and thunder. Immediately an angel proceeded from this flame, with a glittering and flaming sword, with which, at one blow, he killed them all. And then the fire consumed them, leaving no more than their bones and skulls."

This sheds light on the unanswered questions in virtually every giant story told around the world. It explains why the Incas were so horrified by an act of sodomy, that they'd burn you alive along with your wife and children. They'd burn your house to the ground, and destroy every molecule you'd ever touched, as if somehow your possessions could bring you back to life, or cause someone else to travel the same road. They were reacting to the horrific memory of the Peruvian giants.

Garcilasso wrote about several tribes or cities in the same region, though he did not specify whether the others were giants. These other nations were naked barbarians, without laws or gods or civilization, and some lived in hollow trees in the mountains. They had no propriety in wives or children, and everybody mated with everybody, in public, including men with men. They allowed their hair to grow long and matted, never combing it, and never removing the straw or dust that clung to it. They did not cultivate land.

Among them were the natives of the province of Caranque, whom Garcilasso did not describe except to mention them by name, in the midst of all the other barbarians. Other texts describe the pre-Incan people of Caranque as a cannibalistic, barbaric, and brutish race.

Friedrich Hassaurek, who lived in South America for four years, wrote about how in ancient times, a race of giants conquered the Quitu people of what is now Ecuador in South America, in the 900s. As Hassaurek references Garcilasso, he is likely referring to the same giants. He called them a race of cannibalistic giants known as the Caras, or Carans, who came by sea, landed at Punta Santa Elena, and conquered the region.

They brought no women with them, and they:

> "...became so wicked that they were at last destroyed by fire from heaven. Certain ruins of a style entirely different from the architecture of the Incas... discovered in the neighborhood of Punta Santa Elena, are attributed to their Herculean efforts."

In the *Geography of Ecuador*, Villavicencio described a circle of thirty, enormous stone seats with arms, discovered on the summit of a mountain. *The Antiquities of Manabi, Ecuador* stated that many ancient historians believed in this race of giants, though the notion was later dismissed.

In other words, those who came later did not see the giants with their own eyes, so they ridiculed the tales. Even the discovery of massive, sculptured figures of the giants, and their stone seats, did not convince later historians. These seats were unlike anything else that had been discovered in North and South America, at the time of Villavicencio's book in 1858:

> "...each one of which is a sphinx, above which is the seat with two arms, all of stone, well worked, and of a single piece, which may be transported."

There was a table in the center of the circle, and columns of stone. Several seats were removed and sent to various museums including a museum in Guayaquil, and one to the Trocadéro Museum in Europe in 1882. Archeologists who came later found no trace of a circle of stone seats that matched the earlier descriptions. The only stone seats they found were inside houses, and thus Villavicencio's claim was dismissed. They did not entertain the possibility that people had taken the seats, which were out in the open for anyone to carry away.

The stone seats found in houses had crouching human figures supporting the seats, or crouching pumas, a bird or lizard, a bat, a monkey-like figure, or a copper disc. Some also had geometric borders. There is no way to know whether the original seats were moved to the houses, or whether the seats in the houses were simply copied from the originals.

As for the "fire from heaven," volcanoes are prevalent in South America, and it is possible that a volcano produced this "fire from heaven." It's also possible that the fire was extraterrestrial, as that seems to be a common theme during the era of giants, as demonstrated by the story of Sodom and Gomorrah, Cholula, and the evidence of vitrified forts in Europe.

The giants lived side-by-side with the Olmecs, and some historians credit the Olmecs with the invention of writing, the Mesoamerican calendar, the concept of zero, the compass, and the Mesoamerican ballgame. An artifact known as the Cascajal Block suggests that the Olmecs developed the earliest known writing system in the New World. Others believe that the tablet is a fake. The controversial tablet does not negate the other indicators of Olmec invention, however.

The Olmecs, who date back to 1600 B.C., are best known for sculpting a series of colossal heads. The heads appear to be wearing helmets, and are believed to represent Olmec rulers. *Laventa Colossal Head 3* resembles a modern-day football helmet from the side, and it is speculated that the helmeted heads represented ball players. Ancient astronaut theorists propose that the helmets represent astronaut headgear.

The bigger question here, is *who* do the heads represent? Do they represent the Olmecs themselves, or do they represent the Quiname giants who once ruled over them? If there is even the slightest possibility of extraterrestrial origin, as suggested by the helmeted heads, then knowing who they depict tells us which road to follow to unravel our extraterrestrial history.

Mesoamerica had Quiname giants, and 8,800 miles away, the Philippines had Quimane giants. Is this a coincidence? Or is it just another link in the chain of giant legends that all seem to overlap one another regardless of region, race, or religion?

As late as 1849 in the Philippines, in the province of Abra on the island of Luzon, there were wild tribes living in the mountainous regions. These "wild and generally unconverted and unsubdued tribes" included the Quimanes, Ibalos, Busaos, Igorrotes, and Tinguianes. They were all distinct from one another in both mannerisms and language.

Whether the Quimanes of Luzon were the Quimane giants of Philippine legend, the text didn't say, but giant legends, and the skulls of giant's heads, are both a part of Philippine lore.

In one tale of Spanish conquest of the Philippines and Molucca Islands, as soon as soldiers anchored the boat, a company of giants appeared. The giants called out and lifted their hands in the air to show that they were unarmed. The Spanish soldiers did the same. An ensign and four others went ashore, and the giants made signs for him to lay down his leading-staff. As soon as the soldiers were unarmed and on-shore, the giants withdrew to the place where they'd hidden their own bows and arrows. Ten soldiers went after one of the giants, and took him. The other giants attacked, and their arrows flew thick in the air. The Spaniards barely had time to get back to the boat, and the ship's steward was shot in the eye with an arrow.

The Spaniards did manage to capture one giant, which they described as "a giant even among the other giants." The giants were each above three yards high, and proportionately spread and brawny. That would make them taller than nine feet. This tale is related in *The Discovery and Conquest of the Molucco and Philippine Islands* by Bartholomew Leonardo de Argensola in 1708.

Argensola's book talks about Magellan discovering his namesake — the Strait of Magellan — at the southern end of South America. There he encountered giants above fifteen spans high, who ate raw flesh. A span is generally accepted as 9 inches, which makes the giants of Magellan a whopping 11.25 feet tall.

Another reference to giants is when captives on the ship began to weep in fear as they passed through a particular portion of the Strait of Magellan, because they were afraid of the giants who lived there.

Sir Francis Drake sailed the Strait of Magellan on his way to the Molucca Islands in 1566. After several stops they wintered in San Julián's Bay in Argentina. Crewman Thomas Haughton mutinied and Drake cut off his head. Here they saw eight giants so tall, that even the tallest Englishman looked like a dwarf. The giants killed two Englishmen with bows and arrows, and then fled so swiftly it seemed as if their feet didn't touch the ground.

Besides the Quimane giants, Philippine lore includes a sky god whose name in part is Adara, worshipped not only in the Philippines, but in the whole of Malaya of which the Philippines are a part. *Dêwa-pūn-tūrun-deri-adara* is listed in an 1812 Malayan dictionary as a deity who came down from the skies, and the reference breaks down as follows:

> Dêwa = deity, demi-god, goddess.
> Pūn = also.
> Tūrun = to descend, come down from.
> Deri = from, of.
> Adara = the air, atmosphere, or sky.

Another creature in the Malayan skies was the giant Garuda bird. Belief in this mythological "bird" spans several cultures and religions including Hindus and Buddhists, over 3,000 miles away.

The Buddhist Garuda is both a bird, and a divine being, with enormous wings that can span several miles. It can make itself small, or disappear at will, as if with a cloaking device. A Garuda bird can uproot a giant tree, level a mountain, or empty a lake. Garudas have their own cities, and kings, and they have the ability to take human form to have relations with women.

This does not sound like a bird — it sounds like an airborne vehicle that transports humanoids who dress in armor, and wear hinged headgear that resembles a bird, like the Native American thunderbird. Perhaps the aircraft is designed to resemble a bird, and indeed, one of its purposes is to transport others, such as Narai up to his heavenly palace, where Garuda rests on top of the residence like a helicopter on a helipad until he is needed again. The Garuda is also the vehicle of the Hindu god Vishnu.

THUNDERBIRD

Garuda is the Hindu name for the constellation Aquila, which is linked to the legends of the god Zeus and his giant cronies. Aquila is associated with a "giant eagle" that kidnapped the king of Troy and carried him to Mount Olympus — the realm of the giant gods who had access to spacecraft.

The Māori people of New Zealand also held Aquila sacred in their cosmology, and they called its primary star the *pillar of the sky* or *pillar of heaven*, while others called it the flying eagle.

Ancient legends often talk of human-animal beasts, with the body of a man and the head of an animal, and these beasts may be nothing more than a human wearing a hinged, animal-mask that opens to reveal the human inside, like the Native American thunderer, or thunderbird legends, which are represented pictorially with a hinged face mask or helmet.

Is there any connection between the Quimane giants and the Garuda birds that transported deities to and from Earth? We may never know, but there is another giant whose name starts with Q, and this giant takes us straight back to the biblical Nephilim and their ancestors.

Spellings included Qemants, Kemants, and Kamants, and they were descended from Anayer, the son of Arwadi the Arvadite, who himself was the son of Canaan. The *Bible* considered the inhabitants of Canaan to be the descendants of giants who were native to the region — pagan giants who had inhabited Canaan since the Great Flood.

Biblically the Arvadites were grouped with other races of giants including the Amorites, all of which practiced idolatry and were cast out of Canaan. The Arvadite giants who survived the cleansing ended up on the island of Arvad/Aradus off the coast of Phoenicia. Mount Hermon was also in Phoenicia, as was the city of Ashdod where some of the giants fled.

Aradus and Tyrus were two Phoenician islands whose architecture was different from their neighbors. Giants built the walls of Tyrus, which were perfectly fitted polygon blocks and checkered squares. It was the people of Tyrus who provided the materials for King Solomon's temple, and helped to build it. One of Solomon's temples honored the god Molech, as we saw in the chapter on the Fomorian giants who worshipped Molech.

These giants lived in solid cities of stone. When Moses originally sent spies into Canaan expecting to find tents, they found great walled cities such as Hebron, which was inhabited by the giant sons of Anak, called the Anakim.

Ezekiel described the city of Tyre, aka Tyrus, as having lofty houses surrounded by a 150 feet high wall, complete with watch towers. That's as tall as the Statue of Liberty, and a human standing next to Liberty is about as tall as her ankle, to give you a perspective. It would take thirty men of six feet tall, standing on each other's shoulders, to reach the top of the wall in Tyrus.

The giants of Tyrus taught men how to build huts and boats. The giant Chrysaor, whose parents lived on Tyrus, was the ancestor of the mighty Titans, another race of giants.

The Phoenicians worshipped Baal and Ashtaroth, both with ties to giants. The Amorites were giants, and Ashtaroth was not only a deity, but the name of the city where Og, the giant king of Bashan, lived.

According to *The Empire of the Amorites: Yale Oriental Series Researches, Volume VI* by Albert Tobias Clay, published by Yale University Press in 1919, King Og lived in Ashtaroth, and the Rephaim giants were defeated in Ashtaroth-Karnaim. Both Og and the Rephaim were giants. We're back to the giants of the *Bible*, which leads to the Malayan god Adara and his land of god-carrying Garuda birds.

In a text known as the *Onomasticon* which lays out biblical topography, written by Eusebius sometime before 324 A.D., two forts bear the name Ashtaroth, being nine miles apart, and lying in between the cities of Adara and Abila. Ashtaroth, the city of the giant Og, is six miles from the city of Adara. So Ashtaroth is both a city, and a deity, and Adara is both a city, and a deity, though the deity Adara belongs to a people thousands of miles away. Is it even possible that this city of Adara is connected in some otherworldly way with the Malayan god Adara? Or to the Adara deity of the Qemants of Ethiopia? The coincidences just keep piling up where the giants are concerned, and now we're about to connect Adara with Molech, the pagan god of the biblical giants and the Fomorians giants of Ireland, Scotland, the Hebrides, and Scandinavia.

The University Magazine and Free Review, Volume 1 edited by John Mackinnon Robertson in 1894, suggested that Adar was synonymous with Adar-malik or Adrammelech, which meant *Adar the prince*, and the Amarna tablets refer to *Adara*.

The Amarna tablets are a series of letters on clay tablets, sent between the Egyptian administration and its representatives in Canaan. In the second edition of Smith's *Dictionary of the Bible*, Theo G. Pinches says that *Adara* occurs on the Amarna tablets as a by-name of the Babylonian/Sumerian god Hea, and he proposes an original Adara-milku, which means *Adara, lord of counsel*. However, the Hebrew scholar Heinrich Wilhem Gesenius suggests that Adrammelech is simply a contraction of Adar-ha-Melech which means *splendor of the king*, or, *splendor of Molech*.

In the city of Sepharvaim, people sacrificed their children to the gods Adrammelech and Anamelech; but Babylonians had no such deities, or fiery human sacrifices. This was the ordinary form of worship for the pagan god Molech, and it takes us straight back to the Nephilim giants who worshipped the god Molech with human sacrifices. These giants span the entire world, with connecting threads from even the remotest regions.

It was the Molucco Islands where giants attacked a Spanish boat, and these islands are part of the Malay Archipelago where the Quimane and Adara legends exist. Molucco has multiple spellings, just as Molech did, and one of them is Maluku.

A History of Modern Indonesia Since c.1200 by Merle Calvin Ricklefs suggests that *Maluku* is derived from an Arab trader's term for the region, Jazirat al-Muluk, which means *the land of many kings*. Muluk is cognizant with Melech, Molech, and Moloch — three names associated with giants.

Is it possible that the giants of Molucco, aka the Molucca Islands, were related to the giants who worshipped Molech, as the connections suggest?

Mound Builders

Another race of giants came from North America, and they left behind evidence as compelling as the Nazca Lines of Peru, which boast zoomorphic shapes that can only be seen from above such as monkeys and hummingbirds. They predate the Native Americans, and lacking a better name, they've been dubbed the *Mound Builders*. One Mound Builder site was found in Georgia, along with giant mummies.

A Standard History of Georgia and Georgians, Volume 1 by Lucian Lamar Knight in 1917, described a series of mounds surrounded by a deep moat, which was filled by the tide of the Etowah River. The moat varied from 15 to 40 feet wide. Two reservoirs form backup holding tanks, about an acre square and 30 feet deep, that held enough water to fill the moat if the feeder streams ran dry.

Knight marveled at the moat which enclosed nearly 50 acres of land — an obstacle that would hinder enemies. The site has seven mounds, and the largest and most impressive was not built by the known hunter tribes of the Etowah region. Figurines excavated from the mounds do not in any way resemble Native Americans, nor is there evidence that the Mound Builders had anything in common with the Native Americans who followed. They were a race unto themselves.

The central mound is quadrangular. It stands 80 feet taller than the surrounding valley, with an apex diameter of 225 feet east to west, and 222 north to south. The top is nearly flat, and in other discoveries of flat-topped mounds, buildings existed on top. These Georgia mounds became known as the Etowah Mounds.

One Etowah mound was excavated by the Smithsonian, and underneath they discovered a vault, covered by a layer of large flagstones. The flagstones had been dressed by hand, showing that the men who quarried the rock understood their business.

Inside the vault was the skeleton of a giant, though it was one of the shorter giants at only 7 feet 2 inches tall. He had coarse, jet black hair down to his waist. The skeleton was well preserved, and several other skeletons were found nearby. The bodies had been prepared similar to mummies, and the flagstones bore carved inscriptions.

WHO WERE THE GIANTS?

Who were these Mound Builders that mummified their dead? Were they the giants of Native American legend, of a race that predated their own? For awhile, the two cultures lived simultaneously, and in some cases, the giants became teachers and peacemakers, such as Hiawatha. Unfortunately, the Europeans who wiped them out did everything in their power to erase every vestige of their lifestyle, legends, religious beliefs, traditions, and history. In doing so, they erased much of what we might have learned about the giant Mound Builders.

Illinois had mounds as well. The Kincaid Mounds of Illinois were also built in the shape of flat-topped pyramids, with houses on top, and steps leading up the side of each mound. The houses were built with vertical posts, lashed to create a lattice. The lattice was then woven with reeds and grasses, and covered with mud plaster. Finally, the plaster was covered with woven mats inside and out. The finished walls were a foot thick — enough to keep the house cool in summer and warm in winter.

The roofs had rafters, a lattice, and were thatched with grasses. They also had joists which created an attic in which to store corn. Furnishings included benches and beds. These mounds are dated at 1050 A.D., long after the reign of the Fomorians and Nephilim on the other side of the world, right around the end of the Teotihuacán culture.

The Fifth Annual Report of the Bureau of Ethnology, published by the Smithsonian, gave a height of over 7 feet tall for one Illinois skeleton. It was found in East Dubuque, Jo Daviess County, in a large mound. The "unusually large" skeleton was distinctly traceable when first found, but it crumbled to pieces immediately after the removal of the hard earth in which it was encased.

The Twelfth Annual Report of the Bureau of Ethnology provided an image of a stone coffin found in Jackson County, Illinois, on Hale's place. The coffin was 7 feet long and contained three skeletons. They are depicted as being almost as long as the coffin:

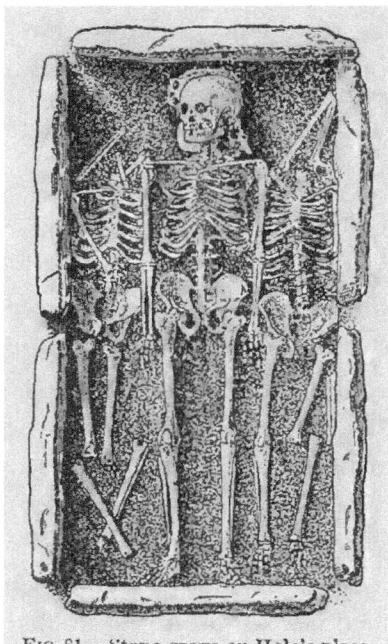

FIG. 81.—Stone grave on Hale's place.

    Carthage, Illinois, is the site of another "mountain" of giants, according to Volume IV of *Stone Magazine* of illustrated articles, published by The D. H. Ranck Publishing Co. in 1892. The skeletons were in all conceivable positions, and were of "unusual size." Their teeth were larger than ordinary human beings.

    The Great Serpent Mound in Ohio is dated at 1070 A.D., and it appears to be built for an aerial view, like the Nazca Lines in Peru. From the sky, the mound looks like a giant serpent of 1,370 feet long, coiling around like a sidewinder snake which culminates in a strange looking head. It is built on top of a plateau, inside of a meteorite impact crater. Nobody knows who built the mound.

    Another reptilian mound is the Alligator Effigy Mound, which is also in Ohio. It was charcoal-dated to 950 A.D. The image resembles a lizard, but the locals refer to it as an alligator. Scholars believe that it was intended to represent Underwater Panther, a fierce creature that lived in the water and ate people.

WHO WERE THE GIANTS?

Far to the south is Poverty Point in Louisiana, which is an odd name for this unusual earthwork construction. Poverty Point consists of mounds, along with a pattern of six concentric half-circles, divided by five aisles at various points. It is dated between 1650 and 700 B.C., making it one of the older constructions.

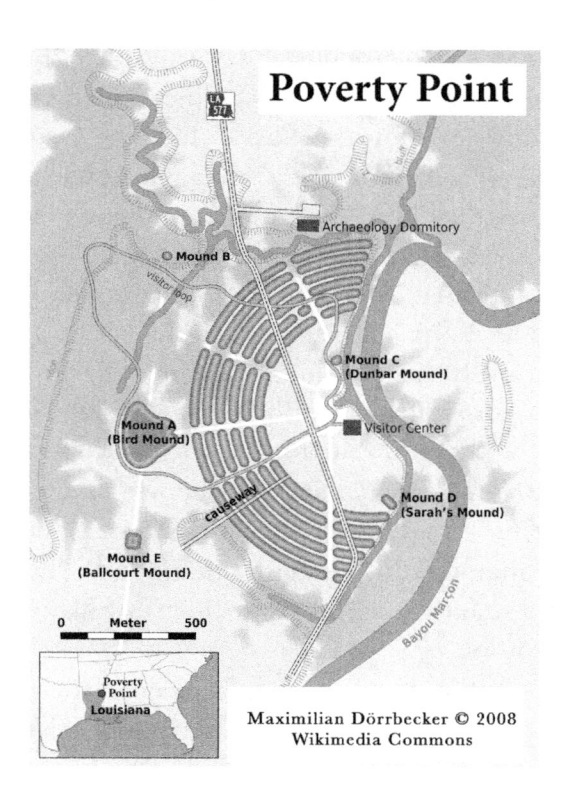

Maximilian Dörrbecker © 2008
Wikimedia Commons

The Mound Builder cultures include the Mississippian culture of the Southeastern United States, who was known for its flat-topped pyramid mounds with buildings on top. This culture, in turn, is associated with the Southeastern Ceremonial Complex (SECC) which has an interesting cosmology, with representations that resemble Norse cosmology.

The cosmological "map" of the SECC has three levels: an Above World or Overworld comprised of heavenly bodies such as the sun, moon, four stars, and thunderers. The Middle World is our Earth, which is Midgard in Norse mythology. Down below is the Beneath World or Under World, which is a cold, dark place. The three levels are connected by a cosmic tree, and each level has its own sub-levels. The beings that live in the various worlds are in opposition with one another, just like the oppositions among the Norse gods and their worlds.

The thunderers or thunderbirds were huge, birdlike beings in the heavens (Above World) who could emit lightning from their eyes, and from the "glowing snakes" that they carried around. They "thundered" when they flew, and created wind.

Sometimes they lived on a mountaintop, or on a mountain that floated in the sky. These thunderers could "shapeshift" into humans by tilting back their beaks like a mask, and removing their feathers as if the feathers were a blanket or garment. This sounds suspiciously like opening a helmet to expose the face within, as an astronaut might do, or an ancient soldier wearing heavy armor, and you've already seen a depiction of this entity and his face mask in the *Mesoamerican* chapter.

Thunderers could intermarry with humans, but woe to the human who attempted to enslave a thunderer. They would don their thunderer suit, which allowed them to take vengeance on the foolish captors.

Images of thunderers exist on ancient artifacts, such as a copper plate discovered in the Etowah Mounds near Cartersville, GA. The plate was engraved with a design "unlike any vestiges of ancient art yet discovered in America." This image matches the description given of the thunderer, with a bird-like mask covering a human-like face, a feathered blanket, and items in his hands.

Titans, Daityas, and Sumerian Giants

These are just a few of the giants that our ancestors feared, worshipped, or intermarried with. The Greeks had an entire pantheon of giant gods, known as the Titans. The lost island or continent of Atlantis was named for a second-generation Titan known as Atlas. The Mycenaean Greeks had a giant named Cronos who ruled over Elysion. Cronos is associated with a Golden Age of longevity, and morality, where everyone does the right thing and no laws are needed. If only Cronos ruled our world today! And don't forget the giant Hercules.

Hindus had the Daityas, a clan of giants so big that the stones on their jewelry were "the size of boulders." They are often associated with demons.

Sumerian texts gave us Gilgamesh and Humbaba, and the Sumerian *Epic of Gilgamesh* is a tale that mirrors several biblical stories up to a point, after which they diverge. Gilgamesh and Humbaba may have been fallen angels of the Grigori. They were associated with the constellation known as the Stars of Ea, and the Square of Pegasus. Whether this pinpoints their origin is an unanswered question about these ancient races. Scholars suggest that Gilgamesh reigned around 2700 B.C. That dates him after Sodom and Gomorrah, Goliath, the arrival of the Mound Builders, and the Fomorians, but before the Mesoamerican giants who terrorized the Olmecs, and the city of Teotihuacán.

Gutians

Following Gilgamesh were the Gutians, who also lived in Sumer. They were a barbaric, ravenous people, who may have descended from giants. They were pale-skinned, blond-haired, and they came into power in Sumer around 2150 B.C., several hundred years after Gilgamesh reigned. They raided Sumer in a series of hit-and-run guerrilla tactics, and crippled the economy. It was not safe to travel, or work in the fields, and this resulted in famine. Once they took power, civilization collapsed. They were terrible rulers, as they did not understand the complexities of running a civilization. They allowed the canals to fall into disrepair, which resulted in even more famine and death.

In 150 A.D., the geographer Ptolemy mentioned a tribe of Scandia that he called the Guti, which some scholars connect to the Gutones/Goths. If they were related to the Gutians, which is a matter of speculation, then they went by many names including the Geats. This inserts them into Norse legends, as Odin's semi-giant son founded the kingdom of Geats. The heathens of England considered Geat to be the son of a god, i.e., one of the original giants, which fits perfectly with Odin. The Jutes of Jutland may also have been Geats.

Ipsolini and Spali

In Bulgaria, there were Ipsolini giants, which were the second race to inhabit Earth, with humans being the third race. In other words, humans followed the giants, just like in the *Bible*, and the Americas, though none agree on the numbering.

The Ipsolini giants reached 9.8 feet tall and had huge heads. Sometimes they were represented as having only one eye. Their voices were so powerful that they could shout across the mountaintops. They lived in caves, and fed exclusively on raw meat, just like the other giants.

Some equate them with the Spali, a race who battled against the Goths, which suggests giants at war with one another. The Ipsolini giants were known by several names including Hellenes, dog-headed people, and blackberry people.

The Hellenes of Hellenic Greece come straight down from the Olympian giant Zeus, via his son Hellen with Pyrrha, which gives us yet another thread that strings together all of the giant legends. Bulgaria is sandwiched in between Greece and Romania, and it borders Turkey.

The Giants of Basque

Just over a thousand miles to the west is Basque, a region in between France and Spain, which has several giant legends. The giants of Basque lived in the hills, and were reluctant to convert to Christianity. Most kept their old ways and lifestyle. Their most outstanding feature was their strength. They were credited with building stone formations, ages-old megalithic structures, and dolmens. There are several varieties of Basque giants.

Jentil: which means "gentile." They were a pre-Christian civilization who built megalithic monuments. They were hairy, and so tall that they could walk far out into the sea, and throw rocks from one mountain to another. They were called the "stone throwers." They may have taken part in the defeat of Roland in the Battle of Roncevaux, where the Basques defeated the Frankish army by throwing rocks at them. These Jentil invented the saw, metallurgy, grew the first wheat, and taught humans how to farm. They were unwilling to move out of the mountains, and instead disappeared into the earth under a dolmen in the Arratzaren Valley in Navarra, when a portentous luminous cloud — perhaps a star — appeared, allegedly the same star that appeared for the birth of Christ.

Basajaun: a huge, hairy creature that lives in the forest. They protected flocks of livestock, and taught skills such as agriculture and ironworking to humans.

Mairu: giants who built dolmens, lived in the mountains, and were associated with Lamia/Lamiak/Lamina — a siren- or nereid-like creature. They were beautiful women who charmed men, and were believed to live underwater. If you left food for them on the shore, they'd eat the food and then finish up one of your chores such as plowing a field. They built bridges, at night.

They went away when men built small churches in the forest, somewhere at the other end of a rainbow, just like the rainbow-bridge wormholes. There were also males, who were strong and built dolmens at night. These males were the Mairu, which means *Moor*. In Spain, ancient monuments were attributed to the age of Moorish domination — the Moors being a remnant of old, pre-Roman deities. These deities could have been Celtic, Norse gods, Minoan, Mycenaean, or Greek — which means they could have been connected to several giants already listed. Pre-Roman inhabitants included Celtici, Gallaeci, and later Greeks.

King of Turan

Not all giants lived barbaric lives — some lived a life of luxury, such as the giant king of Turan. He was Emperor Afrāsīāb, and presumably, Afrāsīāb and his family were giants because in an epic poem, his son was described as being so big that ninety fur cloaks of skin could not cover his legs, which would explain the immense size of Afrāsīāb's fortress and the height of its walls.

The fortress of Hankana was a subterranean fortress, encircled in walls of iron, and brilliantly lit by its own sun, moon, and stars, all fashioned by the magic of King Afrāsīāb himself. It had no "frost of winter" or "heat of summer," like our homes today with their HVAC systems.

Hankana was immune to mortal attack. Its walls were one thousand times the height of a man, and they were supported by a hundred columns. Various histories put Afrāsīāb's longevity at either 400 years or 2,000 years, showing that he wasn't actually immortal as believed, but simply long-lived.

Macrobians

Another long-lived race were the Macrobians in the horn of Africa. The Macrobians were the tallest and handsomest of men, standing at nearly 10 feet tall. The Greek historian Herodotus, known as the Father of History, lived from 484-425 B.C., and he believed that the Fountain of Youth was in Macrobia, which means *Land of Longevity*. The concept of people living for a thousand years, how it was possible, and why it ended, is explored in the book *Ancient Aliens and the Lost Islands: Through the Wormhole* by Lars Bergen and Sharon Delarose.

Macrobian lifespans were counted in centuries rather than decades. Greek tradition speaks of a Hyperborean people called the Macrobii of Macrobia, who lived for centuries in a state of paradisiacal tranquility. Their lifespan reached 1,000 years by some accounts, and the historian Pliny stated that the shortest Macrobian lifespan was 130 years, barring accident or injury.

The Macrobians mummified their dead and encapsulated the bodies in hollow crystal pillars. The sepulchers, or tombs, were made in the following manner: The corpse, after being prepared as in Egypt, was covered in plaster, and painted with a likeness of the deceased. The mummy was placed in a case of native crystal, which they dug up in great abundance. It remained in this crystal coffin for one year, without any disgusting appearance or smell, at the home of the closest relative, who offered sacrifices to it. At the end of one year, the mummy was taken into the city and deposited with others.

Their Fountain of Youth had water that was so insubstantial in nature, that neither wood, nor anything else would float on its surface, but would instantly sink to the bottom. When you bathed in the water, you became shiny as if anointed with oil, and you smelled like violets. In Senegal, the natives used an oil that smelled like violets to prepare their food. It tasted like olive oil, and turned the food into a color more beautiful than saffron.

Macrobian weapons were powerful. A bow which the king of the Macrobians sent to Cambyses was so strong that, of all the Persians, only Smerdis, the brother of Cambyses, could bend it, and then only the breadth of two fingers.

Herodotus listed Meroë as the capital of Macrobia. There was actually a kingdom of Meroë, adjacent to the kingdom of Axum/Aksum, with a location that fits the descriptions given of Macrobia. It was quite a kingdom with hundreds of pyramids, and it was ruled by warrior queens.

Meroë has over 200 pyramids that we've excavated, so the legends are viable. The Kingdom of Meroë lasted from 300 B.C. to 300 A.D., and some of the pyramids date back to before the kingdom itself — to 720 B.C. Herodotus died in 425 B.C., so Meroë's association with the long-lived giant Macrobians predated the later Kingdom of Meroë.

All of these legends give us different pieces of the story, and they've given us a glimpse into the world as it was in the days when giants roamed freely. We've seen two very different sides of these giant humanoids: the first-generation giants who came down from the heavens as our teachers and mentors, who laid with our women to produce a race of human-giant hybrids; and the hybrid children who ended up terrorizing humans.

It may have been simple logistics, being so much bigger than us, and the competition for food. Their ugly nature may have been triggered by the food running out. If their parents were forced to leave, as with the Grigori legends, it would have left them without anyone to guide them toward a more peaceful path. We don't know how old the giants were when their parents were taken away, and no human could have successfully disciplined a child so big. Humans were in the process of learning, and we were sometimes described as savage ourselves, so we may not have been equipped to take on the role of parent or teacher of a species that towered over us. Or perhaps, the giants were just ugly in their nature — period. All we can do is speculate on what happened all those thousands of years ago.

One thing we don't need to speculate on is how big they were. Giant bones are one of the best-kept secrets, and as you read on, you'll find out why.

GIANT SKELETONS

Their size ranged from 7 feet tall, all the way up to 15 feet tall, and the difference is easily explained by the number of generations between the giants and their full-blooded ancestors.

Goliath

The biblical Goliath was "six cubits and a span" tall which is 9 feet 9 inches. He lived over a thousand years *after* the "giant-killer" flood by most accounts. He wore a bronze helmet, bronze greaves on his legs, and a coat of bronze, being scale armor that weighed five thousand shekels or 125 pounds. He carried a bronze javelin. Goliath's spear shaft was as big as a weaver's rod, and its iron point weighed six hundred shekels, or an estimated 15 pounds. Let me repeat — his *spear tip* weighed 15 pounds.

In other words, not including his helmet and leg armor, he carried at least 140 pounds of armor and weapons. Carl Netsch, a blacksmith in New Hampshire, calculated the weight of a full suit of iron armor and weapons as might have been worn in ancient Israel by an average man. His estimate: 60 pounds. Goliath's armor weighed more than twice that.

Goliath's brothers were giants as well, and his brother Lahmi carried a spear that was compared to a large pole on a loom, or a ship's boom.

For events and timelines in ancient history we rarely have a definitive date that we can pinpoint, and if you ask five historians, you will end up with five different dates for a single moment in history. The dates presented here come from various sources and unless they can be tied to a monument that's been carbon-dated, they are just estimates.

Proposed flood dates range from 2105 B.C. to "some time before 2500 B.C." not taking into account archeological dating for the flood which suggests a much older date. Goliath's death is somewhere between 1000 and 1500 years after the flood.

Fomorian Bones

The Fomorians, who lived both before and after Goliath, stood between 10 and 15 feet tall. Their shoes were longer than a human shoe by a whole foot. They were so tall that they had to stand in holes in order to work alongside a human, who stood only as tall as their waist based on historical descriptions.

However, giant bones have been found in Ireland, which was one of their strongholds. In Leixlip, Ireland, two laborers found a giant skeleton while digging a ditch to convey water in a churchyard. *The Dublin Freeman's Journal* of August 1812, said that the man could not have been less than 10 feet tall, and he was thought to be Phelim O'Tool who'd been buried there 1,252 years earlier. That would have dated the skeleton at 560 A.D., though there's no way to be certain that it was Phelim.

Another skeleton was found in Dysart, in County Louth, Ireland, according to *The Spokesman-Review* on April 3, 1914. The remains also indicated a height of 10 feet tall. Three skeletons were found that day, each in a separate grave, and each grave was encased with stones. The skull measured 18 inches from the top of the head to the bottom of the chin.

On December 11, 1950, an article in the *Lodi News-Sentinel* stated that an ancient burial ground had been discovered in County Meath, and that the bones were being studied by officials of the National Museum. Four mounds were revealed with subterranean passages and chambers similar to the world-famous caves at Newgrange, eight miles away.

The skeletons were dated between 1500 and 2000 B.C., based on artifacts found therein, which is in keeping with a Fomorian timeline. They also found evidence of a chamber that was used for cremations, so if these ancient people cremated their dead, it's a miracle that we have skeletons to find. While the actual size of the skeletons was not given in the article, a different article on the same discovery suggested that this might be scientific substantiation for the legendary race of seven-foot giants who inhabited Ireland before the dawn of history.

The discrepancy in size from 7-feet to 10-feet to 15-feet can be explained by generations mixing with humans, so that their children kept getting shorter and shorter as more human blood got mixed in. The Fomorians may have been around for 3,000+ years when the Meath giant died, putting him many generations after the original giants.

Today, you won't find many archeologists or historians holding up giant skeletons for all the world to see, or embracing a definitive YES that giants ever existed. In part, this is due to the loss of evidence which is detailed in its own chapter. It's also due to the devastation that such an announcement would inflict on our society as the age of giants pre-dates Adam and Eve. Just like the great UFO cover-up, there may be a similar cover-up relating to the extensive proof that's been hoarded away on the giants.

The evidence that we do have, however, is almost exclusively dated after 5000 B.C., which is, coincidentally, a date suggested by Robert Ballard for the flood. Using the Masoretic dates for the chronology of the *Bible*, and adjusting for Ballard's discovery, then several families of biblical giants lived both before and after the flood.

The Rephaim, Anakim, Emim, and Zamzummim giants all existed after the flood. The cities of Sodom and Gomorrah, where giants lived, were destroyed after the flood showing that the wickedness that the flood was supposed to eradicate survived, but here is where it gets interesting. Existing archeological monuments are dated AFTER 5000 B.C.:

5000	BC —	Great flood per Ballard archeology
4722	BC —	Fomorian giants, Ireland
4500	BC —	Mound Builders of North America
4000	BC —	Step pyramid, Sardinia, Italy
4000	BC —	Ceide Fields, Ireland
3500	BC —	Stonehenge, England
3200	BC —	Newgrange, Ireland
3100	BC —	Sumerian tablets
2700	BC —	The reign of Gilgamesh the giant, Sumer
2686	BC —	Step pyramids, Egypt
2630	BC —	Saqqara pyramid, Egypt
2584	BC —	Giza pyramid, Egypt
2150	BC —	Gutian giants, Sumer
2100	BC —	Ziggurat of Ur, Sumer
2000	BC —	Caral pyramid, Peru
1650	BC —	Poverty Point complex, USA
1600	BC —	Olmec civilization, Quiname giants, Mexico
800	BC —	Nubian pyramids, Nubia/Meroë
600	BC —	Hanging Gardens, Babylon
550	BC —	Temple of Artemis, Greece
545	BC —	King Ling of Zhou pyramid, China
484	BC —	Macrobian giants, Africa
466	BC —	Statue of Zeus, Greece
150	BC —	Teotihuacán civilization, Mexico

The little-known race of North American giants — the Mound Builders — predated even the great pyramids, and they give us some of the oldest archeological finds for an advanced race of giants. The Mound Builders left behind giant mounds all throughout North America, and we originally attributed the mounds to Native Americans but they pre-date Native Americans. Artifacts discovered in the Etowah Mounds of

Georgia included figurines that did not resemble, in any way, Native Americans, nor did the Mound Builders themselves have anything in common with the Native Americans who followed.

We often associate mummies with ancient Egypt, but several ancient peoples mummified their dead, including the Mound Builders of North America.

Mummies in the United States

Kentucky was known for its mummified giants, and they were not only giants — they had red hair. Remember the red-headed, cannibalistic giants that the Paiute called Si-Te-Cah? The Paiute lived in what is now California, Nevada, Oregon, Arizona, Utah, and Idaho — a long way from Kentucky.

The early settlers of Kentucky discovered mummies in caves, according to a *New York Times* article in 1874, which referenced a book called *History of Kentucky* by Lewis Collins, Judge of the Mason County Court, published by his son, Richard Henry Collins, after his father's death.

The mummified giants reached up to 8 feet tall, and they were found sitting inside cone-shaped recesses with their knees doubled up under their chins. Nearby was a variety of seashells which are found only in the Indo-Pacific which extends from Hawaii to the Indian Ocean. Collins' book gave heights between 7 and 8 feet tall with a jawbone so big that a 6 feet 4 man named John Campbell slipped a jawbone over his face, and his own jawbone fit inside the giant's jawbone, flesh and all.

Another postmortem book was published entitled, *Collins' Historical Sketches of Kentucky: History of Kentucky, Volume 1*. It described a mummy found in Mammoth Cave, Kentucky, in 1813. Keep in mind that these books were written by a judge, not some sensationalist tabloid rag.

The body was wrapped in skins and cloths, with the outermost layer being deerskin, followed by another layer of deerskin, this with its hair cut away by a sharp instrument. Next was a layer of cloth made of twine, doubled and twisted, but the thread did not appear to be made by a wheel, or the cloth by a loom. The warp and filling were crossed and knotted in a manner seen in fabrics of the Northwest Coast, and in the Sandwich Islands. The next layer was a mantle of cloth, similar to the previous but with long, brown feathers, arranged and fashioned with great art, and capable of protecting a living person from rain and cold.

The body was in a squatting position and estimated to be fourteen years old with sorrel colored hair. Sorrel can refer to a light reddish-brown, copper-red, chestnut, reddish-gold, or deep burgundy. Elsewhere his hair color was described as sorrel, fox, and dark red. Other mummies in both Tennessee and Kentucky had hair of brown, yellow, or red.

Then it went into a long diatribe suggesting that the hair changed color due to chemical influences in the atmosphere, and apparently, red-haired Egyptian mummies are given the same explanation. It's unthinkable that a race of red-headed giants might have existed, in spite of the multitude of legends that claimed they did.

According to Collins, the Kentucky mummies strengthened the legends of the Northwest Tribes, who believed that Kentucky was settled by Mound Builders with white skin, a belief that was echoed by several Native Americans, all of whom described the ancient Mound Builders as being white-skinned.

One theory assigned a Toltecan origin to the Mound Builders, and as the Toltec's evidence and legends are unique unto themselves, they are listed in the *Mesoamericans* chapter.

Other theories suggested that these early inhabitants were Mongolian, Malayan, Egyptian, Hindu, Tartar, Celt, Hebrew, Welsh, Polynesian, Viking, Greek, African, Chinese, European, the Lost Tribes of Israel, or the Atlantides, which are associated with the lost continent of Atlantis. Nobody wants to believe that the giants were a race unto themselves — even though they seemed to be one of the earliest peoples to arise after the flood, with historical accounts even before the flood.

Unlike the Kentucky and Lovelock mummies, which appear to be genuine, this next discovery is either an elaborate hoax or con, an elaborate cover up — or both. The drama unfolded just a few weeks after the Roswell UFO crash, and it was big enough to wipe UFOs right off the front page.

The discovery involved giant mummies, Masonic devices, remnants of dinosaurs and other extinct beasts, and prehistoric stoves that cooked using radio waves.

On August 5, 1947, this made newspapers around the country including the *San Diego Union*, *The Neosho Daily News*, *The Waco News-Tribune*, and the *Santa Cruz Sentinel*. News reports mentioned the Colorado Desert, the Colorado River, southern Nevada, Arizona, and Death Valley in California, so the cave system spanned three states, as the Colorado Desert refers to the Death Valley area and not Colorado.

Several giant mummies were found in a region that covered 180 square miles, and boasted no less than 32 caverns. Retired Dr. F. Bruce Russell of Ohio discovered the tunnels in 1931, although the discovery didn't go public until 1947 — the same year as the Roswell crash — and the mummies represented giants of 8 and 9 feet tall.

Russell, along with Dr. Daniel S. Bovee of Los Angeles, found the mummified remains and implements of a civilization that Dr. Bovee estimated to be 80,000 years old. These giants were clothed in medium length jackets, and trousers extending slightly below the knees. The texture of the material resembled grey-dyed sheepskin, but was assumed to be taken from an animal currently unknown.

In one tunnel they found the remains of several well-preserved animals including dinosaurs, imperial elephants, saber-toothed tigers, and other extinct beasts, paired off in niches as if on display. Was this an ancient museum? Another cavern boasted a ritual hall, with devices and markings similar to the Masonic order — devices that suggested an advanced civilization.

The spokesman for the expedition, Howard Hill, described the giants as wearing "a prehistoric zoot suit — a hair garment of medium length, jacket and knee length trousers... Some catastrophe apparently drove the people into the caves," he said. "All of the implements of their civilization were found, including household utensils and stoves which apparently cooked by radio waves." He added that he knew how unbelievable it sounded.

Hieroglyphics were chiseled on carefully polished granite, and the find was compared to what we'd expect from the Lost Continent of Atlantis. Several other witnesses described the caverns as "chock full of bizarre artifacts of all kinds."

Why haven't we heard of any of this today? Just like the Roswell UFO crash cover-up, this was believed to travel the hidden roads, though in a different direction. The bones and other artifacts were sent to the Smithsonian, which seems to be the burial ground for all such ancient finds in the United States. Allegedly the military took control of the region and secured all entrances to the tunnels.

The underground city and its tunnels had several entrances, one being in Wingate Pass, and the tunnels ran up into the Panamint Mountains. Once the government found out about the mysterious underground city, which would have been sometime in the 1930s, the area surrounding the tunnels came under the control of the military. This aspect of the story is easily verified.

In 1940, Fort Irwin National Training Center was built to the south, closing off a large portion of Wingate Pass Road. In 1942, Creech Air Force Base was built to the east, becoming a major military installation. In 1943, the Naval Air Weapons Station China Lake was built to the southwest, and there were several others, including... are you ready for this? — Area 51.

The Nevada Test and Training Range was established in 1940, and it encompassed a vast territory to the east/northeast of

Death Valley, and it's adjacent to another portion of the legend: Scotty's Castle, of Death Valley Scotty fame.

Death Valley Scotty was also known as Mysterious Scott and The Burro Man, according to *Mysterious Scott, the Monte Cristo of Death Valley* by Orin S. Merrill in 1906. He was a lavish spender, yet nobody knew where the money came from. Whenever he'd run low, he'd disappear for awhile, and then reappear with gold. He'd head into the mountains with his burros, as witnessed by other prospectors who were keenly interested in his movements. They'd see his campfire and then POOF — all traces of Scotty would disappear, "as if he had gone up in smoke."

When he came back out of the mountains, his burros were laden with ore. Some believed that he was robbing trains, as he'd been arrested for train robbery once. Others believed he was stealing the gold. It was alleged that he had a partner who disappeared one day, and Scotty was arrested for murder. There was never enough proof to convict him.

The known facts, however, were that he had an abundance of money, and that he made frequent trips to Death Valley and the Funeral Mountain Range. Coincidentally, *Wind Gate Pass* — the very entrance to the giant mummy caves found decades later — is mentioned in conjunction with Scotty's comings and goings. This pass, known as Wingate, Wind Gate, and Kingate, is now part of the military installations.

Volumes 32-33 of the *Los Angeles Mining Review* published in 1912, verify Scotty's legal troubles over a doctor bill for treating Scotty's brother. He was injured in Wingate Pass while frightening mining experts away from Scotty's "mine."

The *Outing Magazine, Volume 48*, published in 1906, quoted Scotty as saying, "Maybe I've got a mine and maybe not. Maybe it's on Furnace Creek, in the Funeral Range, Death Valley, and maybe it's somewhere else, and maybe I ain't got a cent." At the time he'd just come out of his secret hidey hole with a bag of ore. His prosperity was attributed to swindling a New York banker to invest in a bogus gold mine, which Scotty refused to divulge the location of, even to his benefactor.

Financial World, Volume 19, published in 1912, reported that Scotty had finally been outed. His wild spending sprees, his chartering a trip on a "special train" to New York to drink champagne on "other people's money" were nothing more than a ruse to attract investors. His alleged Death Valley Scotty Gold Mining Co. owned no mines, nor had it been sold for a million dollars. He confessed that he'd been paid $200 to sign a fake receipt. *The Los Angeles Mining Review, Volume 32*, added that the "inquiry into the mysterious business relations of Death Valley Scotty" showed Scotty claiming he had $25,000, and seven days later claiming that he had no money. A. M. Johnson, his wealthy financier, claimed that he'd never given Scotty a grubstake, and that Scotty had lied by saying he did. He had, however, paid Scotty a "salary" for work he did.

Mining and Scientific Press, Volume 105, published its exposé that same year. Johnson paid for the chartered train, and gave Scotty $5,000, with the expectation that Scotty would divulge information on his Death Valley mines. He'd receive another $5,000 on arrival, and would be given a substantial interest in the gold mining company they'd form. As Scotty had nothing to divulge, nothing happened.

Johnson, however, funded Scotty for several years, still believing in this gold mine and soon, another family named Girard got in on the deal and made payments to Scotty. These backers intended to send Scotty to the mines, with an armed guard, to collect "a ton of high-grade ore."

Their $15,000,000 corporation would issue shares of stock at $100 each. People will come crawling out of the woodwork when the $$$ signs flash headlines, and Scotty was dragged into court for some $1,000 judgement for "professional services." Scotty refused to divulge any information on money he'd received, and was committed for contempt. He finally admitted to several counts of fraud, stating that he'd never held more than $200 of high grade ore at one time, or acted as a go-between for high graders. He had, however, purchased high grade ore to use in his "grand-stand plays." He was officially unmasked as a con man, and yet his story did not end there.

Travel Magazine, Volume 31, published six years later in 1918, referred to the "sackfuls of rich ore" that Scotty toted to Los Angeles, and how he spent money "by the thousands."

In 1920, Scotty made news again. *The Salt Lake Mining Review, Volume 22*, posted that Scotty, who'd paid $50,000 for that fancy train ride but had more recently been working a regular job, quit the job to go back to his mysterious mine in Death Valley, where he declared that "he could recover his fortune."

Was Scotty a con man? Or did he have access to a vast, underground complex that was full of gold, in addition to mummies and artifacts? Did Amazing Explorations run a con as well, or had they genuinely found the mummies of giants, 8 to 9 feet tall, along with an entire underground complex?

The government usurped that entire area, including the entrance at Wingate Pass. Were they after Scotty's source of gold? Did they confiscate Amazing Explorations' mummies and artifacts? Or was this just an opportunity to divert attention from the Roswell UFO crash? Perhaps the government created the hoax to throw doubt on all of the other giant discoveries that had been made, such as the Lovelock Giant.

If Scotty was just a two-bit con man, why did his associate Albert Mussey Johnson start buying up land in Death Valley, between 1915 and 1927, long after Scotty had allegedly been "exposed" for nefarious dealings? Johnson acquired 1,500 acres, and later built a mansion in Grapevine Canyon that he named Death Valley Ranch. He called it a "gentleman's ranch" for rest and relaxation. Apparently he built another "ranch" for Scotty called the Lower Vine Ranch. This comes straight from the United States National Park Service website.

Scotty had always held his cards close, not wanting to file an official claim that would mark his gold mine on a map for all the world to see. The Death Valley Gold Mining Company, Inc. that never officially owned a mine was still in business in 1927, and this time, they were planning to mine for gold, and had set up the Skookum Mining District. Assays showed a rich source of gold, and by March 1927 they had a carload of ore ready for shipment.

Just when it looked like they'd hit the jackpot, they sold the assets of the Death Valley Gold Mines to World Exploration Company out of Texas, a company whose president was in and out of oil deals, real estate deals, and gold mining deals. Scotty's gold mine, or at least some portion of the land, was now in the possession of a company controlled by Chester R. Bunker and C.R. Lewis. According to an ad selling antique stock certificates from this mine, Goldfield broker Sol Camp, who was the manager of the mine, sold a controlling interest in the mine to Bunker for $100,000. Bunker started the mine back up and the prospects were excellent by fall of 1927.

In October, a large chunk of land was deeded to Albert Johnson by Bev Hunter, which appears to include, or at least border, the Skookum mine that Bunker was working. It appeared to have been a transaction entered into years earlier. One year later Bunker was jailed for fraud, and more deed transfers took place in that vicinity. All talk of gold mining vanished.

Not long after, the underground city enters back into the tale, according to *Death Valley Men* by Bourke Lee in 1932. Somehow Scotty's secret had gotten out, and every prospector in Death Valley had gone searching for it. At that point, Scotty admitted to knowing exactly where the underground city was.

Then two men claimed to have found an ancient, underground city in the heart of the Panamint Mountains, whose entrance was near Wingate Pass. They claimed that the city was a treasure house, a lost city of gold, bigger than any mine could ever be, bigger than the United States Mint. They'd been trying to get the treasure out for years, but they needed help and everybody they tried to partner up with wanted too big of a share. They allegedly offered the whole city to the Smithsonian Institute for $5 million dollars. This is not unprecedented, as the Dueling Dinosaurs of Montana were offered to the Smithsonian for $15 million in 2013.

The many fraud claims suggest a hoax, but you have to wonder about Scotty's access to gold, and his wealthy benefactor setting up shop even after the fraud allegations.

This underground city included caves, treasure vaults, council chambers, a royal palace, and galleries with stone arches. It also had gold statues, gold shields, gold spears, gold bars, bins of jewelry, gemstones, and mummies. It had some sort of lighting and cooking system that used natural gas. Gigantic doors of solid rock swung on hidden hinges, set up with some form of counterweight that allowed you to move the door with one finger.

They'd carried out some of the gold and jewelry, but the discovery was too vast. They allegedly convinced experts from the Southwest Museum to make the journey, but there'd been a wicked rainstorm and they couldn't find the shaft to get in. They'd only been there three times and of course, you don't mark something like that for others to stumble across.

In Bourke Lee's book, the men who "found" the city were Fred Thomason and Mr. White, and they shared the discovery with Bill Corcoran and Jack Stewart. The last anyone saw of Thomason and White was Bourke Lee himself, who saw them in the valley patching a tube for their car tire. The two men disappeared, along with White's wife.

Either Dr. Russell of the 1947 newspaper article was one of the four men using a fake name, or he read the story in Lee's book and adopted it, because he claimed to have found the shaft in the same way as the men who tried to sell it to the Smithsonian. Or maybe Lee used fictitious names to protect his sources, as might be expected.

Russell had a chance to explore more of the city, and measure the mummies, which is where we get the rest of the details. He succeeded in getting investors this time by showing them some of the artifacts, and then the underground city itself, and Amazing Explorations was launched. Was this an elaborate con to scam investors? Had they set up the underground city themselves, as some sort of exhibition to sell tickets to?

They issued a statement to the press, which is the newspaper story that appears on August 5, 1947. A live press conference was supposed to follow, where Russell intended to display one of the skeletons, and enough artifacts to convince even the most skeptical reporter.

He was supposed to deposit the investment capital at the Barstow bank, and retrieve the artifacts from the cave for the press conference, but he disappeared. His car was found with a busted radiator in a remote area of Death Valley, with a suitcase inside. Everyone thought he'd absconded with the money, even though it was a pittance compared to what was in the caves, and what they could make exploiting the discovery as one of the Wonders of the World. Of course there's always the possibility of robbery. Either way, Russell was gone, and the investors, who'd only been there once, could not find the entrance again.

Whether Amazing Explorations out of California had any connection to World Exploration out of Texas, isn't clear, but Chester R. Bunker was associated with the Texas company, and he was involved in several lawsuits over land deeds in San Bernardino County, California, where Wingate Pass is located.

In *Dickens v. Bunker: 169 Cal. App. 2d 383*, Bunker had agreements dated September 1, 1947, to buy land; and others dated 1952 to sell it on payments. He was apparently a middleman. When the payments were completed in 1956, he never turned over the deeds, because "there had been a sale to the state" by the owner, attorney Lester Peterman. *Marks v. Bunker, 165 Cal. App. 2d 695* was much the same. A big newspaper spread in 1951 which advertised the lots for sale, and named both Peterman and Bunker, links Bunker to "the development of this desert region since 1934" — or three years after the caves were found, north of his development.

The lots were in the southern part of the county, however, and not the mining district where the entrance to the caves was located. It does potentially link the mining company that took over from Scotty, and the big, public announcement about the underground city and mummies.

The military did indeed block off several areas that may have provided entrances, including the main entrance at Wingate Pass. The dates given for the three adjacent installations are 1940, 1942, and 1943 — several years prior to the 1947 newspaper article — but 11 years after the discovery of the entrance by men who allegedly contacted several museums and government agencies. So was this a hoax, or a cover-up?

Russell and Bovee had hoped to cash in on the underground city when they launched Amazing Explorations, Inc. This is verified in the files of archeologist Jesse L. Nusbaum, as mentioned on the National Park Service website. Nusbaum's résumé is exhaustive, covering his archeological travels through Mexico, Central America, and the American Southwest, and his name appears in the *Directory of American Scholars* in his day.

Nusbaum was the southwestern lead archeologist for the NPS, and his reports cover a period from 1920-1958. Of particular interest is what he labeled the *nut file*, which consists of a file labeled "Nut File" plus six folders labeled "740-17 Nut File." This file covers everything that Nusbaum investigated on the "crackpot" cases, and it included Amazing Explorations, Inc. Newspaper clippings, correspondence, and periodicals on each case were neatly categorized, including his replies to letters from anthropologists enquiring about a particular case.

Nusbaum's files also include the Lovelock Cave discovery, where it crosses paths with the *Native American Graves Protection and*

Repatriation Act (NAGPRA) — a law whose goal is to gather up all of the skeletons and artifacts that have been unearthed, and return them to their prospective tribes. Museums and other archeological depositories are expected to post an inventory of their collections, and items can be requested by the descendants. Tens of thousands of skeletons have been repatriated.

This law pits archeologists, anthropologists, ethnologists, and other scholars, against the descendants of unearthed skeletons. On the one hand, you have respect for the dead — on the other you have scientific study and the advancement of human knowledge. In the middle are the skeletons in a legal tug-of-war. NAGPRA gives agencies an ample reason to lie about their holdings, if it means the loss of prehistoric evidence that cannot be replaced.

All of North America was once divided into tribal lands, so each discovery correlates to the lands once ruled by a particular tribe. It puts the government in a pickle where giant bones are concerned. They aren't ready to acknowledge the existence of giants, and yet that's the only way to hang on to skeletons that clearly do not belong to a Native American tribe. They have to publicly declare those skeletons as not Native American.

Why would the government want to cover up evidence of giants? Simple. The original giants were extraterrestrial. They came down from the heavens, mated with humans, and begot human-giant hybrids. As time passed, the gene pool would have been diluted and later giants wouldn't have been as tall as their early ancestors, but the DNA of these giant skeletons might be the smoking gun of proof that extraterrestrials came to Earth, and we know how keen the government is on sharing that info.

As for Lovelock, this comes from a *Notice of Inventory Completion: Department of Anthropology & Ethnic Studies, University of Nevada Las Vegas, Las Vegas, NV,* for human remains and other objects collected from Pershing County where Lovelock Cave is situated, along with reports for several other counties:

GIANT SKELETONS

"In 1989, human remains representing a minimum of one individual were collected from Lovelock, Pershing County, NV, by the under-sheriff for that area (AHUR 120C). No known individual was identified. No associated funerary objects are present. Analysis determined that the human remains are that of a pre-contact or early historic Native American adult. No additional information is available regarding the circumstances surrounding removal."

These remains clearly have no relation to the Lovelock Cave excavation, with its plethora of mummies and thousands of artifacts. The single skeleton was found decades later.

Final thoughts on the Lovelock excavation were extracted from a publication by the Phoebe A. Hearst Museum of Anthropology entitled, *Lovelock Cave Formerly Known as Sunset Guano Cave (NV-CH-18).*

The report states that archaeological materials from Lovelock Cave were acquired by the museum over a 65-year period in 21 accessions. Some were excavated by L. L. Loud in 1912, some came from a private collector, and there were others. Apparently, there was a "joint claimant" to the cave, who prohibited excavations in his end, according to Loud and Harrington. The museum referred to Lovelock Cave as "one of the most important sites in the history of North American archaeology." They wouldn't make this statement unless Lovelock was indeed genuine, though it doesn't verify that giants were involved, only that ancient human remains were discovered.

Loud salvaged thousands of specimens relating to human skeletal material, and vegetal material, but he devoted less than a paragraph of detail in his published report. "Specimens" does not necessarily mean full skeletons — it can refer to pieces of a skeleton which need to be matched to other pieces.

The archeological specimens collected from the Lovelock Cave were divvied out to countless museums, and one of note was the Museum of the American Indian, Heye Foundation. This museum was transferred to the Smithsonian in 1989. The

Smithsonian, according to their own website, is not subject to NAGPRA, though they are subject to The National Museum of the American Indian Act (NMIA). Either way, remains of giants would not qualify for repatriation, not being an ancestor of the Native Americans.

So the underground city mummies give us a possible hoax, or a diversion from the Roswell UFO crash, or a giant cover-up, while the Lovelock Giant is most likely the real deal.

Calaveras Skull of California

This brings us to the next big-discovery-turned-hoax which also involved the Smithsonian — the Calaveras Skull. Nobody denied that the skull itself was genuine, but the entire story catapulted into the sphere of hoaxes simply because the giant skull was used to play a practical joke. The skull was planted in the mineshaft of a gold mine in Calaveras County, as a joke on Prof. Josiah Whitney, the head of California's geological survey.

Due to its location, the skull was thought to be millions of years old, as it was found among extinct plants and animals. As a prehistoric find, the skull was ground-breaking, but when they discovered that the skull did not exist millions of years before Adam and Eve, and that they'd been the butt of a practical joke — the skull itself was treated with derision.

Several people were involved in the find: miner James Mattison who found the skull; John Scribner, the store clerk who cleaned the skull; and William Jones, who received the skull after it was cleaned. Dr. William Jones, physician and natural history buff, sent the skull to Josiah Whitney.

Thirty years *after* the discovery, William Henry Holmes, an archeologist from the Smithsonian, traveled to Calaveras to investigate, and Holmes debunked the find. By then the skull was at Harvard's Peabody Museum, where the first-ever fluorine analysis was run on it. The skull was dated to 5,000 years ago instead of millions.

The jokesters confessed to their dupe, with store clerk Scribner being the one to plant the skull in the mine. The skull was originally found in Salt Spring Valley west of the mine. To further complicate the issue, the skull that was sent to Whitney may not have been the Salt Spring Valley skull, as the descriptions did not match. Somewhere along the way, the skull had been switched out, further supporting the hoax theory. Jones was so disgusted at falling for the practical joke, that he threw his skull into the street; then he had second thoughts and retrieved the skull.

Was it the skull of a giant? As there was a switch out, there's no way to know. The skull as it exists today does not suggest a giant, but the original skull was compared to other gigantic skeletons, so someone did believe it to be the skull of a giant. Whether that was also part of the hoax, or whether there was a skull that got spirited away by someone along the chain, us puny humans will likely never know.

So what happened to the Calaveras skull that we have today — the skull that is not a giant? In 1992, the skull underwent radio-carbon dating, which dates it to about 1252 A.D. — the beginning of the Medieval Inquisition in Europe. The skull was genuine and it lives at the Peabody Museum, at the Harvard University, in Cambridge, Massachusetts. Dating the skull at 1252 A.D., versus the original skull being fluorine dated at 5,000 years old, suggests that there was, indeed, a switch out.

Appletons' Popular Science Monthly, Volume 56, published in 1900, has an article about the Peabody Museum of American Archaeology and Ethnology, and the transfer of its property to the corporation of Harvard College. The artifacts and bones were used in teaching students about anthropology. Among the items transferred: the Calaveras skull and artifacts found with it, gifted to the museum by the sister of Professor J. D. Whitney. The package included all of the original documents that related to its discovery and history. It would represent the 1252 A.D. skull.

In a side note, the Mewuk Indians of the Calaveras region believed in a cannibalistic "stone giant" or "rock giant" called Che-ha-lum-che, who lived in caves and came out at night to hunt for food. His favorite prey: Humans.

He preferred to kidnap women. To lure a woman close, he'd make a crying noise like a baby. As soon as they were in range — BAM! They were his, to be carried off to his cave and eaten. He also ate dead people that others left behind, so the Mewuk burned their dead to prevent the bodies from being eaten.

Mound Builders of Georgia

According to a story in the *New York Times* dated April 5, 1886, the Georgia giants were 14 feet tall. This estimate was based on the length of two thigh bones found among acres of skulls and bones that were exposed after heavy flooding in Tumlin Mound Field. The find was described as a *mine of archeological wealth*, and as with similar discoveries, the Smithsonian arrived on the scene to collect the evidence. News of this amazing discovery spread like wildfire, reaching all the way around the world, even as far as New Zealand.

The Tumlin Mounds are now known as the Etowah Mounds, *Tumlin* being the name of the man who owned the land when the discovery was made, and *Etowah* being the name of the nearby river. Many news stories refer only to the nearest city, which is Cartersville, Georgia, so all three references point to the same region, and the same collection of giants.

The Antiquarian Magazine & Bibliographer, Volume 6, published in 1884, gave a height of 7 feet 2 for the famed giant that was found buried in a stone vault, while several other publications gave a height of 9 feet 2 inches. He was laid out carefully on top of animal skins, over a thick matting of reeds and dry grass. The underside of the heavy flagstone that sealed his vault from above was carved with inscriptions. This giant was thought to be a king, because his head was encircled with a copper crown. His coarse, jet black hair reached down to his waist, and he had no whiskers. The skeleton was remarkably well-preserved. The Smithsonian reports substantiate the shorter stature, as *Smithsonian Institution, Bureau of Ethnology, Issue 5* stated that the frame of the skeleton was heavy, and "about 7 feet long."

His bones, along with the rest of the skeletons and artifacts, were forwarded to the Smithsonian whose spokesperson declared it the most interesting collection ever found in the United States. The Etowah discovery was detailed in the book, *A Standard History of Georgia and Georgians, Volume 1*, published in 1917. The book was written by Lucian Lamar Knight, who was the Compiler of the State Records of Georgia. He wrote about mounds discovered along the Etowah River near Cartersville, mounds in the vicinity of Rome which also borders the Etowah River, and mounds in southern Georgia near the town of Blakely.

Other giants were found in Sea Island, Georgia — these also of the shorter variety. Archeologist Dr. Preston Holder gave heights ranging from 6 feet 5 inches, to 7 feet tall, for the giants whose bones were found in the sand dunes. They were uncovered while dynamiting to build an airport, which exposed several shattered skulls and skeletons. The Smithsonian Institute was called in, and they sent Dr. Ales Hrdlicka to study the bones. Hrdlicka was the first curator of the museum that became the Smithsonian, which was originally called the United States National Museum. Hrdlicka also founded the *American Journal of Physical Anthropology*.

Another witness to this find was Dr. F. M. Setzler of the United States National Museum, who took part in the dig after the others sent word out of this amazing discovery. The arrival of so many indicates that this find was genuine, else the original archeologist on the scene would have prevented the others from wasting their time.

Holder commented that "this fellow couldn't fit into a motor car." The evidence in one mound convinced Holder that the site was a temporary camp rather than a permanent village. The mound was composed of three layers of shell, each layer being six inches to a foot thick, separated by layers of clean sand from one to three feet thick. There wasn't enough domestic garbage in the shell layer to suggest a village.

A skeleton of six and a half feet tall was determined to be a teenage male, presumed to be the son of a chieftain, or even a chief himself. Great care had been taken with his burial which included several artifacts: three small bone awls, three large deer-bone awls, three split bones in the process of becoming tools or weapons, four mussel-shell pendants, a chipped stone spear-point, and a string of approximately 80 seashell snail beads. One skeleton wore an apron woven of 225 olivella seashells.

Some skeletons were found curled up with their knees under their chins; others were found with a coating of red hematite pigment. From the arrangement of the burials, archeologists concluded that this was a popular fishing hole, and that if a fisherman happened to die, he was buried on-site. A nearby village yielded tribal pottery and cooking utensils, turtle shell pendants, and bear's teeth.

They also found "bundle" burials, where dead bodies are exposed in trees or temples until they decompose, and the remaining bones bundled together in mass graves. Our ancestors couldn't have predicted how interesting their bones would be to later generations, else maybe they'd have taken greater care.

Swamp Giants and Cannibals

As recently as 1877, based on the initial estimates, giants roamed the swamps of Florida, and they lived on shell foods which they cracked with their teeth, according to archeologists who unearthed a burial ground on a gulf island. The bones were believed to be of the "Garib" tribe, native to the West Indies. The skulls, many of which were battered and crushed, were larger than ours today, as were the body bones, indicating that

GIANT SKELETONS

they were "veritable giants." Their bones were sent to the Smithsonian Institution. This story appeared in the *Lawrence Journal-World* on August 5, 1927.

Today we list two tribes of a similar name: Carib and Galibi, so they were likely referring to one of those, though neither tribe today would be considered giants. However, a Spanish explorer named Alonzo de Ojeda discovered what he called an "Isle of Giants" on a voyage in 1499. He found the Caribbean West Indies island of Curaçao, according to the book *The West Indies* by Amos Kidder Fiske, published in 1899. A 1907 book entitled *Amerigo Vespucci* sheds additional light on the giants. Vespucci was a Florentine merchant who joined the 1499 voyage to seek his fortune in the New World.

According to Vespucci, they stopped at Maracapana where natives offered food and assistance in the hopes of gaining favor. The natives pleaded with Ojeda to rid them of a tribe of ferocious cannibals who were plaguing them. The cannibals lived on a distant island, and they regularly raided coastal regions. Their mission: kidnap whoever they could get their hands on, and carry them off to be eaten. Ojeda agreed to help, and sailed for seven days to reach a chain of islands which were believed to be the "Caribbee Islands."

A great battle ensued, and once they were refreshed and recovered from their wounds, they sailed to Curaçao where they found giants: "every woman appearing a Penthesilia, and every man an Antei." Greek mythology lists *Penthesilia* as being a queen of the Amazon warrior women. Antei, or Antheus, was a giant who did battle with Hercules. After a dangerous encounter with the giants, Ojeda and his men retreated, and went on their way.

Later historians couldn't figure out which port he referred to as *Maracapana*, but assumed it to be current-day Barcelona, Venezuela. A different chapter in the Vespucci book expanded on the run-ins with both the cannibals and the giants, and it gave a slightly different version of accounts. Apparently they'd encountered the cannibals independently of the harassed coastal natives, and the cannibals were quite friendly. They were naked, and did not eat one another, but took their canoes to the islands or countries of their enemies, and captured their "meals" from the ranks of enemies. They rarely ate women.

The ship left the island of cannibals and encountered more friendly villages, and then they sailed farther away into regions where people became unfriendly and attacked them. They fought a great battle and were about to give up, but one Portuguese sailor spurred them on to victory. They slaughtered the natives and burned their homes, and that's when they rested and healed their wounds.

From there, they sailed to an island which at first seemed deserted, so eleven of them landed and walked inland. They came to a village with twelve houses, and met seven women who were no less than "a span and a half" taller than the sailors. A biblical span represents 9 inches, which indicates that the women were a foot or more taller than the sailors.

The giant women were afraid of the sailors, but they extended hospitality nonetheless. The sailors were plotting to kidnap two of the giant women as a present to the king, but 36 giant men arrived. The men "were of such great stature that each one was taller when upon his knees than [Vespucci was] when standing erect." They were armed with giant bows and arrows, and immense clubs. At that point, the sailors became frightened, but they conversed with the giants in the friendliest manner possible, and departed as quickly as they could.

Were these the same giants believed to have lived in the Florida swamps? Or were the giants in Florida kin to the giants in the neighboring state of Mississippi? Perhaps all three shared the same genetic seed, though they would have had to travel over 2,000 miles to reach Mississippi from Venezuela.

In January 1841, *The Polynesian* in Honolulu reported that a giant human skeleton was unearthed on the eastern shore of

Pascagoula Bay in Mississippi, along with the ruins of an ancient fortification built primarily of seashells. The skull was so big that it could fit loosely over a modern human head.

It was the first French settlers that made the discovery, according to *Besançon's Register of the State of Mississippi*. Also found were fire-coals, and fragments of a "peculiar" kind of earthenware. All evidence that may have shed light on the origins had long since disappeared by the time Besançon's report came out, but the tradition still lingered among the older French settlers that the fortification had been built by a tribe known as the Biloxies, "long since extinct."

The Biloxies were at war with a powerful neighboring tribe, and after many defeats were driven to the seashore where they built the seashell fortification. They were besieged until their supplies ran out, and when all hope was lost, they marched into the ocean and perished.

Like the fairies of ancient Ireland, strange music was often heard near the ruins — only in the summer on the most serene of evenings, and just after sunset. The music was melodious and sounded like several instruments playing in concert. Sometimes it seemed to come from the water, sometimes the air, sometimes it died out after a few moments, only to be revived with increased energy after which it played for hours.

The Biloxies, or Biluxies, called themselves the "First People" just as the Quiname giants were the "First Race." The early Europeans called the Biloxies by many names including Annocky, Annocchy, and Annochi. Is it possible that these "Annocky" giants of Mississippi were related to the Anunnaki deities of Mesopotamia, whose name meant "those who from the heavens came to earth?" The Anunnaki appear in the Epic of Gilgamesh, already mentioned with its race of giants. It seems that wherever you find giants, you find coincidences and a similarity of names.

Traditionally, the Biloxi tribe is not known for building fortresses like the one of seashells, so connecting them to the giants who did build the fortress may have been a European error. We just weren't familiar enough with the tribes to always get our facts straight.

The Pascagoulas believed that historically, a small tribe of Indians of lighter complexion, with different customs and manners, lived in the Pascagoula River region. These ancients "emerged out of the sea" and were a peaceful, kind race that spent their leisure enjoying public festivals. They built a temple where they worshipped the figure of a sea god whenever the moon passed from its crescent to full. They sang and danced and played instruments to celebrate their sea god.

When Hernando de Soto arrived in 1541 and destroyed Mobilla, a white man with a long, grey beard appeared to the sea god worshippers. He wore flowing garments and held a book in his hand, which he kissed over and over again, and he held a cross in his hand. He spoke of the contents of the book, and one night, the river rose up in mighty waves all along the channel, and on the crest sat a woman with magnetic eyes, singing. The robed white man, and the entire tribe of pale-faced Indians, rushed to the river to listen to the siren's mystic song.

One by one, the tribesmen leaped into the waters, and as soon as they were all in, a loud and exultant laugh was heard. The waters immediately returned to their normal level, leaving behind the white man, who died of grief and loneliness. This legend of 'Mobilla' comes from *History of the Choctaw, Chickasaw and Natchez Indians* by Horatio Bardwell Cushman, published in 1899. Mobile, Alabama is only 40 miles from Pascagoula, which in turn, is only 20 miles from Biloxi.

Mobile, Alabama is on the Gulf Coast, and up in the northern part of the state is Town Creek, Alabama, where archeologists discovered not only skeletons of above-average height, but evidence of cannibalism. *The 44th Annual Report of the Bureau of Ethnology*, published by the Smithsonian, mentioned several skeletons:

GIANT SKELETONS

- a man much above the average size
- a young person of very large stature
- a middle-aged person about 6 feet high
- a large adult (estimated just under 6 feet tall)

This indicates that "large" equates to about 6 feet tall, so "very large" would be well over 6 feet tall. Countless skeletons were found, and since the bones of many skeletons were all jumbled up together, few were given an estimate of size. Many of the bones fell to pieces when touched, and all evidence pointed to the piles of bones being "remnants of a cannibal feast." In other words, the majority of these skeletons represent the victims, rather than the cannibals.

There was a third tribe who lived alongside the Biloxies and Pascagoulas, except that several names are listed and nobody knows if they were one tribe with many names, or many tribes that we just got mixed up with one another. All we know is that they disappeared from history, leaving behind only a whisper of a tribal name. They were the Capinans/Capinas, or the Moctobi, or the Annochy — three radically different names to describe this elusive tribe. Did they build the Mississippi seashell fortress?

As the Annochy tribe of Mississippi, they offer a coincidence of names — a coincidence that comes straight from a text entitled, *Smithsonian Institution, Bureau of Ethnology, Issues 21-23*. Several spellings and synonyms are listed for *Annochy*, one of them being Anaxis. This just happens to be the name of a giant in Greek mythology. Traveling up the family tree of Anaxis takes you to the Olympians — the second tier of giant gods in Greek mythology. The first tier was the Titans, one of which was Atlas who ruled over the Lost Continent of Atlantis. Why was a tribe in Mississippi — who may have built a seashell fortress where a giant skeleton was found, and then disappeared into the sea from whence they came — named for an ancient Greek giant? And what about the giants of Arkansas, a state that borders Mississippi to the north?

Giant Skulls That Fit Over Your Head

Incredible stories abound when it comes to the giants of antiquity, and a race of ten-footers made their home in Arkansas, according to the *Memphis Daily Appeal* in 1870. The story was so incredible that the lead-in made reference to a *roorback* — a word coined for Baron von Roorback whose fictitious travelogue included an incident damaging to James K. Polk, just before Polk became the 11th president. The article declared that what we were about to read was strictly true, without any exaggeration about the giant skeleton, and that the article was not a *roorback*.

The location of this unexaggerated discovery: a 25 feet tall mound in Chickasawba, Arkansas, used by Chief Chickasawba himself, possibly as a place of worship. He was a trader, and a friend to the European settlers. He was also a man of "gigantic stature and Herculean strength." It was common to see him carrying 20 gallons of honey to the trading post.

A giant skeleton was unearthed from his mound, of a man between 8 and 9 feet tall. The skull was so big that it slipped right over the head of a man noted as one of the town's best citizens.

This seems to be a common thread with the old giant skulls — trying them on for size, slipping them over your own head to the amazement of onlookers.

Also found was a peculiarly shaped earthen jar that did not in any way resemble Indian pottery of the region. It appeared to be a round-bodied, long-necked carafe or water decanter. Even the clay was described as *peculiar*, and the workmanship "very fine." The body of the carafe was adorned with images of proportionally sized human hands and thigh bones.

Similar skeletons had been found buried with vases that were almost identical to the carafe, but which were thought to be funeral vases. Several skeletons and their vases existed in the city at the time of the news report, and one skeleton measured between 9 and 10 feet in height.

The article went on about how many giant skeletons had been misidentified in other parts of the world, being actually the fossils of mammoths and mastodons, but made it clear that the Chickasawba bones were indeed giant humans.

The article continued with descriptions of still-living giants, or giants in recent memory: Cotter O'Brien at 8 feet 7 inches, Byrne at 8 feet 6, McGrath at 7 feet 9, Miss Henrion at 7 feet 9, and Chang the Chinese giant at over 8 feet.

Eleven years later, on Halloween night 1881, a note was made in the Arkansas Historical Report that the owner of the property did not want the mound disturbed any more than it had been, because he wanted to use it as a cellar for his house.

The Third Annual Report of the Bureau of Ethnology, published by the Smithsonian, verifies that skeletons were found in Mississippi County, Arkansas, though it doesn't specific sizes. Locations mentioned include the Chickasawba Mound, Carbon Lake Township, Pecan Point, Menard Mound, and Indian Bay.

The United Methodist Free Churches' Magazine also published a tract in 1881 about "Pre-historic Races in America" and their mounds which clustered into villages. Ancient wells of regularly-cut stone, the remains of underground workshops, and round towers in an excellent state of preservation were among the remnants of the Mound Builder civilization.

They were "as skilled as the ancient lords of Egypt, and judging from their implements and utensils, they appear to have been larger than ordinary-sized men." In addition, the skulls were peculiar, and did not resemble the skulls of the Native Americans who followed.

Reverend J. Boyes wrote about these ancient giants in a letter to the young folks. The giants burned their dead in a furnace, which left no wood ashes to mingle with the bone material. The ashes were stored in urns of burnt clay, and the urns were buried with walls built up around them as if to protect the ashes forever.

The urns were of a quality and design that was not duplicated by the people who later lived in the region. The giants built canals, fortifications, and double walls that extended for miles, or sometimes enclosed buildings. When the Native Americans were specifically asked who built the Chickasawba Mound, they answered that the builders were NOT a Native American tribe, but were of the race of men from long ago — a race who built mounds, and houses, and cultivated the land. These men all migrated south, which fits in perfectly with the seashell fortress giants, and other evidence of giants found along the southern coasts of the United States.

Another giant gives us a look at how some of the evidence disappeared, according to *Smithsonian Institution, Bureau of Ethnology, Issue 44*. The Taylor farm in Scott County, Arkansas was excavated by S. R. Sherrell after a schoolteacher and pupils had torn the mound all to pieces in their eagerness, and destroyed most of the skeletons and artifacts therein. Sherrell, however, managed to examine a small portion that they had not attacked. "In this he found a skeleton which, by measure, was 8 feet long… Doctor Bevill and Mr. Sherrell are men who know what they are doing and what they are saying: and their statements of what they did and what they saw are beyond question."

A few months after the Arkansas skull was being "tried on for size," the same was occurring in Kern County, California. Workmen were digging on the banks of the Kern River when they found a 7 feet 5 inch skeleton buried with flint-heads and spear-heads. A full grown person placed his head inside the skull.

Not to be outdone, the *Louisville Courier-Journal* reported the exhumation of a 12 feet tall giant, while excavating a new fire-cistern in Jeffersonville. Though the skull was badly damaged by the workmen, enough was left of the skull and other bones to determine the size.

Other California skeletons were reported in 1908 and 1916. The Santa Monica beach giant was over 9 feet tall, and he had thirteen buddies. They were put on exhibition, and examined by scientists who put their age at hundreds of years old — this from *The Washington Times* on July 13, 1908.

At the Frank Wallace ranch near San Leandro, California, an 8-footer was found. Deputy Coroner Robert Morgan took charge of the skeleton, and it was sent to the anthropological department of the University of California, according to *The Pittsburgh Press* on December 23, 1916.

Trying on the giant skulls was big news in Ohio as well, which brings us remarkable tales of the giants who came before us. These giants pit independent historians against academia.

Athens County and the Ohio Valley are home to numerous mounds, and skeletons ranging from 7 to 9 feet tall. They are attributed to the Allegewi tribe, which the Allegheny River and its mountains are named for, although there is dispute as to whether such a tribe ever existed.

Academia claims that we don't know much about this tribe archeologically, and that most of what we have comes from the folklore of other tribes such as the Lenni-Lenapes and Mengwes who attacked the Allegewi and drove them south. From legends, we can deduce that they were tall, but not giants. Skeletons pulled out of mounds tell a different story, however, especially when the skulls fit over a modern, human head.

Two 7-footers came out of the banks of the Hocking River at Roach's Mill, a half mile east of Athens. A 9-footer was found by W. C. Fry in a gravel pit east of Dayton in 1904. A giant skeleton was dredged out of the east bank of Lake St. Mary's in 1918, though a size was not given beyond the description of "giant human."

Three others were unearthed during the construction of the Toledo and Ottawa Beach Railroad in 1898. These were roughly 7 feet tall, and they were found in solid yellow clay, eight feet below the surface. Several tomahawks of a "large size" were also been found in the vicinity.

Woolverton Farm near Tippecanoe City produced an 8 feet tall skeleton, with a skull big enough to "fit as a helmet over the average man's head" according to the *Janesville Daily Gazette* on April 7, 1904. It was one of seven skeletons found buried in a circle with their feet toward the center.

Some believe that the Allegewi built the earthworks found in Ohio, which date from 300 B.C. to 300 A.D., and others credit the Adena or the Hopewell. A third view puts forth that the Allegewi are none other than the Adena or Hopewell, a view which is not shared by academia, especially as both the Adena and Hopewell skeletons appear to be of average height.

According to *Anthropological Series, Volume 6*, published in 1922 by the Field Museum of Natural History, Hopewell represented a culture, a way of life that was different from other known tribes. They built terraces or platforms that resembled flat-top pyramids, and lived in fortified towns. They built stone walls cemented together with clay, and the walls appear to have been "destroyed by the action of fire" in some places, creating a striking difference between the original wall and the burnt wall.

Mysterious circles, sacred mounds, and strange monuments were their hallmark, created by immense feats of labor. Not less than 3,000,000 cubic feet of earth went into the composition of the Hopewell Mounds at Paint Creek. Mound #25 was described as "too large to have been the work of human hands."

Remarkable tablets were found, which "suggested the famous Cincinnati tablet." One was originally enclosed in sheets of copper, but a local resident, intent on removing the copper, broke the tablet, and portions were lost.

Jawbones were found with precision cuts, made with an instrument so sharp and precise, that the nature of the cuts were "deemed to be impossible." Some skeletons were found in such a state of decay that they could not be saved, and charred or decayed skeletons appeared to be the norm. Many skeletons were charred, either laid out on stone hearths, or directly in a fire. Two types of skulls were found in the mounds, representing two distinct races. Of the multitudes of skeletons found, only one was described for its size, being 5 feet 11 inches tall. Descriptions were focused on artifacts that were found with each skeleton, or whether the skeleton appeared to have been buried or cremated, and its state of decay.

Dr. Thomas Wilson of the Smithsonian visited the mounds in 1891 and 1892, and his notes "were never published," though we have the notes of others which include the discovery of 8,185 flint disks arranged in a herringbone pattern. Obsidian, mica, crystal, and copper were found in abundance, along with sheet copper, and a cloth made of vegetable fiber, doubled and twisted and about the size of fine pack-thread, along with ivory bone needles. The obsidian is believed to come from Yellowstone Park, which represented a 3,000 mile journey by canoe, or an overland journey through lands of hostile tribes.

If the obsidian passed from Yellowstone to Ohio via trade, then artifacts would be found in between, but there was no trace found along the way. The 8,185 flint disks were believed to originate in Tennessee, and it seemed a marvel that they transported such a large quantity across several hundred miles. So how did they transport the obsidian and the flint? By canoe, in a monumental journey? Or could there be an extraterrestrial explanation, from a race with "flying canoes" such as Hiawatha?

The Hopewells appeared to have an inexhaustible supply of meteorites. Either meteorites were falling more frequently in the area, or they had access to a large deposit somewhere. This report obviously wasn't aware of the Great Serpent Mound in Ohio that was built inside a meteorite impact crater, which suggests that the same culture is connected to both.

They had fossils that weren't native to Ohio. Approximately 100,000 pearl beads were unearthed, carefully drilled and with an estimated value of $1 million dollars. "In the age of the Mound Builders, there were as many pearls in the possession of a single tribe of Indians, as existed in any European court" and some were nearly an inch around. Whoever these Mound Builders were, their extermination took place long before the Europeans arrived. Dates for the Hopewell mounds fall somewhere between 500 and 1500 A.D., depending on the source, and based on European settlement, 1500 A.D. is unlikely.

The Antiquarian, Volume 1, a monthly journal of archeology and ethnology published by Landon in 1897, described the Hopewell artifacts as "belonging to a high and strange civilization" in contrast to the Native Americans.

Skulls were found that represented "short-headed" and "long-headed" races. *Primitive Man in Ohio* by Warren K. Moorehead in 1892, pointed out that archeologists in the United States had sorely neglected the study of the skeletons and skulls, in spite of the large number of skeletons found. Moorehead and his associates traveled to the Smithsonian a "couple of years" prior to publishing his book, and they were allowed to examine the crania and skeletons of the Ohio mound collection by Dr. Thomas Wilson, Curator of the Prehistoric Anthropology section of the Smithsonian Institution.

They offered great detail in describing the skulls, but of the skeletons, most were found flattened during excavation as if they'd been drawn between iron rollers. The short-headed people of Hopewell ranged from 5 feet 4 inches to 6 feet 1 inch, and "no skeletons of gigantic size were discovered" in the short-headed skull group. Whether this statement encompassed the long-headed skull group wasn't clear. Both the Hopewell and Adena mounds were attributed to races that were generally less than six feet tall. In the middle of the debate, archeological discoveries keep on surfacing.

National Geographic posted a story entitled "Wooden 'Stonehenge' Emerges from Prehistoric Ohio." Made of wood instead of stone, the site appears to be a series of incomplete, concentric circles spanning 200 feet, and it's surrounded by earthworks that are attributed to the Hopewell culture who reigned for the first 900 years A.D.

Not all archeologists agree on the relationship between the Adenas, Hopewells, Allegewis, and the Ohio Mounds. The Allegewis are most often credited for the mounds and the advanced culture that they represent, which suggests that the amazements attributed to the Hopewells were actually Allegewi.

History of Crawford County, Pennsylvania, published by Warner, Beers & Co. in 1885, stated that the Allegewi were wiped out by the Lenni-Lenapes and Mengwes in a bloody war that lasted many years, and that the Allegewi survivors were driven south.

Several Indian tribes told early settlers about a "larger and more powerful race" who once occupied the region, and they were the Mound Builders. Sometimes they were described as "tall" and even "gigantic." Tales of Allegewi giants are attributed to legends that grow taller with every telling.

How does this account for giant skeletons that were found in Ohio? It doesn't. We've already seen reports of seven, eight, and nine footers. *The Smithsonian Institution, Bureau of Ethnology, Issue 12* gives us another glimpse into the Ohio debate. Prehistoric mounds in Ohio, Indiana, Illinois, and Missouri are remnants of a culture that was more ancient and advanced than the Native Americans. They had developed the art of making glass, along with rolls of sheet copper of such uniform thickness and flatness, that there was no evidence that they'd ever been hammered.

The same issue mentioned stone graves in Franklin, Ohio, which enclosed skeletons of "a very large size." Ripley, Ohio, produced skulls with a half inch in thickness, and femurs of 22.5 inches in length (which represents humans a little over 7 feet tall.) Most of the bones were in such a state of decay that they could not be taken out. On the farm of Colonel Pren Metham in Coshocton, Ohio, a stone box-grave contained a skeleton over 7 feet long. One example of a stone grave comes from Brown County, Ohio, where Ripley is located.

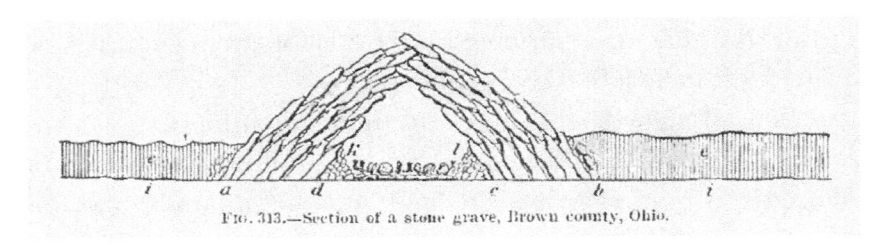

FIG. 313.—Section of a stone grave, Brown county, Ohio.

The state of West Virginia borders Ohio to the southeast, and giants skeletons were the highlight of the Kanawha Valley, as detailed in *The Fifth Annual Report of the Bureau of Ethnology*, published by the Smithsonian.

A mound on the farm of Colonel B.G. Smith was excavated, and a "large and much decayed skeleton" was found inside a stone vault, along with a nearby skeleton of "ordinary size." The giant skeleton measured 7 feet 6 inches, and was enclosed in a wrapping or coffin of bark. Except for the left forearm, none of the bones could be saved. A separate mound produced "two very large skeletons, in a sitting posture, with their extended legs interlocked to the knees."

The Twelfth Annual Report of the Bureau of Ethnology mentioned well-preserved skeletons found in bark coffins on the farm of Peter S. Crouch in Mason County, West Virginia. Many of them were "very large." A large skeleton was also found in the McCullough Mound in West Virginia:

> "The rock heap had been disturbed by parties who found a very large skeleton with stone weapons. Beneath it, sandstone slabs as heavy as a man could lift, were scattered through the shaft and at the bottom, enough of them standing and laying at all angles to have covered the vault, and appearing to have been hurled thus by the caving in of the roof."

The fifth annual report gave honorable mention to the T. F. Nelson Mounds of North Carolina, where an unusually large skeleton of not less than 7 feet fall was found in Mound #16.

More interesting than the size of the skeleton, is the manner in which it was buried.

FIG. 25.—Appearance of T. F. Nelson mound after excavation.

Clearly this does not represent an ordinary burial, and similar graves have been found in other mounds. Most mounds have multiple layers of burials, with the bottom layer housing intricate burials such as the Nelson Mound, along with the bones of giants. Europeans weren't the only intruders to these mounds, as we are sometimes led to believe. Native Americans also disturbed the mounds to add their own burials, which is why the origin of the mounds became convoluted.

The added skeletons are described as "intrusive burials" by archeologists, and are not buried as deep. Neither are they buried with the same care as the originals. The twelfth annual report mentioned several "intrusive burials" and seemed divided in its opinion as to whether they represented Native Americans intruding on the burials of other Native Americans, or whether the intrusion was on the mounds of an earlier, unrelated race.

While the following image from a Tennessee mound does not represent an intrusive burial, it does give you an idea of what an intrusive burial might look like if these skeletons had been found in a layer above the stone cones of the Nelson Mound.

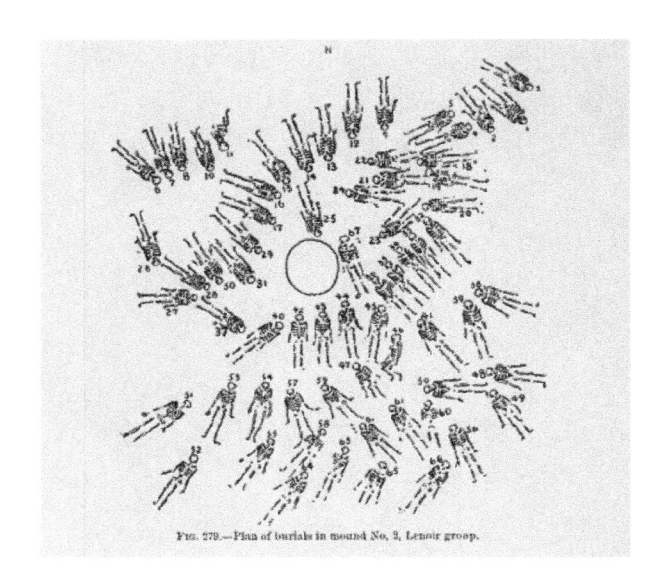

FIG. 279.—Plan of burials in mound No. 2, Lenoir group.

The Wild West

No region has more tall tales than the Wild West, and archeologists in New Mexico went chasing after a 12 feet tall giant, according to the *New York Times* in February 1902. The skeletons were found in Guadalupe, New Mexico, where an ancient burial ground yielded a multitude of enormous skeletons.

Luiciana Quintana, who owns the ranch where the giants were found, discovered two stones with curious inscriptions and giants buried underneath. Quintana predicted the discovery of many more based on ancient traditions that a race of giants once inhabited the region, along with detailed accounts given by early Spanish invaders.

The state of Nevada also brought forth the skeleton of a veritable giant, according to January 1904 articles in *The Wichita*

Daily Eagle and *The Saint Paul Globe*. Workmen were digging gravel when they found bones about 12 feet down, and Dr. Samuels determined that the bones of were from a man of 11 feet tall.

South Dakota is famous for its Badlands, and the Black Hills Bandits outlaw gang of 1876-1877. South Dakota also sported a mound with nine giant skeletons, between 7 and 8 feet tall. They were found in Brown County on the farm of S. H. Elliott.

They were buried in an unusual manner: face down, with the bodies doubled backward so that the heels rested on, or next to, the back of the head. A child was found buried with his dog. Flint arrowheads and stone pipes were also unearthed — pipes which were different than those normally found in the region. They were not made of the traditional red pipestone, but were a type of stone similar to flint, which would have been difficult to work with. Even the form of the pipes was different, having a hole for the stem in the bottom, instead of at the side.

Another Wild West state is Utah, which was terrorized by the Hole-in-the-wall gang as led by Butch Cassidy and the Sundance Kid. Among their hideouts: Robber's Roost in Utah, somewhere far south of Salt Lake City. Giants also lived in Utah, which some archeologists believe were Mound Builders. One such giant measured 8 feet 6 inches, and was found near the Jordan River in the vicinity of Salt Lake City.

When found, he was standing bolt upright with his head eight feet below ground. It took nine more feet of excavating to reach his feet. The bones were severely decayed and they crumbled at the slightest touch. The skeleton was adorned with a copper chain necklace that had three engraved medallions of unknown hieroglyphics.

Texas gave us the "giant on the beach" in 1940, when a skull was unearthed in Victoria County. The *San Antonio Express* said that it was "believed to be the largest human skull ever found in the United States, and possibly in the world." That's what you call a tall tale!

Archeologist W. Duffen excavated the mound, which produced a normal-sized skull, along with a skull twice the size of a normal human. The giant skull was in pieces, and it was reconstructed at the WPA laboratory under the supervision of physical anthropologists. They hoped to determine whether the skull belonged to a tribe of extraordinarily large men, or just a single member of abnormal size — a case of gigantism.

Another skeleton was found in Diablo Mountain, Texas, according to the *Fort Worth Daily Gazette* on December 31, 1887. The skull itself seemed to be of ordinary size, but the jawbone and vertebrae were exceptionally large. They were discovered in a natural tunnel or cave about 700 feet above the level of the plain.

Six inch long bone needles, cooking utensils, and fragments of pottery were also found. It was described as the "first systemic archeological expedition" in the United States, and archeologists believed that the facts would support a theory that all of the southern valleys had been densely populated by a people who "mysteriously disappeared," based on other discoveries that had also been made in the region.

Sierra Diablo, Texas, is about 50 miles from the Mexican border, where it crosses over into Chihuahua, Mexico. The *Superstition* chapter covers this region in depth.

Montana was crawling with explorers after gold was discovered at Gold Creek in 1852, followed by placers near Deer Lodge and Helena. An 1866 newspaper spoke of rumors that a huge streak of gold-rich gravel was paying out at Blackfoot City, Ophir Gulch, and several gulches off of Elk Creek. Gold was so abundant that the county seat was moved from Silver Bow to Deer Lodge and prospectors appeared in droves. Nobody is more thorough than a gold miner on the hunt for the elusive nugget, and many caves were explored in those exciting days.

One discovery that hit the headlines and then went dead silent was 'King Solomon's Cave' in Ophir Gulch, Montana, according to the *Sacramento Daily Union* on November 28, 1873, and the *Otago Daily Times* on February 12, 1874. Explorers including Lon Whittier, Abe Echols, George Barnard, and a fourth man traversed hundreds of feet of narrow passages, sometimes crawling, to reach a "most magnificent chamber" with an ancient fireplace, next to which charcoal had been stacked. The blackened floor and smoke-stained wall indicated that the fireplace had been much-used. Leaning against the wall was a massive copper shield of 57 inches by 36 inches. Also, about eight feet up, there was a cavity in the wall.

They stacked the stones and George Barnard climbed up to look in, and when he shined a light in the cavity, he quickly descended in a state of alarm. Inside was a petrified giant.

Of course the others climbed up to see for themselves and sure enough, there was a giant of 9 feet 7 inches tall covered in carbonate of lime. He wore a helmet of copper or brass, which "the corrosive elements of time had sealed to his brow." Two mammoth spearheads were also found, one with a socket of silver, along with a large bone hook.

Strange lettering was on the wall, and pictures of three-masted ships. One picture of a ship included a big man holding a spear, this being on a flat stone in the wall.

The flat stone was removed to expose yet another chamber, with bones of several more giants, a primitive quartz crusher, and a number of copper tools. The consensus was that they were mining in the cave, got trapped by a landslide and died there. The article ends with the cave being pre-empted.

Pre-empted means that either the explorers camped out in the cave to establish a claim, or the federal government came in and took it over. Whatever happened, the story disappeared after the initial report. Even Lovelock Cave and Death Valley Scotty left behind clues, but Ophir Gulch went silent.

Bulletin 105 of The Bureau of Mines and Geology for the state of Montana describes Ophir Cave as being on Cave Gulch, which is a tributary of Ophir Creek, also known as Carpenter Creek. The entrance is under a low limestone ledge. A small hole at the base of a sink leads down a talus cone into a room that's 60 feet by 80 feet. This room has a man-made shaft sunk 38 feet into another room, which is a hundred feet long.

The cave made national news in the 1950s when reports indicated that it was 3,000 feet deep, but the cave was later explored to find a depth of only 184 feet. *The National Speleological Society Newsletter* for October 1960 included a "Report from Montana" by Howard McDonald settling the discrepancy. An exploration was made in December, in spite of deep snow, and after nine hours inside the cave, the depth was determined to be highly exaggerated.

However, rumors often have a grain of truth, and according to *The History of Northwest Caving to 1972* by Tom Miller, the cave really was that deep in the early 1940s. Captain Greenfield of the U. S. Air Force explored Ophir Cave to a depth of 3,000 feet between 1940 and 1944.

The original news report stated that the giants may have been trapped by a landslide, and couldn't get back out of the cave. That tells us two things: that the cave is subject to landslides and cave-ins, and that the 1873 explorers may have had to move rubble or dig into a wall to discover the passages.

Several earthquakes have hit Montana, which is the most seismically active state in the United States. The region which includes Ophir Cave has been hard hit, which means that the cave as it existed in 1873 when the giant was found, may be radically different than the cave as it exists today. Earlier descriptions also referred to the cave as having a "large number of massive chambers" as well as fracturing from earthquakes.

Today the cave is described with two rooms, one of which is accessible via a man-made shaft. If someone hadn't excavated a shaft, all we'd know about is a single room. This further supports the suggestion of the four 1873 explorers or miners that the giants became trapped.

While it doesn't substantiate the original claim of giant skeletons, it does demonstrate that debunking a rumor doesn't always prove that the rumor is false. As for the skeletons — according to the *Exposition Records of the Smithsonian Institution and the United States National Museum, 1867-1940*, the Smithsonian did make an expedition to Montana between 1875 and 1878, and external sources date this trip to 1875, within two years of the original discovery of the giants. We can only speculate as to whether the trip included Ophir Cave.

Lost Cities

Sometimes giants are associated with lost cities, as was the case in Cayuga, Canada, in 1871. Workmen digging on Daniel Fredenburg's farm found a pit full of gigantic human skeletons about five feet below the surface. They estimated at least 200 skeletons measuring up to 9 feet tall, with only a few shorter than 7 feet. Each skeleton wore a string of beads around their neck, and some had stone pipes in their jaws. The teeth were in an almost perfect state of preservation, but fell out soon after being exposed to the air. Several of the pipes, which were similar to cutty pipes, had been engraved with dog's heads. The skulls completely covered an ordinary man's head.

The farm itself consisted of 150 acres and had been cultivated for nearly a century. The pit was covered with several centuries' growth of thick pine, which indicates that it predated the Indians known to the region.

This big story made news everywhere, including the *North Otago Times*, *Toronto Telegraph*, *New York Herald*, and *West Coast Times*. Surprising for today, but not uncommon for the 1800s, the pit "and its ghostly occupants" were left open to the view of anyone who wanted to have a look.

On maps of the Township of South Cayuga for 1876, Fredenburg is spelled Fradenburgh, and there's a tract of land called the Fradenburgh Tract that runs adjacent to the Grand

River, which Daniel shared with his brothers. The news stories don't mention his brothers, so presumably the ancient city was found on Daniel's segment of the tract.

Other discoveries were made on Fredenburg's farm over the years. Dozens of similar pits were found at various times, along with the remnants of mud-homes with chimneys, and even a blacksmith's shop with two tons of charcoal. Large shells were found, almost petrified, and were thought to be used for holding water. The report stated that if the area were to be thoroughly explored, the results would be "highly interesting." However, the skulls and bones of the giants were fast disappearing — taken away by curiosity hunters.

When discoveries were made on private property, it was only by permission from the owner that archeologists could come in and excavate. This might take several acres of land out of use, and when those acres are feeding your family or are part of a farming business, permission might not be given. Look out the window into your back yard. Would you be willing to give up the use of your property for an indefinite period of time, or allow someone to dig it all up after you've planted flowers and trees, built garages and sheds, and so forth?

Around the World

These reports are just a handful out of the countless discoveries made all around the world, and our ancestors who found the bones didn't always take world history into consideration. *The Oxford Companion to Archaeology*, edited by Brian M. Fagan and published in 1996, gave us an interesting look at the "History of Archaeology From 1900-1950" with articles by several authors.

They noted that archeology became more professional after 1900. We took greater care to preserve artifacts that were not as spectacular, but that helped us fill in the details of the big finds. Prior to 1900, excavations were minimal, noting only the most obvious points. The bones of large mammoths were collected, but accompanying material was often discarded. Even prehistoric cave art had been previously dismissed, but was now coming into prominence. Archeology was further advanced by humans becoming airborne, and seeing sites such as Stonehenge from a loftier perspective. Radio-carbon dating was embraced as a godsend by some, but discarded as invalid by others. To complicate it further, wars got in the way. In other words, just like the rest of humanity, scholars do not always get along, or agree with one another.

The article alleged that in 1929 Russia, archeologists were arrested by the secret police, their work being condemned by the Communist Party. It was considered important to gather evidence that supported Marxist principles, and the non-Marxist scholars were being purged. Eventually the tides turned and archeology was embraced once again. A similar story involved Italy under Mussolini, who "kept tight control over its own past." In Greece, the doors were wide open, but preference was given to the Classical Period at the expense of the post-Roman period.

You can't help but wonder how common this is. Everybody, including archeologists and the institutions that they represent, comes to the table with specific beliefs. Maybe it's political, or maybe it's religious, such as a concept that all humans evolved from a single base pair, and so all science must support that belief.

Perhaps it's a stubbornness in wanting to cling to an outdated view of history, such as our notions of where mankind began, and how he spread across the world. Even the concept that ancient mythology may have been based on physical beings, and not just stories that someone made up, is a hard pill for many to swallow. Scholars forever argue on whether the *Bible* is a history book to be taken literally, and whether the Greek gods, or the Roman gods, or the Norse gods, and others were physical beings. We've been taught that giants are fairy tales, and we label both giants and gods as mythology or folklore, which is just a polite way of calling it fiction. The dictionary defines mythology as a story that concerns a hero or event that often lacks a basis of fact. Myths are inventions of the imagination.

In addition, we're often too busy annihilating a population at the expense of preserving history. Conquerors love to destroy history, and they will rewrite history to glorify themselves and downplay the achievements or contributions of others. This is not limited to any single country or religion — we are all guilty of it.

An unfortunate side effect of studying human remains and attempting to differentiate the various races is in how the information gets used. Hitler used archeological findings to justify doctrines of racial superiority. In doing so, he may have set us back decades in the government acknowledging cannibalistic giants, or giants that came down from the stars. He demonstrated the ugliest side of bringing historical facts to light.

With so many hidden agendas and wars, it's amazing that we've got anything left to show for the early discoveries. So many of our giants were unearthed in the 1800s, before archeology really came into its full glory, and we often had a complete lack of respect for races or religions other than our own. Case in point, the theft of a skull.

The headlines in January 1910 read, in part, "Captain Chittenden of Santa Barbara… Invaded Savages' Burial Ground at Night…" The story was featured in *The Washington Post*, in honor of Chittenden's donation of a giant aboriginal skull to the Smithsonian, which he'd stolen twenty years earlier.

Chittenden gave up a "lucrative law practice" to study and explore Indian nations, and to that effect he'd traveled to Vancouver Island in British Columbia. He encountered a settlement of Flat Head Indians and stayed among them, which suggests that he was their guest.

He came across a partially exposed grave in their cemetery, which revealed the skeleton of a "gigantic savage" — an ancient chief of the tribe who'd been dead for more than 100 years.

Chittenden coveted the giant skull for his archeological collection, and he plotted on how to acquire it. Even knowing how sacred the skeleton was to his hosts, he devised a daring plan under cover of darkness to steal the skull.

With a canoe at the ready, he crept into the burial grounds at great peril to his own life, and stole the skull. Then he fled the island by canoe, not stopping until he reached the United States.

The story was told as if he were a hero, accentuating the risk he took in order to acquire this valuable specimen. Over the next twenty years, several anthropologists offered great sums of money for the skull. He turned them all down and kept the giant skull as his most prized possession. When he finally decided to part with the skull, he gifted it to the Smithsonian with great fanfare. The article closed by mentioning the many donations he'd made to museums over the years, to their Indian collections.

Dr. Ales Hrdlicka, Assistant Curator of the anthropological division, said that the skull surpassed all similar skulls in the museum's possession.

The Flat Heads may not have been giants, but their ancient chief certainly was, along with their legends of a giant ogre. He was a mighty man, with rugged limbs, and thick, matted hair which fell in tangles over his shoulders. He had sullen eyes that remained transfixed in a permanently angry stare.

One day a boy came down from heaven, who possessed weapons more potent even than the giant's brutal strength. When the giant saw the boy, he became enraged, because the boy did not fear him as everyone else did. The boy killed the giant, and made sure that his bones were crushed into powder.

Flat Head legends also included thunderbirds or thunderers, whose movement through the skies created a great thundering noise, and whose eyes emitted bolts of lightning.

Giants lived in the legends of British Columbia, and they lived in the cemeteries and caves of France, where an 11 feet 6 inch tall skeleton was discovered in Castelnau, France, in 1890.

Four years later, more giants were found in Montpelier, France, which indicated a race of giants between 10 and 15 feet tall. Professor Kiener studied the bones, and admitted that they were of a very tall race, but thought them to be abnormal in dimensions and morbid growth rather than suggestive of an actual race of giants.

The Popular Science News and Boston Journal of Chemistry, Volume XXIV, published in 1890, featured the Castelnau discovery. The cemetery that housed the bones was dated back to the Polished Stone and Bronze Age, which agrees with the timeframe of when giants were common on Earth.

The article stated that authorities disagreed as to whether the bones represented an anomaly of growth, or an actual, genuine giant. It mentioned local legends of a giant that once lived in a cave in the valley.

Giants were also found in Egyptian tombs, according to the *Arizona Weekly Citizen* in 1896. Professor Timmerman made the discovery in 1881 in the Temple of Isis, where he found a row of tombs. The smallest skeleton measured 7 feet 8 inches, and the largest 11 feet 1 inch. The tombs were thought to date back to 1043 B.C.

A race of giants lived in the Canary Islands off the coast of Africa, according to Issue 644 of the *Otago Witness*, published on April 2, 1864. They'd reprinted a story from the *Evening Bulletin* entitled, "Human Fossils in California."

> "The historians of the Canary Islands have also gravely related accounts that those islands were once inhabited by a gigantic race of men, and one of these is stated by them to have been found, as quoted in "Prichard" (1855), which measured 15 feet in length, and the skull contained 80 teeth, and the back and breast of others were covered in hair."

These are just a few of the giant legends and skeletons that have been reported around the world. In addition to those already listed, eight-footers were found in Maryland, Oklahoma, and New Jersey. Nine-footers were found in Indiana, Tennessee, and Wisconsin. Ten-footers were found in Iowa and the Ozark Mountains, and a whopping 10 feet 9 inch tall skeleton came out of Sauk Rapids, Minnesota. Pennsylvania pulled in the lead with an 11 feet 3 inch skeleton taken from Mr. Neese's tan-yard, as reported by Judge Atlee in 1798, and don't forget the 11 feet 6 inch giant found in Castelnau, France. Of course, none can match the 15-footers of the Canary Islands.

The fate of all these giant bones is just as interesting as the possibility of giants themselves, but there's one more detour before we go down the Road of Bones — a detour of engraved stone tablets that have also been found in North America with some of the giant bones.

Engraved Stone Tablets

Woven throughout the news articles are mentions of hieroglyphics engraved in stone, with rarely a comment on what the messages might mean. Newsmen are savvy enough that if an archeologist on the scene offered insight, it would become part of the article:

"This is ancient Greek…"

"It resembles Egyptian, but it isn't…"

"The message is in Hebrew, and it says…"

"Unintelligible…"

That's the word used in a Michigan discovery where the skeleton was found with an engraved tablet: "Unintelligible."

A petrified body of no less than 12 feet 7 inches made front pages all across the country on September 6, 1919, including the *Middletown News-Signal* and the *Border City Star*. The location of the body: Jackson, Michigan.

Patrolman Nierman found the body while digging in his garden on North Street, and when he got down about two feet, he discovered what looked like a human hand. He summoned assistance and they unearthed a well-preserved body.

Dr. H. B. Neagle, the city health official, examined the body and determined it to be human. The legs were six feet long from the thigh to the sole of the huge feet. The toenails were still in place, the nose was small and broad, the teeth were big and protruding, and there was black hair still on the skull. The body was petrified.

This was big news in 1919. A huge crowd gathered and police were called in to hold the people back. Nierman was offered $500 for the body, but he turned it down.

Less than 100 miles to the west, and 25 years earlier, a giant was found inside a mound near Diamond Lake, Michigan. The *Daily Public Ledger* reported the discovery in September 1894. The lower jaw was so big that the jawbone of a human today would easily fit inside. A doctor who measured the bones estimated the giant at 11 feet tall.

The mound did not appear to have ever been disturbed, as there was a pine stump that was three and a half feet across. Along with the giant skeleton bones, they discovered an earthen tablet with unintelligible characters.

Engraved stone tablets that nobody on-site could read were common in the digs that unearthed giants, and as we know, once the evidence is carried away by officials, its secrets aren't always shared with the public. You can bet that somebody has a hoard of tablets squirreled away that they are deciphering, or have deciphered. For the common man, however, the evidence is no more than a teaser. Ohio gave us a bit of extra skin with its teaser, providing more than a brief mention of the hieroglyphs.

A mound in Brush Creek Township, Muskingum County, was opened by the Historical Society under the supervision of Dr. J. F. Everhart. Inside the mound, a coffin housed an 8 feet tall female skeleton, plus a child. The mother-child coffin was made of a peculiar yellow clay, which did not exist naturally in the township, and it must have been brought in from a distance. They also found a 16 inch figurine of an infant made of the same yellow clay, and a roll of peculiar black substance that was 12 inches long by 4 inches around, which crumbled to dust when exposed to air. The artifacts were also in the coffin.

ENGRAVED STONE TABLETS

Nearby were the skeletons of a man and woman, measuring 9 feet tall, and 8 feet tall, respectively. The female was face down and the male face up, buried back-to-back. Seven other skeletons all measured between 8 and 10 feet tall. There wasn't a single tooth found in the eleven skeletons, or the mound itself.

At one end of the mound was a stone altar, 12 feet long by 4 feet wide, and charred human bones. Other artifacts included the handle of a large vase, nicely glazed, almost black in color, and burned to hardness.

Leaning against the mother-child coffin was an engraved stone tablet of unfinished sandstone. One description gave its dimensions as 12.5 x 11 inches, and 4 inches thick; another put it at 12 x 14. The stone had not been squared, nor the surface leveled, and the only sign that tools had been used on it was in cutting the hieroglyphics. The tablet had passed through fire.

There were two rows of hieroglyphs, with a groove and circular indentations in between each row. The characters were skillfully engraved.

Three of the characters were V-shaped, and similar to those found in the Great Pyramid which are generally believed to symbolize power and distinction, as if the remains were those of important persons.

Some characters suggested an old Greek alphabet, while others resembled Egyptian or Hetruscan, and Punic was also mentioned. Dr. Everhart believed that the circular depressions referred to heavenly bodies, and concluded that this was a giant race of sun worshippers.

Robert Clark, Charles L. Low, and Dr. H. H. Hill examined the mound and its artifacts, and gave a written statement:

> "We have examined this stone very carefully after hearing Mr. Everhart's statement concerning it, and we are satisfied that it is not of recent production, but has every appearance of being a veritable Mound-Builder's relic, and is well worthy of a serious effort to unravel its mysteries."

This discovery elicited mentions in several newspapers, along with a more detailed account in *1794, History of Muskingum County, Ohio*. An interesting comment suggests that the public is frequently excluded from the proof found in archeological digs:

> "The above report contains nothing but facts briefly told, and knowing that the public has been humbugged and imposed upon by archeologists, we wish to fortify our own statements by giving the following testimonial:
>
> "We, the undersigned citizens of Brush Creek township, having been present and taken part in the above excavations, do certify that the statements herewith set forth are true and correct, and in no particular has the writer deviated from the facts in the case.
>
> "[Signed.] Thomas D. Showers, John Worstall, Marshall Cooper, J. M. Baughman, S. S. Baughman, John E. McCoy."

Similar statements were made regarding the engraved tablet, of which photographs were taken and sent to all the best known writers on the subject, along with savants in the United States, England, and Canada.

The first two glyphs on the tablet were the Greek Alpha and Omega, followed by a numeral, and a scepter with a number above it. More numbers followed, and then a serpent symbol of life spirit, followed by the sign of addition. After that came Delta, and the Greek sign of the infinitive.

Circular depressions in between the rows were believed to represent the sun, moon, and stars, and the first character in the second row represented a stamp or seal commonly used in the 3rd century B.C., according to a table of Semitic characters. Next came another form of serpent associated with a numeral, and then a ligatured character repeated, and numerals of order, and angle marks.

The inscription was composed of three forms: Demotic or Enchorial, hieroglyphic, and Greek. Demotic fell out of use in 525 B.C., and hieroglyphics in the 3rd century A.D. By this measurement, the inscription was dated at 425 B.C. A translation was given as:

> "I am the Alpha and the Omega, saith the Lord God, which is and which was, and which is to come, the Almighty; giving first, power on earth; secondly, the spirit, added from heaven without ending."
>
> "The heavens declare the glory of God," as a seal of His power to bless, first, with life, and forever, these servants.

Translations of these ancient texts is an interesting topic, with different results depending on the translator. In Los Lunas, New Mexico, there's an 80+ ton boulder of volcanic basalt dubbed *The Mystery Stone, Commandment Rock*, or the *Los Lunas Decalogue Stone*, with an inscription that is nine rows long.

This stone is not related to a discovery of giant bones, but it is so big that archeologists couldn't tote it off to be forever hidden from public view. Thus, attempted translations are more public.

In 1949, Robert Pfeiffer of Harvard's Semitic Museum determined the language to be Paleo-Hebrew, which is a mixture of Greek, Moabite, and ancient Phoenician. He translated it as an abbreviated *Ten Commandments* which began:

> "I am Yahweh, the God who brought thee out of the land of Egypt, out of the house of bondage. Thou shalt not make unto thee a graven image..."

A non-biblical translation by Robert Hoath LaFollette presented it as:

> "We retreated while under attack... then we traveled over the surface of the water; then we climbed without eating, just when we were greatly in need of water, we had rain... In the water we sat down."

This is the translation shown on a handful of websites that claim that it's based on Phoenician, Etruscan, and Egyptian.

Robert LaFollette is listed as a "lawyer and dabbler in archeology" who wrote a Navajo translation as well as an English translation in the year 1964. His translation seems to have disappeared from most websites, as if being summarily dismissed for lack of credentials. Robert, however, may be closer to the source than the scholars whose translations appear everywhere, although you have to dig pretty deep to find out why.

The August 1973 issue of *Desert Magazine* had a feature entitled, "New Mexico's Mystery Stone." Robert H. LaFollette is listed as an "Albuquerque petroglyph expert" who studied the strange Phoenician characters, believed them to be Navajo, and translated the stone with the help of a Navajo interpreter. There is "no written language" for Navajo according to the article, and the connection to Navajo was made based on the phonetic sounds for each character.

His translation is summarized as an epic journey of a people pursued by enemies, who flee across the water. There was an account of a battle, and an ordeal of hunger and thirst. The travelers met other tribes, were assisted by those tribes, and they finally arrived at a river where they built homes.

The March 19, 1999 issue No. 87 of *Ruidoso News*, a local newspaper in New Mexico, printed a story called "New Mexico's Mystery Stone." It referred to Robert LaFollette as an attorney in Albuquerque who made a phonetic investigation of the inscription, and claimed that it was the Navajo language written in Phoenician. The article was more interested in Dixie Perkins' translation, and claimed that both the Semitic and Navajo translations had been disproven. Across the internet, Robert's translation is usually attributed to Etruscan, Egyptian, and Phoenician, and sometimes describes a freak rainstorm.

Robert LaFollette has a deeper connection to Native American lore than most people, depending on which LaFollette was involved in the translation. There are four different Robert LaFollettes, and one of them was born to an Oneida Indian woman. This Robert not only had a law degree, but went on to become the Commissioner of the Bureau of Indian Affairs. His entire adult life was dedicated to Native American issues.

All of the Robert LaFollettes appear to be connected. Robert Marion LaFollette, Sr., was a Wisconsin senator who ran for president of the United States. His son Robert Marion, Jr., was also a senator, and his name is listed as being on the Committee on Indian Affairs, according to a document that came before the 79th Congress regarding *S.J. Res. 79* on May 14, 1946. The bill is entitled, "A Bill Establishing a Joint Congressional Committee to Make a Study of Claims of Indian Tribes Against the United States, and to Investigate the Administration of Indian Affairs."

Robert Hoath LaFollette is listed as the nephew of Wisconsin politician Robert M. LaFollette, and he managed his uncle's presidential campaign. Robert M. Jr. had a brother Philip, who named his son Robert, but no details are given on whether this is Robert Hoath — the attorney in New Mexico who ran for Congress three times unsuccessfully.

The fourth Robert was born on November 16, 1912, in Wisconsin, and he died in Albuquerque in 2002. His name is given as Robert LaFollette Bennett, and his mother was Lydia Doxtater Bennett, a full-blooded Oneida Indian woman. His father was a "white farmer," according to the *Encyclopedia of the American Indian in the Twentieth Century*.

This is the Robert who devoted his life to helping Native Americans, and he was handpicked in 1966 by the Secretary of the Interior to become the Commissioner of the Bureau of Indian Affairs. Among his many credentials: He served on the Navajo reservation in Arizona, and he was the first Director of the New Mexico Native American Law Center in Albuquerque.

His appointment as BIA director was big news, because he was the first Native American to head the bureau in a hundred years, except that his father was not Native American, but either a white farmer, or a white mail carrier, depending on the source. You have to dig deeper for the name of his father.

Lydia Doxtator, aka Doxtater, married Fred H. Bennett on January 31, 1912 in the Oneida Mission Church, Hobart, Brown County, Wisconsin. They had a daughter named Prudence, and a son named Robert, who was born on November 16, 1912. Both Fred and Lydia were mail carriers, and maintained a small farm, according to *The Oneida Indian Experience* published in 1988 by Syracuse University Press. At various times Lydia was a maid, seamstress, and interpreter.

Nowhere will you find an explanation as to why two mail carriers, one being Native American, would name their son "Robert LaFollette" after one of the most powerful political families in the state — a son who was later handpicked by the Secretary of the Interior for his directorship.

Whatever the reason, he might very well have been involved in the translation of the Los Lunas stone, if not as the Robert LaFollette who translated it, then as someone who assisted behind the scenes. The point being that everywhere you find his translation, the only credit given is that he is a "lawyer and dabbler in archeology" — a phrase copied from one website to another, easily used to discredit his contribution. If nothing else, you can be sure that the two Robert LaFollettes knew each other, born 12 years apart, both with legal connections in Albuquerque, one born into a prominent family in Wisconsin, and the other born into an ordinary family in Wisconsin.

Other translations have appeared as well, including one by Dixie Perkins, and some even consider the stone to be a hoax. Virtually every stone inscription that we can't neatly explain ends up embroiled in controversy: the Kensington Runestone, Dighton Rock, Newport Tower, Bat Creek Inscription, Newark Ohio Decalogue Stone, Keystone, and the Johnson-Bradner Stone.

The Bat Creek Stone came out of a burial mound in Tennessee which was excavated by the Smithsonian in 1889. The director of the project, Cyrus Thomas, identified the inscription as being "beyond question letters of the Cherokee alphabet." Eighty years later, the inscription was identified as Paleo-Hebrew by Semitic scholar Cyrus Gordon, who looked at it from a different orientation, and other Hebrew scholars agreed. Wood fragments found with the stone were radio-carbon dated between 32 A.D. and 769 A.D. This was the status in 1988.

Fast forward a couple of decades, and suddenly the Bat Creek Inscription is shadowed in doubt. Two archeologists argued that the inscription was copied from an 1870 Masonic reference book, and thus, was a forgery that they pinned on the Smithsonian field assistant. There is a major discussion on the controversy around this artefact in *The Bat Creek Stone Revisited, a Reply to Mainfort and Kwas in American Antiquity*, by J. Huston McCulloch in 2005.

Mainfort and Kwas had published a report in *American Antiquity* in 2004 declaring the Bat Creek Stone to be a fraud, perpetrated by Smithsonian field agent John Emmert. The allegation stretches far beyond this one controversy, according to the 2005 rebuttal. A single proven fraud or error could send a shadow of doubt over every single discovery ever documented.

McCulloch goes into detail on all of the points made by Mainfort and Kwas, and supports the possibility of a Paleo-Hebrew translation, as well as the authenticity. He also refers to Cyrus Thomas as the "chief debunker" of allegedly Old World inscriptions, and makes reference to the Smithsonian performing a "house cleaning" sometime around 1920 by discarding field notes and photographs, possibly because they'd already been compiled into a published account.

Of a particularly interesting note is a comment he made in closing, in regards to the mandible of the human skull that was found with the Bat Creek Tablet, which was unfortunately lost. He speculated that it had been lent to another institution for study, and never returned.

In the middle of the Bat Creek debate, another translation surfaced from the opposite side of the globe. Alan Wilson, Baram Blackett, and Jim Michael identified the characters as being from the Welsh Coelbren alphabet, with the Bat Creek tumulus as the possible burial place of Madoc, a Welsh prince who allegedly sailed to America in 562 or 1170 A.D.

Among the various translations:

"Only for Judea"
"Only for the Judeans"
"Holy to Yahweh"
"Madoc the ruler he is"

In other words, translators will filter the inscription through their own personal beliefs. One sees a biblical message, while another sees a weary traveler, or a Welsh prince, or a Cherokee message. By the same token, giant bones are either singular instances of people with abnormal growth, or they represent a race of giants that roamed the world prior to, and alongside, modern humans. The opinion given will match the preconceived beliefs of the person making the statement.

Today, the Bat Creek Stone controversy rages on — still embroiled in allegations of fraud, hoaxes, and finger pointing. If archeologists and other experts cannot agree with one another, how on earth can we ever know the truth behind a single artefact, or discovery of bones? Especially when evidence vanishes, such as ancient skeletons or field notes?

Another important point is that several archeologists, studying the same site, the same giant bones, and the same artifacts, will present different opinions. They do not agree amongst themselves, so when you use an expert opinion as a basis for your own opinion, keep that in mind.

Coincidentally, there was a Native American tribe known as the Modocs, who were driven out by gold miners. Joaquin Miller wrote a book in 1874 entitled, *Unwritten History: Life Amongst the*

Modocs. The Bat Creek inscription was found in Tennessee, while the Modocs lived in the western states. His book was not well-embraced as it portrayed life from the point of view of the Modocs, rather than their oppressors.

The Modocs shared a valley with the Paiute, and they had a village on Tule Lake. Remember the red-headed Si-Te-Cah giants of Paiute legend who were called *Tule Eaters*, who lived on a raft in a lake? The Modocs also had legends of a red-headed tormenter that they called Yahyáhaäs, minus the raft.

They didn't call him a giant, but he was tall and naked with a great head of bushy, bright red hair. He could put you into such a deep sleep, that it appeared as if you were dead. He also cut off the fingers of living people, and wore the fingers on a necklace around his neck. He stole men's wives, and he could disappear "like a flash." He carried a cane that emitted a "streak of fire."

The name of this frightening man whose power seemed almost magical was Yahyáhaäs. Compare that to the giant Nephilim brothers from the *Book of Giants*: Ohyah and Ahyah or Hahyah. These Nephilim brothers were connected to the Grigori, and to the Yaksas who begot the giants who brought ruin to Earth and its humans. This is yet another one of those odd coincidences where entities on opposite sides of the globe share similar names, like the Quiname and Quimane giants. And speaking of coincidences, is there any connection between the inscription that mentions a Madoc ruler, and the Modocs?

As for the necklace of fingers, this is not unprecedented. The *Smithsonian's Ninth Annual Report of the Bureau of Ethnology* highlighted two finger-necklaces as worn by medicine-men of the Cheyenne in Wyoming and Montana, which included a picture of a necklace with its blue and white beads, and fingers with long, yellowed fingernails.

One of the necklaces was buried, and the other was sent to the U. S. Military Academy at West Point, and later forwarded to the National Museum in Washington, where it could "fulfill its mission of educating students in a knowledge of the manners and customs of our aborigines."

WHERE ARE THE BONES?

One of the biggest questions is, "Where are the bones?" If we've found this many bones around the world, what happened to them all? Why aren't there exhibitions of giant skeletons, with scholars coming forth to declare that yes indeedy, giants were once the dominant race on Earth?

Several newspaper articles stated that the Smithsonian Institution was called in, and that they took the bones away. That indicates that an anthropologist, who is a specialist in the study of ancient humans and their remains, traveled to the site and studied the bones on-site before whisking them off to the Smithsonian for further lab study.

Anthropologists are trained recognize human bones, and these bones were found before DNA testing, so they relied on what they could assess visually. If bones found in the 1800s survived into our century, today's anthropologists might very well be studying them. However, there are many elements that could have destroyed the bones, and some of them may surprise you. There is also a possibility that the bones are genuine, but the government doesn't want us to know the truth.

If an ancient race of giants towered over us, it would completely overwrite Earth's history and religions. So let's look at the fate of old bones.

Crumbled to Dust

You've already read several instances where the bones crumbled as soon as they were exposed to air, or were touched. In case you missed it, here are a few more, all taken from an *Annual Report of the Bureau of Ethnology* of the Smithsonian. The numbers denote which annual report it came from, and none of these relate to giants. They simply attest to the fact that ancient bones don't always survive the passage of time.

> 2 — Nashville, TN: "It was found near the head of a skeleton, which was much decayed, and had been so disturbed by recent movements of the soil as to render it difficult to determine its original position."

> 3 — McMahon Mound, TN: "…in which numerous skeletons had been deposited. The bodies had been interred without order, and the bones were so intermingled, and so far decayed, that no complete skeletons could be collected… In the earth surrounding the ashes and clay, a number of skeletons were found; these were in such an advanced stage of decomposition that only a few fragments of skulls could be preserved."

> 3 — Taylor's Bend, TN: "…two very much decayed skeletons. A part of one cranium was preserved."

> 3 — Kingston, TN: "Three feet from the surface, six very much decayed skeletons were found, no parts of which could be preserved… Opposite Kingston, on the Clinch River, are three mounds, located on the farm of T. N. Clark. They are all small, and, with the exception of two much decayed skeletons…"

> 3 — Fain's Island: "Four feet below the surface were found the remains of thirty-two human skeletons. With the exception of seventeen skulls, none of the bones could be preserved."

12 — Pipestone County, MN: "In this was found a single skeleton lying at full length upon the right side, head north, on the original surface of the ground... and was so much decayed that the bones and even the teeth crumbled to dust when exposed to air."

37 — "The skeletons were found with the head pointed in an eastwardly direction, and were all so greatly decomposed that it was impossible to preserve any of them for measurement and study, the bones in most cases consisting of only a pasty mass."

Skeptics in Charge

There is no single answer for what happened to the old bones, and sometimes it was done to control information. Not every era in man's history was on board with gaining new knowledge, especially if that knowledge was disagreeable. Hence, the common practice of burning reams of literature just because it was pagan, or belonged to a race of people that you were at war with. Sometimes people just wanted to stay warm on a cold winter's night, and would burn anything flammable.

Issue 644 of the *Otago Witness*, published on April 2, 1864, reprinted a story from the *Evening Bulletin* entitled, "Human Fossils in California." The article stated that the science of studying human fossils to unravel human history was "making a revival." That suggests that prior decades were not particularly interested in getting to the truth, or preserving the truth if it conflicted with their beliefs.

The lengthy article claimed that theologians had entered into a furious war with savants regarding terminology that was irrelevant to anyone who just wanted the plain truth — separate from "domestic theories."

Savants stood at the forefront of a theory that man existed in every epoch that sustained vertebral animals, long before written history. They blasted everyone who held tight to a theory without ever allowing a speck of new evidence in:

> "Everybody, forty years old, knows that the theories of the abstract and physical sciences have changed, like the quarrels and opinions of the doctors over cholera and yellow fever, every decade, and that national libraries are becoming too small to hold their interminable discussions."

"Interminable discussions" — that's what the article said before it exposed the plight of fossils found in California. Miners were accused of carelessness with historical evidence, and the recording of evidence, which is now lost to the rest of us:

> "The miners of California, with their wonder-working mining expedients, have made some additions to this new study of Human Fossilology since 1848, but from carelessness and want of knowledge on the subject, their discoveries have been loosely recorded, without leaving any visible proofs of their labors to be discussed in detail by philosophers."

One man who attempted to take care with his discovery was Jesuit missionary Rotea in the mid-1700s, who discovered a gigantic skeleton in San Joaquin. He was in the process of digging it out, and had unearthed the entire spinal column, a shin-bone, a rib-bone, some teeth, and part of the skull. He would have succeeded except for a flash flood that destroyed part of the evidence. The skeleton was estimated at 11 feet tall.

Rotea also found 50 feet long caves that were 15 feet wide and high. Inside the caves were statues of men and women, as large as life, painted with bright colors, and dressed in nice clothing. The clothing was different from any race known to the Spaniards since the discovery of California, and presumably belonged to an ancient nation.

Then the article moved to "neophytes." This is important, because definitions for *neophyte* include heathens, heretics, and non-believers. In other words, their opinion was treated with skepticism because they allowed for the possibility of giants that predated Adam and Eve:

WHERE ARE THE BONES?

"Our Californian neophytes, however, unanimously affirm that they were a gigantic people who came from the North. This is a tradition which we do not contend should be credited; still it cannot be doubted that the remains of human beings of disproportionate size to the present ones have been found, as related by the Father Rotea… [who] may have transferred these human fossils to some College of his Order in Bavaria or Italy, on the expulsion of the California Jesuits in 1767, or even before that period."

The source was listed as *History of the California Peninsula* by Father Baegert in 1772, for the fate of the giant skeletons. In other words, it's finders-keepers, and the bones may have been taken to Europe. With the many wars that ravaged Europe in the centuries that followed, it's unlikely that the bones still exist. War has a way of destroying everything in its path, including archeological evidence as you'll see in the segment on *Casualties of War*.

Mexico has been a source of amazing discoveries of human bones, skulls and entire skeletons of prodigious size, indicating that its first inhabitants were men of gigantic proportions. Mexico City sits in the middle of one of the great seats of the ancient giants.

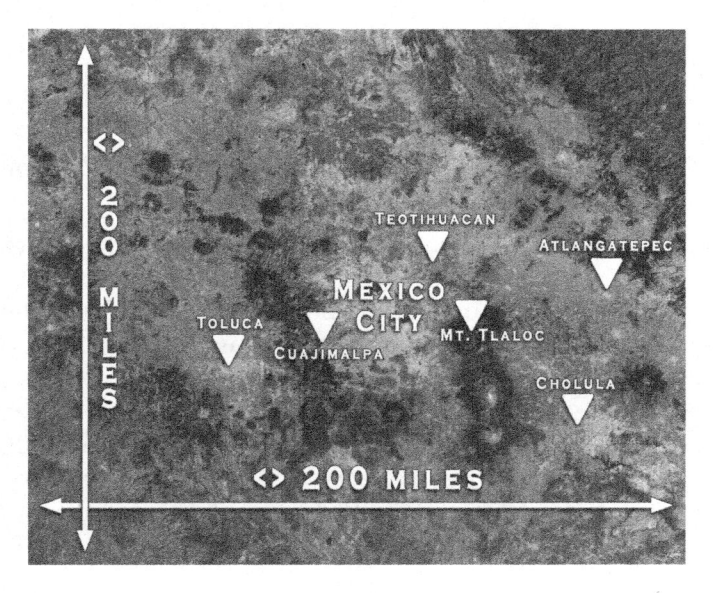

Gigantic skeletons have been found in Toluca, Cuajimalpa, and Atlangatepec. A Jaguar God named Tlaloc is associated with the Pyramid at Cholula which was built by giants. Mt. Tlaloc was also named for him. The ancient city of Teotihuacán has tunnels full of pyroelectric balls. It also has pyramids which boast images of a vehicle that is supposed to represent Tlaloc. All of these places are clustered around Mexico City.

D'Acosta spent time in Mexico City, and he was described as someone whose opinion should hold weight:

> "Hernandez and D'Acosta, who were men of learning, correctness and veracity, affirm that human skulls and even whole skeletons of astonishing size have been found in Mexico."

D'Acosta refers to José de Acosta, a Jesuit missionary and naturalist who traveled extensively through Mexico and South America. He visited archeological sites such as Cuzco, which was the capital of the Incan Empire. He spoke to men who had sailed through the Strait of Magellan, where a tribe of giants lived. They were pursuing Sir Francis Drake, whose encounters with giants are in the *Mesoamerican* chapter. D'Acosta devoured information everywhere he visited, including Mexico City. He compiled his knowledge into a series of books, which include legends of giants whose bones he personally saw.

Not everyone agrees with D'Acosta, or that giants should be accepted as anything but myth. The article referred to him as a "man of learning" but then discarded his opinions on giants:

> "We know that some of the bones mentioned have been found in tombs, which appear to have been made on purpose to hold them, and among the civilized nations of America it was a common tradition that a race of men existed in former times of extraordinary height and bulk. But, that a race of such people existed as a nation, and not as exceptions, is a matter indeed of great question, and not at all to be accepted."

WHERE ARE THE BONES?

"Not at all to be accepted..." It didn't matter that "men of learning" traveled through regions where giants left evidence, and *witnessed* that evidence. Once a man makes up his mind to believe or disbelieve, then no bulk of facts will sway the man, short of a horde of giants descending from the heavens today and traipsing through his back yard. That's why lawyers can take the same set of facts and twist them to prove totally opposing views on the guilt or innocence of a person.

Thus if the man holding the evidence doesn't believe in it... if he believes that the bones are just a fluke of nature, an abnormal growth in one person, do you think he's going to come forward and say, "Hey look! It's another set of bones from the ancient race of giants!" No, he will quietly hoard the bones away and label them as a medical anomaly.

At the other end of the spectrum is carelessness. Gold miners were the demise of untold numbers of giant skeletons. In Sierra County, California, a gold mine known as *Smith's Flat* made news in the 1800s for its output of gold. The Keystone Company had a cleanup of 104 ounces from Smith's Flat, and the mine was so rich that you could see gold in the dirt. Other clean outs were 40 and 80 ounces. Smith's was one of the more prolific mines with a quoted yield of $2 million, in a list of mines where the output was often only $100,000.

The 1800s sent waves of miners to California, three hundred thousand by one estimate, all on a search for gold. They had no interest in preserving any artifacts that they found, and old bones were just a nuisance to be discarded — cleared out of the way. Such was the fate of a human collarbone found in Keystone Tunnel of Smith's Flat.

The bone was found in November 1857 by miners who were drifting for gold in the tunnel. They were one thousand feet beneath the forest-covered surface of the mountain, and as many feet above nearby Canon and Oregon Creeks, and about 4,000 feet above sea level.

The collarbone was discovered in the gravel drift of an ancient river bed under the mountain, in a perfectly sound state of preservation. The fate of this particular giant bone went the way of so many others during the gold rush:

> "Strange to say these miners knew not the value of such a remnant of humanity, and that, if it had been properly authenticated, it was worth its weight in gold."

Miners at the Dexter and Peters' claim at Blanket Creek in Tuolumne County, found the thigh bone and skull of a giant in 1855. The bones were found on a ledge, in a jumbled mass with other human skeletons, accompanied by mortars and pestles. This giant was estimated at 12 feet tall, or twice the size of a human. The gruesome significance of this discovery is detailed in later segments, where human bones were ground into powder for use in medicinals, or as flour to bake bread.

Miners in Jacksonville, Oregon found a pair of human jawbones that were 7 inches wide, and the width of the face when alive was calculated at 9 inches.

In 1863, bones were found in the sea-cliffs of California, near the Rincon, a few miles from San Buenaventura Mission:

> "They were of immense size; but falling into careless keeping, as usual with such matters in California, they were lost to the disciples of Lyell and Agassiz, and museums and quidnuncs missed a grand specimen."

Quidnunc is an archaic word for "gossipmonger," and Lyell and Agassiz referred to Sir Charles Lyell and Louis Agassiz. Lyell's passion was geology, and he was a close friend of Charles Darwin. He believed in the theory of evolution, though he struggled with how it fit in with his religious beliefs. He wrote extensively on geology, and its evidence of the antiquity of man.

Louis Agassiz was also a geologist and paleontologist, as well as a physician. He did *not* embrace Darwin's theory of evolution.

He advocated polygenism — a theory which suggests that we all did not stem from a single lineage. Polygenism suggests that various races of man were either living prior to Adam and Eve, or that there were multiple Adams, created at the same time in different places around the world.

Giants mated with humans and produced a hybrid species, according to ancient texts and the bones we've found, and they weren't the only extraterrestrial race to do so.

Unfortunately, theories such as this are used to promote racism, and there's even a term for it — Scientific Racism. Instead of accepting the notion that we can all be different, but equal, our differences are used to promote hatred and war. It does not negate the theory itself, however. It just shows the ugly side of humans who'll use any tool in their power to justify the ill-treatment of others.

A side effect of this hatred is that it interferes with the study of ancient human remains that might prove multiple lineages. It is yet another reason for the government to keep the discovery of giant bones under wraps. Humans are not evolved enough to embrace a theory without using it as a weapon. First we must learn to get along with one another, and we're a long way from that. Has there ever been a century, or even a decade, devoid of a war somewhere on Earth? Perhaps the government is wise to keep its secrets.

Make Room for Daddy

Miners and skeptics may have destroyed evidence, but so did everybody else — each for a different reason.

Our ancestors were well aware that you didn't waste precious real estate until the end of time, by burying bodies who would own that tiny plot of land forever. Churches often had charnel houses near graveyards, where they deposited bones that were unearthed while digging a grave. Time limits might be put on how long bones could claim a piece of greenery, after which time they were dug up and dumped in the charnel house or ossuary. Sometimes the remains were moved to a permanent, shared location, and sometimes they were cremated.

Eventually the charnel houses became rank and disgusting, or were abandoned until nobody cared about them anymore. Ancient tombs were bought and sold, dug up and repurposed.

The Louvre Palace dates back to the 12th century and has undergone countless renovations and alterations. It was originally built as a military fortress and later became a royal residence.

In 1363, King Charles V ordered a chateau to be built, and the builder, Raimond Dutemple, bought ten ancient tombs from the churchwardens of the Innocents. He wanted the stones for masonry. Another segment of the cemetery was sold and became a marketplace, according to *Military and Religious Life in the Middle Ages and at the Period of the Renaissance* by Paul Lacroix in 1874.

Even in those ancient times, the cemetery was a mass of stones, crosses, human remains, and filth. Grass grew up among heaps of skulls, and the floors of the charnel houses bent beneath vast piles of decomposing bones. Graves had been dug in every available space of ground, and the smell was unbearable.

Over two million bodies were buried in the Innocents' cemetery in Paris, and in the reign of King Louis XV, the unsanitary conditions at the cemetery affected the surrounding businesses. The cemetery was cleared out in 1786, and the bodies were moved to catacombs. As part of the cleanup, body fat was collected and turned into candles and soap. In other words, the bones were cleaned and the flesh removed.

A charnel house in Rothwell Parish, England, was discovered under a church by workmen. If it was "discovered," that means it was long forgotten. It was piled very carefully from the ground to the roof on two sides with human bones, mostly just the larger bones and skulls. There was an aisle down the center to walk through. The bones "mouldered down to half their former height" once the air hit them.

WHERE ARE THE BONES?

A similar collection of bones was found in Hythe, Kent, and in Ripon, Yorkshire, according to *History, Gazetteer, and Directory of Northamptonshire* by William Whellan and Co. in 1849. If the remains of humans a thousand or more years after the reign of giants were not protected for posterity, then how can we expect ancient remains to come down through the eons unscathed?

A charnel house that belonged to the Knights Hospitallers later passed through many hands. In the early seventeenth century, it was rented by the Armenians from the Turks. Bodies were still being added in 1818, but it had the appearance of being abandoned not long after:

> "The field or plat is not now marked by any boundary to distinguish it from the rest of the hillside; and the former charnel house, now a ruin, is all that remains to point out the site... An opening at each end enabled us to look in, but the bottom was empty and dry, excepting a few bones much decayed."

Let's take one final look at the fate of bones in charnel houses, from *The History and Survey of London and Its Environs: From the Earliest Period to the Present Time* by B. Lambert in 1806.

Somerset House was built in 1549 by the Duke of Somerset. He demolished the palaces of the Bishops of Chester and Worcester, plus an inn of chancery called Strand Inn, and the Church of St. Mary, in order to get building materials.

He obtained additional building materials for Somerset from the Church of St. John of Jerusalem with its tower, and cloisters on the north side of St. Paul's Church, together with the chapel and the charnel house, all of which he destroyed for the singular purpose of building a grand house for himself.

Another text describes the fate of the bones from the various churches: they were "flung into Finsbury fields." The owners of the bishop's houses and churches received no compensation, and no atonement was ever made.

The Bone Collectors

Bones were a hot commodity in the days of yore. They were *useful*, and worth more money sold to bone collectors than buried in the ground for all eternity. This was the fate of the bones unearthed in Strood, England, according to the *History of Strood* by Henry Smetham in 1899.

On excavating a cellar for the New Fountain Inn in Strood, thirty-one skeletons were found buried therein, including the skeleton of a giant. They were presumed to have died in the hospital which had once been located there. These gruesome fragments of humans past were not taken to a graveyard and given a proper burial as one would expect; they were conveyed to a bone merchant who collected the carcasses, bones, horns and hooves of dead animals, and they were treated the same as animal remains. While a reputable bone merchant would purchase only animal bones, a disreputable bone collector would not be so discriminating.

Fat could be extracted and turned into tallow for candles and soap-making. Low quality tallow would have a greenish-brown color and was used for laundry soap and lubricants. High quality tallow, which was not contaminated with stomach waste, could be used for personal soaps, candles and cooking lard.

Hooves were turned into buttons, hair pins, fertilizer and glue. If the entire carcass was available, the intestines and bladder became sausage casings, brewer's hose and snuff packages. Tail hair produced stuffing for mattresses and upholstery. Bones were turned into buttons, glue, polish, and leather dressing. Other body parts were used as well, and no part of an animal carcass went to waste. Carcasses and bones were a profitable business.

Glue could be sold to a drysalter, which was a merchant that specialized in glue, varnish, dye, salt, pickles, flax, hemp, potash, and dried meat. Tallow was sold to the soap-boilers, who were good customers of a bone merchant.

WHERE ARE THE BONES?

The big soap-boiler operations used iron boilers called soap pans or coppers which could hold up to thirty tons of material. They could produce a variety of soaps including curd soap, mottled soap, yellow soap, marine soap, silicate soap, soft soap, toilet soap, arsenic soap, and medicated soap. In London alone, soap-boilers produced up to 5,000 tons of soap per year, so you can imagine their need for raw ingredients.

Bone merchants sold their wares to several manufacturing businesses, not just soap-boilers. They were also known as "rag-and-bone men" or "bone grubbers" who collected items such as scrap metal, rags, and bones. The items were then sold and recycled. Bones were made into knife handles, toys, ornaments, or used in chemistry and soap-making. Some bones were crushed for agricultural purposes, or as animal charcoal for sugar refiners.

According to *Reports From Committees, Volume 7: Poor Removal; Public Health Bill and Nuisances Removal Amendment Bill*, from Great Britain's House of Commons for the period 12 December 1854 to 14 August 1855, one bone merchant had the following to say about his own activities:

> "You are a bone-merchant; where do the bones come from that you purchase?"
>
> "I purchase bones coming from Australia and from South America: I purchase more bones in London than any other man in London."
>
> "Do you buy from persons in London?"
>
> "Yes, a large quantity."
>
> "Where are the bones that you purchase generally brought from?"
>
> "They are brought from the bone-boilers' yards in London; the process is this: first of all they are bought by what we call rag shops; they are the purchasers of the bones in small quantities of 5 hundred weight and 10 hundred weight and so on; from thence they are conveyed to the bone-boilers' yards, and there they are boiled down and thrown into heaps, after being divested of the meat and the noxious matters."

What are the odds that he sifted through the bones to make sure that none were human? An interesting look into the gruesome business of recycling human bones comes from the book, *Twenty-Four Lectures on the Book of Revelation* by James Wells, Minister of the New Surrey Tabernacle, published in 1870. While he does not appear to be quoting directly from the *Bible* in this passage, he is undoubtedly drawing on knowledge of the bone merchant business:

> "Is he not a very great bone merchant? Have there not been tons of human bones sold, and have they not brought great riches to that merchant?"

In *The Zoologist: A Popular Miscellany of Natural History, Series 2, Volume 9* by Edward Newman in 1874, an archeologist lamented the loss of bones to a bone collector. A large number of bones were excavated from the Valley of the Thames, between the Kennet and Thames rivers. His anguish:

> "An immense number of bones were turned up during this excavation, but few of these have unfortunately been preserved; but from the accounts of eye-witnesses, I believe at least one perfect human skeleton and several skulls were exhumed."

It goes on to talk about other artifacts that were dug up, including the antlers of a deer that were repurposed as tools. Then it says:

> "I do not know from what depth this was obtained, it having been rescued from the stores of a bone merchant, to whom most of the fossils found their way, I fear."

He and his associates were hoping to retrieve the bones of an extinct species of wild cattle from the bone merchant. If you still aren't convinced that human bones were a hot commodity, Volume 5 of the 1832 publication of *Fraser's Magazine* had an articled called "The Climax of Cemeteries!" It chronicled funerary practices, including tribes "who piously entombed their deceased ancestors in their own filial stomachs." In other words, they ate their dead. Others used human bones in various "useful and ornamental purposes," while the Egyptians took great care to entomb their dead. Unfortunately, these mummies were an excellent source of fuel for later generations, who did not have access to lush forests or coal mines.

Several publications bespoke of this mummy-fuel, including *The History and Description of Fossil Fuel* published by Whittaker and Co. of London in 1835, and Volume 1 of *The Elevator Constructor*, published by the International Union of Elevator Constructors in 1903. Even the Troglodytes left evidence of their mummy-fuel, according to *Letters from the Red Sea, Egypt, and the Continent* by Mes Esdaile, M.D. in 1839. Herodotus described the Troglodytes as the swiftest running humans of the known world, with a voice that sounded like screeching bats. These cave-dwellers left behind dismembered, half-burnt mummies.

In 1798 Ireland, dead bodies weren't converted into fuel — they inadvertently became food for pigs. Ireland was ravished by war, and slaughtered peasants lay exposed on the ground, where roaming pigs ate the bodies. Decent folks didn't want to eat the pigs, so a canny merchant bought thousands of these pigs. He smoked and pickled them, and sold them to the British. Such merchants were called "pig-jobbers" according to *Fraser's Magazine for Town and Country, Volume V*, published in 1832.

The chemical stage of decomposition made for a great fertilizer, and this was the fate of bodies at the Battle of Waterloo in 1815. London dentists carried off soldiers' teeth in hogsheads, and Yorkshire bone-grubbers took the skeletons of the soldiers and their horses, to be ground to dust in Kingston-upon-Hull, and drilled with turnip-seed in the chalky districts of Yorkshire.

Artificial dentures were made with human teeth even into the 1800s, and the teeth collected on the Waterloo battlefield were so plentiful that they "glutted the market." Merchants at Waterloo made more money selling human teeth than they did robbing dead bodies. In England, dentists were regular customers of the "tooth man" who carried human teeth in a green baize bag, according to *Dental Items of Interest, Volume 43* published in 1921. Poor people even had their teeth pulled, and sold them.

French chemists found another use for human corpses — they converted them into candles. In Italy, bodies were promised a full year of not being dug up. A cemetery in Naples had 365 cells — one for each day of the year — where bodies were kept. This dating system ensured that departed cavaliers were not disturbed for a full twelve months.

Cremated humans were converted to charcoal, which was used in the clarification of wine and vinegar, and the purification of sugar and sea water. It also made for an excellent boot polish.

Bone collectors were not limited to Europe. In Teotihuacán, Mexico, archeologists found thousands of human bone fragments that prove beyond a doubt that ancient peoples repurposed human bones into tools and household items. Apparently the bones had to be sculpted soon after death, lest they become too brittle to work with. They did not get a twelve month reprieve.

As for skeletons, a book entitled, *The Ancient Cities of the New World: Being Travels and Explorations in Mexico and Central America from 1857-1882,* by Désiré Charnay in 1887, claims that the skeletons of the rich were burned, and their ashes entombed. More recent discoveries include buttons, combs, needles, spatulas, and dozens of other utensils manufactured from human bones.

Across the world in Tibet and India, the Buddhist, Shaviite, and Tibetan priests turned human thigh bones into bone flutes or trumpets known as "kanglings." Other ritual implements included human skullcaps. In Guyana, the Carob people also repurposed human bones into flutes, as did the Polynesian Māori of New Zealand. The word *tibia*, that we now use for the human shinbone, was the Latin word for "flute."

The *damaru* was a two-headed drum made of bones for Hindus and Buddhists. While today it is made of wood and leather, in ancient times it was made of human skulls.

The Chamorro people recycled human bones into tools and weapons, and the longer the bones, the more valuable they were. Long bones were whittled into a razor sharp tip, and then carved to create a triple row of barbed teeth so that the spear head would penetrate with ease, but be nearly impossible to pull out. It was usually the bones of enemies that were used, so families took care to bury their own loved ones close to home, and out of the reach of enemies.

Skulls, however, served a different purpose. It was common to display the skulls of your ancestors inside your home, and bow toward them as a gesture of respect.

Human Relics

Some human bones are kept as relics. For example, the bones of saints were kept as holy relics. Their bones were treated differently than the average human bone. They were not burned or buried — they were venerated, and fought over.

The lives of the saints were full of miracles, and their bones were believed to hold the same power to perform miracles. People flocked to the churches that boasted of saint's bones, so possessing a bone was a benefit to the church, and great lengths were taken to protect the bodies from theft. Thus was the scene over the body of St. Thomas Aquinas, according to *St. Louis and Henry IV* by John Hampden Gurney in 1855.

It was dubbed "the battle of the monks for the bones of Thomas Aquinas" and in its original version, the tale took up 15 pages of narrative. Aquinas wanted to bequeath his bones to the Dominicans of Toulouse, France, being his own order, but he died at the abbey of the Benedictine monks in Fossanova, Italy.

Fossanova became a place of pilgrimage for the sick, as it was rumored that his bones were a source of miraculous healing.

A legal battle began over the bones, with the Dominicans begging the Pope to grant them rights to the bones of their own monk. This battle raged on for *decades*, with Fossanova still in possession of Aquinas.

When Fossanova thought they might lose his body to the Dominicans, they cut off his head, and later, removed the flesh from his bones which was still in a state of perfect preservation — uncorrupted and unspoiled.

They boiled the body in aromatic liquid, and put the fragments in a box that would be easy to carry "from place to place when danger was abroad." By separating the head, and making the body easier to move, they ensured that if one part were stolen, they'd still have the other part, and that if someone came to take the bones, they could be quickly and easily whisked away to safety. *Short Lives of the Dominican Saints* by John Procter in 1901, states that the head was given to the Count of Piperno.

Seventy-five years passed, with Fossanova still in possession, when the story heated up. The Count of Fondi — neighbor to the Fossanova monks — convinced them that the bones were in grave danger of being stolen according to rumors, and that he could protect them in his castle, so the bones were moved.

Word got out, and the king of Sicily sent an entire embassy to beg for the body, promising a great fortune to the donor. Fondi and Fossanova both refused the offer, and Aquinas stayed put, but not for long. The Count was uncomfortable being in the middle of such a fuss, so he gave the body to Raymond of Toulouse, general of the Dominicans.

The monks at Fossanova were livid, and brought suit against Raymond for theft and sacrilege. Kings and queens came before Popes and Cardinals, and in the end, the body was officially granted to the Dominicans of Toulouse by the Pope.

The body in Fossanova, and the head in Piperno, were moved to Toulouse, in a two month journey with miracles taking place all along the way. Tens of thousands of people accompanied the decades old body of Saint Thomas Aquinas, carrying lighted candles and torches, in a grand procession.

The bones of the saint, which had been "hacked, boiled, borrowed, stolen, [and] disputed about like a chattel," finally came to rest at Toulouse, except for the right hand, which had been "chopped off and sent as a present to the sister of Aquinas, eighty years before."

Other portions of his body were given out as well, presumably by the Dominicans when they finally gained possession. His arm went to the Dominican Church of Saint James in Paris, and an unnamed body part was given to the Convent of Saint Dominic in Naples. During the French Revolution, the bones were moved from Toulouse to the crypt of the Church of Saint Sernin, and later, moved again.

This is just one account of holy bones or holy relics, as they are most often called. The skull of St. Ivo of Kermartin is displayed at Tréguier's cathedral in France. The skull of St. Titus is in the Church of St. Titus in Heraklion, Greece. The skulls of St. Peter and St. Paul are in the Basilica of St. John Lateran in Rome. The body of Buddha was divided up and divvied out, and his tooth is in a temple in Sri Lanka which is appropriately known as The Temple of the Tooth. Your life had to be pretty miraculous for your body to be treated as a holy relic, and there are countless of these sacred human relics all around the world.

We've gone out of our way to preserve the bones of the saints, but what about the giants, who were often depicted as our enemies? Their bones were important during the age of giants, but as time passed, we stopped worshipping the giant gods.

King Pelops of Pisa, in ancient Greece, was descended from giants. His mother was Dione, the daughter of Atlas the Titan. His father was Tantalus, who was the son of the Olympian god Zeus. The Titans were giants, and the Olympian gods were giants, so Pelops had pure giant's blood on both sides of his parentage — yet he died at the hands of his own people.

Pelops did not meet a pleasant end, as he was offered up as a human sacrifice by his own father. Pelops was killed, cut into pieces, and the pieces boiled into a stew as a banquet for the gods. When the gods (who were all giants) discovered the contents of the stew, they refused to eat it, although Demeter absentmindedly ate part of Pelop's shoulder. Later, at the Shrine of Pelops in Olympia, his bones were stored in a chest with the exception of one shoulder blade, which was put on display.

We have no way of knowing whether the bones existed — all we have is the word of Pausanias, an archeologist who lived from 110-180 A.D. He wrote extensively about his travels through Greece, taking care to notate geography, archeology, culture, architecture, mythology, art, nature, and other aspects of Grecian life. He was particularly fascinated by anything related to the gods, holy relics, and other sacred and mysterious objects.

Pausanias wrote that the bones of Tantalus were kept in a bronze vessel, and that the bones of Pelops were preserved in a bronze box at Pisa, which was a town in ancient Greece. In a different book, he wrote that Pelops' bones were in a brazen (brass) coffer, in a small building not far from a temple in Pisa.

The city of Megalopolis, Greece, had bones of superhuman size from a giant who defended Rhea, the mother of Zeus. Ancient Megalopolis was the site of the War of the Titans — a ten year battle between the giant Titans and the giant Olympians. Today we consider these beings as mythological figures. In Pausanias' time, they were as real as Blackbeard the Pirate, and just as famous for their larger-than-life exploits.

One thousand years from now, will our descendants think of Cochise, Hiawatha, Jesse James, Wyatt Earp, Davy Crockett, and Wild Bill Hickock as mythological figures? Are YOU even aware that they were real people, and not just tall tales that somebody made up as a bedtime story?

Pausanias also stated that Hercules — of our own legends — was the great-grandson of Pelops. Other giants that Pausanias mentioned by name were Thurius, Polybotes, Enceladus, Antaeus, and Mimas. Antaeus was mentioned in the *Swamp Giants and Cannibals* segment, as a comparison to the giants of Curaçao, though the name was spelled Antheus.

Pausanias mentioned a war between the giant Athenians and giant Amazons, and elsewhere of a battle between the gods and the giants. There was also a war between the giants who lived in Thrace, and the giants who lived on the isthmus of Pallene. Are any of these battles related to the war between the two factions of Grigori in the *Bible* — those who kept their distance from humans, and those who got up close and personal with us? If the Titans and Olympians represented giants and their offspring, then their battles become an echo of the battles between the Grigori and their Nephilim children, and Elioud grandchildren.

Historians and archeologists today attribute the legends of giants' bones to our ancestors finding the bones of prehistoric animals and misinterpreting them. Sometimes the bones were skulls, however, which would be pretty hard to confuse with a dinosaur. The skull of Orpheus was displayed at an oracle in Lesbos, while his bones were in a stone vase in Thrace. Orpheus was descended from the giant Greek gods. In other words, his bones were treated with the same veneration as the bones of St. Thomas Aquinas, back when the giants of Greece were looked up to as gods.

Not all bones are preserved as objects of worship. Sometimes the bones of famous people take on a power of their own, just to be able to hold up a bone and say, "This skullcap used to belong to outlaw Big Nose George, but now it's just my ashtray!"

Big Nose George was not a giant, but the fate of his bones demonstrates what happened to bones in the olden days, when they belonged to someone of renown.

George Parrott was an outlaw in the 1800s whose deeds were so nefarious, that after he was caught and hung, his skullcap was used as an ashtray and his skin was turned into a pair of shoes. What did he do that was so incredibly evil that his corpse was treated with such disdain?

The wilds of Wyoming were the stomping grounds for Big Nose George and his outlaw gang. Some claimed that he rode with Butch Cassidy for a spell, while George himself boasted that he once rode with Frank and Jesse James. Whatever tall tales surrounded George's gang, one fact remained undisputed: Big Nose George Parrott was an outlaw.

Like the plot from an old western movie, George and his gang started out as two-bit horse thieves and cattle rustlers, soon graduating to stage coaches and pay wagons where they stole mail, gold, whiskey, and supplies. Stage coaches and wagons were easy pickings for an outlaw gang in the old west, but it wasn't until his gang upped the ante to train robbery that the road to his infamy and downfall began. Big Nose George and his gang attempted to rob the No. 3 Westbound Union Pacific train in Wyoming. They didn't get the gold, but they caught the attention of Sheriff Robert Widdowfield, and Union Pacific detective Henry "Tip" Vincent.

The outlaws led the lawmen on a merry chase through the wilds of Wyoming, finally coming head-to-head in a showdown at Elk Mountain. The lawmen caught up to the outlaws at their camp in Rattlesnake Canyon, where the remnants of a campfire still glowed hot.

The outlaws were hiding in the bushes nearby with the intent of letting the riders pass unmolested, until they discovered that the riders were lawmen hot on their trail. They opened fire on the lawmen and shot Sheriff Widdowfield in the face, killing him instantly. Tip Vincent realized that he was outgunned and attempted to flee, but he was also shot dead.

When the lawmen failed to return to town, a search began. Their dead bodies were found and a whopping $20,000 bounty was put on the heads of the outlaw gang, an incredible amount of money for the late 1800s.

WHERE ARE THE BONES?

The outlaws got away, but Big Nose George Parrott made the fatal mistake of boasting about the killings one night in a joyous round of drinking. His big mouth got him caught, tried, and sentenced to hang.

While waiting in a Rawlins, Wyoming, jail cell for his execution, George tried to escape the hangman's noose. Using a piece of sandstone and a pocket knife, Big Nose George was able to free his ankles from their shackles. When jailer Robert Rankin entered his cell, George took him by surprise, struck him over the head with the shackles, and fractured his skull. George failed to escape. Rankin survived but now there were two dead lawmen to account for, and the almost fatal assault of a third.

The attempted escape of Big Nose George so riled the citizens of Rawlins that a vigilante party of thirty masked men dragged him from his jail cell, intent on hanging him from a telegraph pole.

A gathering of 200 townspeople watched as George stood on a kerosene barrel with a noose around his neck. The hangman's rope broke when the barrel was kicked out from under him, and Big Nose George fell to the ground where he begged to be shot instead of hung. While he was begging for mercy, George managed to loosen the bindings around his hands, unbeknownst to his executioners. Mercy was not granted.

Another noose was placed around his neck, and George was forced to climb a ladder which they'd leaned against a telegraph pole. The ladder was pulled out from under him, and George grabbed hold of the pole and clung to it for life, begging for someone to show mercy and shoot him. No one did.

Eventually George grew tired, let go of the pole, and slowly strangled to death. Big Nose George Parrott died at the hands of the lynch mob in March of 1881.

Shortly after his burial, the coffin was dug up and his body given over to science, so that they could study his criminal brain. Doctors Thomas Maghee and John Osborne were hoping to find physical signs in the brain for criminal tendencies. They sawed off the top of George's skull, and gave the skullcap to a 15 year old medical assistant named Lillian Heath. Imagine giving part of someone's skull to a 15 year old girl as a souvenir? Lillian used the skullcap as a doorstop, pen holder, and ash tray.

Other parts of George's body also became bizarre objects of use. Before the removal of the skullcap, a plaster of Paris death mask had been made of George's face. The mask had no ears, because George's own ears had "worn off" during the long, drawn out hanging. George's skin was made into a medical bag and a pair of shoes. Dr. John Osborne later wore the shoes at the celebration of his election as Governor of Wyoming. Yes folks, human body parts were made into purses and shoes just like alligators and snakes, and worn just as proudly.

The remains of Big Nose George's body were stored in a whiskey barrel, which was filled with a salt solution in order to keep the body viable while doctors performed additional experiments. The whiskey barrel was eventually buried behind the office of Dr. Maghee. Big Nose George's story didn't end there, however. The barrel was dug up in May of 1950 during the construction of a bank.

Inside the barrel were human bones, a bottle of vegetable compound, a skull with the crown sawed off, and a pair of shoes made of human skin. Lillian Heath, the original recipient of George's skullcap, was now Dr. Lillian Nelson, and she was still alive. Lillian had gone on to become the first woman doctor in Wyoming, and she was in her eighties when the whiskey barrel was unearthed.

Lillian still owned the skullcap, which turned out to be a perfect fit for the remains of the skull that was found in the barrel. DNA tests proved the match, and the various body parts of Big Nose George Parrott went on display at the Carbon County Museum in Rawlins, Wyoming, and at the Union Pacific Museum in Omaha, Nebraska. If the remains of an ordinary, two-bit outlaw were important enough to dissect, and turn into shoes and ashtrays, what do you think our ancestors would have done with a dead giant?

In Volume 48 of the *St. Louis Medical Review* published in 1903, the fate of one set of giant bones was its utter destruction. When found at Holbeach during excavations for two houses, the skeleton was complete. Every bone was in perfect condition and not a tooth was missing. Where is the giant skeleton now? It was immediately broken into fragments, and several townspeople seized the pieces as mementos. The skeleton was seven feet two inches tall.

Destruction of Bones in the Bible

Several biblical passages talk about the fate of bones — usually as a matter of destroying the bones of enemies. In *2 Kings 23*, a king went after the worshippers of the evil god Baal, destroyed all of their wicked paraphernalia, and then destroyed their bones. Keep in mind that enemies in the *Old Testament* were often giants, including the Rephaim, Anakim, Emim, Amorites, Zamzummim, some Canaanites, and there were others:

> ASV: 2 Kings 21:36 — "... he spied the sepulchers that were there in the mount... and took the bones out of the sepulchers, and burned them upon the altar."

A *sepulcher* is a tomb, a place of burial for human bones. In this passage, the tombs of those who worshipped Baal were emptied of their bones, and the bones were destroyed. Baal, as we've seen in the Grigori segment, was a god that the biblical giants worshipped. *Ezekiel 6* promises a similar fate to the wicked:

> KJ21: Ezekiel 6:4-5 — "... your altars shall be desolate, and your images shall be broken: and I will cast down your slain men before your idols. And I will lay the dead carcasses of the children of Israel before their idols; and I will scatter your bones round about your altars."

This is a call to action, and it would have been acted upon in the battles against the Grigori, Nephilim, and Elioud giants. Their bones would have been decimated. The extra-biblical *Book of Enoch* expands on the sins of the giants. Chapter 7 describes how the Nephilim giants consumed all of the acquisitions of men, and that when men could no longer sustain the giants, they turned against one another, and against men. They ate all of our food and when the food ran out, they became cannibals. They devoured one another's flesh, and human flesh, and drank blood. *Micah 3* of the *Bible* also mentions cannibalism:

> KJ21: Micah 3:2-3 — "... who pluck off their skin from off them, and their flesh from off their bones. Who also eat the flesh of My people, and flay their skin from off them; and they break their bones, and chop them in pieces, as for the pot, and as flesh within the cauldron."

These cannibalistic giants threw their own kind, along with us, into a cooking pot just as we'd cook up rabbit stew. Giants destroyed the bones of their own people, because they were ravished with hunger. They did not plant crops, or tend livestock — they sustained themselves by rustling ours. They ate everything that we produced, which was one of their biggest sins because it left us to starve. We couldn't produce enough to feed them, and have any left for ourselves. They destroyed their own remains, and we went after the bones that were left.

Destroyed to Prevent Resurrection

Our ancestors literally believed that a dead body could come back to life, and that to prevent it, you must stake it through the heart, or completely destroy the bones.

In 1786, Charles Vallancey in his book, *Collectanea de Rebus Hibernicus, Volume III*, wrote how the Dadananai of Mycenaean Greece used their magic to raise dead Athenians back to life, as fast as they were slain in battle by the Assyrians. This was a very effective ploy, because the Assyrians were disheartened to kill an Athenian one day, only to fight that exact same Athenian again the next day. Vallancey believed that the Dadananai fled to Ireland, where they became known as the Tuatha dé Danann.

Vallancey was a British surveyor who was sent to Ireland, and he became an authority on Irish antiquities. His theories were not well received, and his contemporaries stated that Vallancey "wrote more nonsense than any man of his time" calling his works "absurdities."

Vallancey did, however, have access to some of the oldest documents of Irish history to draw his conclusions from, and in those days it was common for history to be "rewritten." *A Dictionary of Miracles* by Reverend Ebenezer Cobham Brewer in 1894, states in its introduction:

> "It was customary in religious houses for someone to read aloud during meal time, and a favorite amusement was to adapt some heathen tale and spiritualize it. Popular adaptations would be remembered, and handed down, and in time these traditions would be lifted into the national hagiography."

We can't know for certain where Vallancey drew his "absurd" conclusions from, or if all of his sources still exist. Both the Tuatha dé Danann and the Fomorian giants they battled were considered heathens. Vallancey drew parallels between the Mycenaean Danaans and the Irish Dananns, going so far as to claim that the Irish were none other than the Mycenaeans who had fled the city of Athens in the province of Achaea.

The *General History of Ireland* published in 1723 by Jeoffry Keating and Dermod O'Connor, expands on the story of the undead, stating that instead of giving up, the Assyrians sought advice from a druid on how to battle this resurrection magic. The druid told them to drive a stake of *quick beam wood* through the body, after which they could no longer be revived.

Vallancey's Dadananai were no longer able to bring the dead back to life, and decided that it was prudent to move out of the country. They left Athens and sailed to Lochlon, and later made their way to Ireland, where they either burnt their ships upon arrival, or flew in from the heavens in dark clouds.

The Tuatha dé Danann were not giants, nor were they evil. They were one of the most beneficial races in our history, bringing wisdom, and laws, to mankind. They came to an Ireland ruled by Fomorian giants, and they drove those giants out, killing most of them. They did away with human sacrifice. They built great castles, and schools, and they were renowned teachers. They were a race of tall, blonde, humanoids, who came down from the stars — a theory explored in depth in the book *Ancient Aliens and the Lost Islands* by Lars Bergen and Sharon Delarose.

The point here is that in both Greece, and Ireland, they were credited with the ability to bring the dead back to life. That is explored in the ancient alien book, along with credible theories that it was nothing more than misunderstood, advanced technology, similar to our technology today. We 'raise the dead' with heart paddles, surgery, and other feats of medicine. We repair broken bones and replace broken hearts. If extraterrestrials were living on Earth alongside humans, then the "magic" and "marvels" that we witnessed probably did take place, except that they were no more supernatural than medicine today.

Extraterrestrials took part in our ancient wars. Zecharia Sitchin wrote about this in his book *The Wars of Gods and Men*. Their medical advances, as seen on a battlefield in 1600 B.C. when Mycenaean Greece came into power, would have stunned human witnesses, and filled us with terror to go up against beings who seemingly couldn't be killed.

No race terrorized us more than the giants, and the last thing a human would want was for that giant to come back to life. There's no telling what might have been done to the body or bones to prevent that from happening.

WHERE ARE THE BONES?

Superstition

An article published in 1930 gives us another glimpse at the destruction of giant bones out of fear. It appeared on the 4th of December in The *Border Cities Star*, and it was entitled, "Superstitious Natives Destroy Relics of Prehistoric Supermen: Scientists Hope to Save Skeletons of Giant Men Found In Mexico and Prove That Humans Have Deteriorated Physically."

> "Preparations for a hasty expedition into the Mexican state of Sonora were made by University of Arizona archeologists today, after they received reports that superstitious natives were destroying valuable relics of a prehistoric race of supermen.
> "Dr. Byron H. Cummings, head of the university archaeology department, expressed the fear natives may destroy all the relics — and the wealth of scientific knowledge they hold — unless stopped at once."

It was hoped that the prehistoric skeletons would prove a long-held theory that giants once roamed the Yaqui River region, and that man had degenerated physically from his previously giant stature.

Acquiring the bones that might prove such a theory was dangerous for archeologists, however, due to the fear and superstition of the Sonorans. They were so intent on destroying the giant bones that they attacked scientific parties to prevent them from collecting the bones. Why were the Sonorans so afraid of the bones? Did they believe that the giants could somehow be brought back to life, if the bones were not completely obliterated? Whatever their fear, the story made newspapers around the country after a miner discovered skeletons as tall as 8 feet 3 inches.

Byron Cummings was the 9th president of the University of Arizona. He held positions including Head of the Department of Archeology, Director of the Arizona State Museum, and Dean of the UA College of Letters. He even held a doctor of law degree, which indicates that he was adept at sifting through facts and evidence. This was a man of learning and prominence, and the newspaper articles quote him, and his hopes of proving this giant race as one of the greatest discoveries of archeological history.

The skeletons were found buried near the Yaqui River, 160 miles south of the United States-Mexico border. As facts were uncovered, more news reports came out including one on December 9 in *The Telegraph-Herald and Times-Journal:*

> "Traces of a lost race of giants, who wore oriental turbans and mummified their dead in a manner similar to that of the ancient Egyptians, have been found in the Yaqui Indian country in Sonora, Mexico.
>
> "Announcement of the finding of thirty-seven bodies of men and women, all more than seven feet tall, in a perfect state of preservation, was made by Dr. Byron Cummings, at the University of Arizona here."

Ethnologist Paxson C. Hayes traveled to Mexico and witnessed the site as well. The mummies were encased in stone crypts, and Hayes believed that an entire city of these lost tribes might be found under the debris and dust of centuries.

Tables were buried near the Mexican mummies — tables that were nearly identical in size and design to tables found buried with mummies in the Gobi desert that borders China and Mongolia, on the other side of the world. Also bordering the Gobi desert are the Altai Mountains, where a giant tooth and finger bone were found in Denisova Cave in 2008. Now we have a piece evidence, as small as it is, in our own lifetime, studied by our own scientists and archeologists.

The 40,000 year old finger and tooth have been identified as belonging to a previously unknown race of humanoids, according to genetic studies. We've dubbed these humanoids as *Denisovans* for the cave in which they were found, and their distinct DNA puts them in a different category from both *Homo sapiens* (humans) and *Homo neanderthalensis* (Neanderthals) though experts don't want to come right out and say it because of an issue with hybrid children. Instead, they are calling the Denisovans a "sister race" of the Neanderthals.

Hybrids should not be able to reproduce, and yet Denisovan DNA has been found in people who are living today, which means that the Denisovans mated with ancient humans, just as Neanderthals mated with humans, and Grigori mated with humans, all generating offspring that reproduced.

We have ample evidence that hybrids do reproduce in other species, a topic covered in the nature book *King of the Forest: An Acre of America Backyard Nature Series*. Highlighted are numerous hybrid species of big cat, such as lions with leopards, lions with jaguars, lions with tigers, and the offspring of those hybrids.

So how is this relevant to giants? The Denisovan tooth is 50% bigger than a human tooth of today, with a root structure that sets it apart from both humans and Neanderthals. They are not calling the Denisovan woman a giant. Instead they refer to the tooth as being abnormally large, explaining that even *Homo sapiens* can have big teeth and not be a giant — the same explanation that we give for every giant bone ever found — that it's simply a fluke of nature in that one individual.

Modern genetics and DNA help us tie some of the isolated facts together that wouldn't otherwise be connected. Denisovan DNA has been found in several populations including aboriginal Australians, Melanesians, the Mamanwas of the Philippines, the Bougainville islanders, and Papua New Guinea. Not all people in these islands have Denisovan DNA, but some do. The islands are in the same region, with Australia to the immediate south of the other islands. This is the same region that the following giant legends come from:

- Luzon, with its Quimanes wild men
- the Malay Archipelago and its Quimanes giants
- the Moluccos giants who attacked a Spanish ship

Here we have a giant tooth, whose DNA can be traced to a region where giants once roamed free — giants that were seen, and described, by Spanish explorers. Coincidence?

Sonora, Mexico, is adjacent to Chihuahua, where another series of skeletons was unearthed in a cave. Paxson Hayes was on the scene of that amazing dig as well. *The Deseret News* ran an article on November 9, 1950 entitled "Mexico Cave Find — Clue to Past Ages" by Prescott Chaplin of Central Press, reporting on 34 giant skeletons that were estimated at 10,000 years old, along with evidence of an ancient civilization.

The cave was in Barranca de Cobre, Mexico, more commonly known as Copper Canyon. Six canyons span a range of 37,000 miles and are longer and deeper than the Grand Canyon in the United States, with Copper Canyon being named for its copper-and-green colored walls.

Each skeleton was in its own basket wrapped like a silkworm. Nine were mummified, and they ranged from 7 feet 6 inches to 8 feet tall. The burial robes had powder-blue designs that resembled latch hooks and pyramids. "The ancient buildings in the cave," Hayes said, "were constructed of a cement-like masonry mixed with bamboo. The huts looked much like mosques."

There are legends of a race of giants that go hand-in-hand with the 34 skeletons. The Tarahumara people lived in the many canyon caves, and sometimes built mud-and-stone walls about breast-high as partitions for families or livestock. Wooden fences were also used for livestock. Each cave had a fire in the middle, without a hearth or chimney. Other cave dwellers included the Pimas, Tepehuanes, and Huarogios.

According to *Unknown Mexico, Volume 1* by Carl Lumholtz in 1902, the Tarahumaras excelled at long distance running, up to 200 miles in 24 hours, and they could run down a deer or a wild turkey. They also brought us legends of a race of giants.

The giants taught the Tarahumaras how to plant corn by cutting down trees and burning them, but the giants also ate children, and ravished the Tarahumara women. Sometimes the women gave birth to giant children, and the birthing process killed the mother.

Eventually the Tarahumaras grew angry with the fierce giants, and brewed up a concoction from the chilicote tree that they mixed with corn for the giants to eat, which suggests that they were feeding the giants, as did other humans around the world.

The chilicote seeds of the *Erythrina* species can be toxic, though they were used medicinally by the Tarahumaras and the Yaquis. The seeds are paralytic, and they've been used to poison fish, rats, dogs, and noxious animals in Mexico, according to *Toxic Plants of North America* by George E. Burrows and Ronald J. Tyrl.

The Tarahumaras and their giants may have a connection to the Mound Builders in the United States, although the evidence that would link them is embroiled in controversy. This comes from *The American Antiquarian and Oriental Journal, Volumes IV-V*, in 1881-1882, in conjunction with the Davenport Tablets — a discovery which is also detailed in *Mound Builders of Ancient America: the Archeology of a Myth* by Robert Silverberg in 1968.

Three tablets were found in mounds near Davenport, Iowa in 1877 by Reverend Jacob Gass. The Smithsonian and others initially embraced the tablets as genuine, but later retracted their blessing from the tablets, much like all of the other tablets found around the United States. One theory was that Gass had planted the tablets himself, and another suggested that the tablets were planted for him to find, in order to cost this 'foreign-born man' his post at the Davenport Academy.

The tablets were found in the Cook Mounds, named for the farmer whose land the ten mounds were on. One tablet showed a hunting scene and a cremation scene. Another tablet became known as the Calendar Stone. The tablets suggested that the Mound Builders predated the Native Americans, which in itself was controversial as several tribes were attempting to lay claim to the mounds as belonging to their ancestors.

Deciphering the Davenport Tablets included Hittite and Aztec decryption notes, as well as a comparison to other Mound Builder engravings, which were believed to be of Hittite origin. John Campbell's translation claimed the language to be Aztec, of the Sonora family which includes the Tarahumara, Cahita, Pima, Opata, and Cora people. Thus it reads:

> "Sacrificed to Caal, Lord of Heaven, Sataba… Sapoca the female slave… Caal, Lord of Heaven casata in the men, in the women, the maidens, the boy's poma utica."

Here we have slaves sacrificed to Caal, the Lord of Heaven, with Caal being the chief deity. Campbell compares the hieroglyphics of the Davenport Tablet to a stone in Hamath, which was the capital city of a kingdom in Canaan. Hamath was founded by the Amorites — a race of biblical giants — in Canaan, which was itself the land of giants.

Consul General Johnson and Reverend Jessup took charge of the four Hamath Stones in 1870 and moved them to the museum in Constantinople. The hieroglyphics were identified as *Hittite*.

Campbell's belief that the Davenport inscription was partially based on Hittite is interesting. The biblical Hittites are grouped with all of the other giants. While the Hittites are not specifically labeled as giants, they lived alongside giants, they fought alongside giants, they were treated in much the same way as the giants, and thus, they may also have *been* giants. Among the Hamath inscription is a passage that reads:

> "Khintiel, King in Hamath, sacrificed the chief Caba to Baal."

This is eerily similar to the Davenport inscription of the Iowa Mound Builders, who were not only giants, but left behind tablets in a language that may link them to biblical giants who were exiled from Canaan. The Canaan survivors had to go *somewhere*. Is this a coincidence?

WHERE ARE THE BONES?

Campbell also compares the Davenport inscription with the language of the Yukahiri people of Siberia, who call themselves Andon Domni, and he links the Yukahiri to the Aztecs. He made several other connections, and believed that the Davenport Tablets would destroy the "many false ethnological theories" and give us a truer science of our history. The current status of the Davenport Tablets is that they are fake, just like every other discovery that might prove an alternate human history with giants.

As for superstitions, the bones of giants were destroyed in the *Bible*. In Mycenaean Greece, hearts were staked, or bones were destroyed to prevent the dead from rising again. In Sonora, Mexico, bones and mummies were destroyed by superstitious natives. Not everyone wants the bones preserved.

In *The Origin of Primitive Superstitions* by Rushton M. Dorman in 1881, Dorman talks extensively about the power of dead bones, and the belief that bones could be used to resurrect the dead, or carried as omens of good or bad luck. An Aztec legend told of a single bone, sprinkled with blood, growing back into a person. The Choctaws believed that the spirits of the dead would return to their bones in the bone-mounds, and flesh would knit together over the joints, and that they would again inhabit their ancient territory. Elsewhere, when a whaler died, his body was cut into small pieces and distributed among the other whalers, dried and preserved as good luck charms.

In Mexico, body parts were believed to carry great power when used in witchcraft and sorcery. Brazilian tribes ground human bones into a powder and mingled it with bread, as a show of love for the deceased. The Tapuyas ground up human bones and used it in marriage feasts, being the most precious thing that could be offered.

When you grew old and withered, you offered yourself up to your children, who killed you, and then devoured you. The Xomanas and Passes burned the bones of the dead, and drank the ashes, as did the Arawaks. You can read some of this in *The*

Antiquary, Volume 11, published in 1885, under the chapter "Cannibalism and Sacrifice."

Then there were the many zombie resurrection beliefs. In Peru, they believed that the dead could rise up out of their graves and walk among the living — and feel, eat and drink as when alive. The Chibchas and Quimbayas had similar beliefs, but if a body was burned to ashes, it would not come back to life. Even the bones of animals would rise again, covered anew with flesh, and restock the Earth at some point in the future. In South America, sorcerers had the power to bring the dead back to life, or so the natives believed.

These superstitions caused the bones of loved ones to be preserved to the greatest extent possible, while the bones of enemies — such as giants — would be destroyed.

Casualties of War

The Etowah Mounds near Cartersville, Georgia, included not only giant bones, but artifacts that stunned archeologists. They did not resemble what one would expect from Native American burial sites, and they were believed to pre-date the Native Americans.

A discussion about the Etowah Mounds exposed another fate of ancient relics — their destruction in wartime. A book entitled, *The Antiquities of Tennessee and the Adjacent States: And the State of Aboriginal Society in the Scale of Civilization Represented by Them; a Series of Historical and Ethnological Studies* by Gates P. Thurston of the Tennessee Historical Society in 1897, takes us deep inside the mysteries of the Etowah Mounds. Among the artifacts were pipes unlike anything found previously:

> "They were obviously very old, and, in all likelihood, antedated, by an indefinite period of time, the occupancy of this valley by the Cherokees. So far as recorded observation extends, nothing like them was noted in the use or possession of the modern Indians."

Two of these pipes were given to the author by Mrs. J. C. Rice of Nashville, and her daughter, Miss Ada Rice. The elder Mrs. Rice was the daughter of Colonel Lewis Tumlin of Bartow County, Georgia, the owner of the plantation on which the Etowah Mounds were located. She brought the pipes to Nashville at the close of the war. Colonel Jones described the pipes from recollection, stating that:

> "...amid the devastations consequent upon the invasion of Georgia by the Federal armies, in 1864, these, with other valuable relics, were either destroyed or carried away by the soldiers."

This gives us conflicting stories about the fate of the pipes, but it also gives us another look at the fate of ancient relics in general. It demonstrates that casualties of war do exist.

Even today, war wreaks havoc on our most precious and ancient relics. During the military action known as Operation Iraqi Freedom in 2003, the Iraq Museum was looted, as were local archeological sites. The library was set on fire, destroying 25% of its books, including some very rare specimens. The same thing happened during Operation Desert Storm.

The Colorado State University website for CEMML, which is the Center for Environmental Management of Military Lands, posted an article entitled, *The Impact of War on Iraq's Cultural Heritage: Operation Iraqi Freedom*. Among its sources was a 1992 article entitled, *AIA [Archaeological Institute of America] Resolution Regarding War and the Destruction of Antiquities*. Several additional sources were listed.

One of the great losses was the theft of at least 15,000 ancient relics, including the cuneiform tablets and cylindrical seals of Ancient Sumeria. Even the records of archeological digs disappeared, dating back several decades. Clay cuneiform tablets from Nineveh and Nimrod disappeared as well. These tablets contained some of the oldest texts in the world regarding the first recorded days of humans on Earth, and the gods who came down from the heavens. The stories told on the tablets completely upset history as we know it, and they offered tangible, physical proof of an alternate history of origin.

Who took them, and why? Was it a random act of theft? Were they taken to protect them from destruction, in case the war couldn't be contained? Or was there a darker plan to eliminate or hide physical proof of an ancient, extraterrestrial race?

We do have public translations of portions of the texts, and scholars such as Zecharia Sitchin often draw on the Sumerian tablets as proof of ancient astronaut theory.

As for the stolen tablets, war is destructive. The Ziggurat of Ur was damaged by missiles or machine gun fire. The Sumerian city of Ur is one of the oldest cities in the world, and it is mentioned in the *Old Testament* and ancient Islamic texts.

Ur is listed as the city of birth for Haran, the father of Lot — the same Lot who later lived in Sodom and Gomorrah, and whose wife became a "pillar of salt" for looking back or lingering when the cities were destroyed by fire and brimstone.

We first excavated the Ziggurat of Ur in the 1930s, and we dated it to 2100 B.C. We know how important these ancient structures and tablets are, and yet, we destroy them, and steal them. In some cases the destruction would include ancient bones.

War Trophies

Ancient civilizations often kept the bones of their enemies as war trophies. Heads on pikes, fingers and teeth as necklaces, heads used as kickballs, shrunken heads, and the bones of a giant would have possessed great value as war trophies.

One monumental war trophy was a tower in Serbia, built of human skulls. It was called the *Skull Tower* or *Tower of Skulls*, and it dated back to the battle for independence at Niš in Serbia, on May Day in 1809, according to *Travels and Politics in the Near East*, by William Miller in 1898.

WHERE ARE THE BONES?

Serbian rebels, when facing defeat, committed mass suicide to avoid capture. The Turkish ruler, as was the custom, ordered the heads of the dead men to be collected. They were embedded in the walls of a tower, built specifically to show off the skulls. The ten-foot tower was composed of 952 skulls, arranged in 56 rows of 17 skulls each.

Sixty-seven years later, *Littell's Living Age, Fifth Series, Volume XV*, published in 1876, stated that the skulls had been removed within reach of a man's arm, though there were still a few skulls remaining at the top.

Through the Lands of the Serb by Mary Edith Durham in 1904, claimed that originally, they were embedded flesh and all, with their "faces staring horribly forth, till the flesh rotted and nothing but the bare skulls remained." Skulls were removed from time to time and buried. By the time Miller's book came out, only one skull was left in the tower.

Most of us don't think of skulls as war trophies to be displayed, but historically, skulls were used as a deterrent to frighten off enemies, such as skulls on pikes.

The Hindu goddess Kali was intricately linked to skulls. Her staff was topped with a skull, and decorated with a garland of skulls. Temples built in her honor often featured skulls. She is sometimes represented as holding the gory head of a giant in one hand, and the sword that killed the giant in the other hand.

The Mayans decorated the branches of dead trees with the severed heads of their enemies. Some displays featured freshly severed heads, while others used the bony skull, which could be displayed on a wooden rack, or embedded in a wall. The Aztecs were particularly noted for these skull walls, and Spanish soldiers once counted 62,000 skulls embedded in a wall. Archeologist Rubén G. Mendoza wrote extensively about these gruesome relics in his article, *The Divine Gourd Tree*. Another gruesome piece of artwork was the bone mobile, which greeted visitors with skulls hanging from the ceiling via looped cords.

Spanish conquistador Pascual de Andagoya wrote about a battle he witnessed between two tribes in Panama, led by the Chiefs of Escoria and Paris (aka Pariza or Parita.)

At the battle site, Andagoya "found a great street entirely paved with the heads of the dead, and at the end of it a tower of heads which was such that a man on horseback could not be seen from the other side." This is detailed in *The Narrative of Pascual de Andagoya* published by The Hakluyt Society in 1865.

"In Escoria," he wrote, "there was a race of Indians, much larger and more polished than the others... by the side of whom the other Indians looked like dwarfs."

Giants who made others seem like dwarfs — just like all the other giants who lived on Earth prior to, and alongside, modern humans. Sacrificial burials at the Temple of Quetzalcoatl in the ancient city of Teotihuacán demonstrated that warriors wore necklaces of human teeth, probably those of their enemies. The Aztecs worshipped Quetzalcoatl, though this was not their city. The Aztecs were known for their gruesome display of enemy heads on a tzompantli, or skull rack.

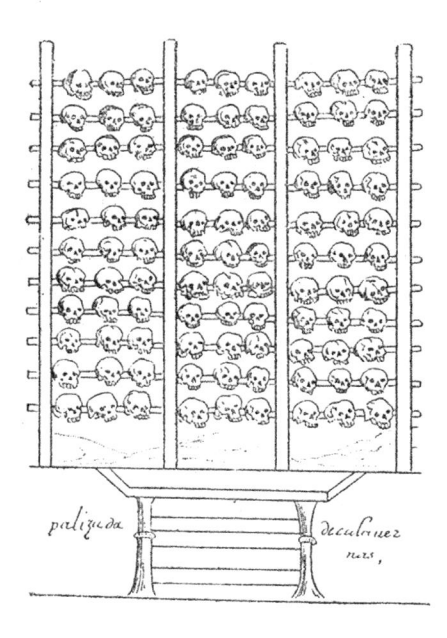

WHERE ARE THE BONES?

A similar rack was described by Diego Durán Bernardino de Sahagún, a Franciscan friar and priest in the 1500s who spent most of his adult life studying the Aztecs. According to Sahagún, the skull rack in Tenochtitlan was constructed with 60 or 70 massive upright timbers that were woven together with horizontal cross beams which displayed tens of thousands of decapitated human heads — or, by another description, about 60,000. On these racks, the heads were impaled in their full regalia of flesh, and allowed to rot for all to witness. Older heads were removed and burned to make way for more heads.

Skull racks were displayed by several Mesoamerican cultures including the Aztecs, Toltecs, Zapotecs, Mayans, and Mixtecs, but some took it even farther, and linked games to the severed heads. There was an ancient version of a Mesoamerican ball game where the losers literally lost their heads. They may have been captives, forced to entertain prior to their deaths, or they may have been warriors. Those were bloody days of history when the bones of the dead were not revered in the same manner as they are today. It's no wonder that the bones of our giant predecessors are so hard to come by.

6th century King Alboin of the Lombards was famous for drinking from a cup made of the skull cap of his father-in-law, though drinking from the skulls of your enemies was also common. Skull cups date back thousands of years, and were used across Europe and Asia.

English poet Lord Byron drank from a skull that his gardener discovered. The "giant size" skull was in a perfect state of preservation when found, and it was his favorite after-dinner cup. Byron had it polished, rimmed with silver, and inscribed with a 20-line poem that he wrote, that began:

> "Start not — nor deem my spirit fled:
> In me behold the only skull,
> From which, unlike a living head,
> Whatever flows is never dull."

Shrunken Heads

Shrunken heads were a particularly inventive form of war trophy, prized by the tribes of the Amazon rain forest. First, a careful incision was made in the back of the neck, and all of the skin and flesh was peeled off of the skull. Red seeds were placed under the eyelids, and the lids were sewn shut. The mouth was held together with palm pins. Once the skin was readied, a wooden ball was placed inside to help hold the form. The head was boiled in specially prepared water, and then dried with hot rocks and sand, all the while molding it to retain its human features. Finally, the skin was rubbed down with charcoal ash.

When westerners encountered these tribes and coveted the shrunken heads, the head hunters started killing just to keep the supply of shrunken heads flowing for tourists. A shrunken head was worth a pound of Peruvian gold in 1910, and you could still buy genuine shrunken heads as recently as 1930. Sometimes, corpses were stolen for their heads.

The Polynesian Māori people of New Zealand preserved the heads of their enemies, and sometimes their friends. *The Māori Race,* by Edward Tregear in 1904, describes it thus:

The brains, tongue, eyes, and so forth were removed. The interior was stuffed with flax, and the skin of the neck drawn together like the mouth of a purse.

A couple of long hairs were passed through the upper eyelids, and the lids drawn down, with the hairs tied together under the chin. This was done to prevent anyone from staring into the empty eye sockets, and becoming bewitched. The lips were sometimes fastened together with stitches, but not always.

Then the heads were steamed or roasted, either in an earth-oven, or by wrapping them in green leaves and spiked on a stick in a shallow hole full of hot stones. The heads were basted with oil to prevent them from becoming charred. This was followed by cycling the heads through the smoke of a wood fire, and the rays of the sun. This preserved the heads, and protected them from insects. As a final touch, the hair was oiled and fastened up into a knot, and sometimes adorned with feathers.

The finished heads were easily recognizable. Enemy heads were exposed on poles, housetops, and the palisades of forts. They were even put on loom-posts so that weavers could mock the heads while working.

A number of these preserved heads are in the possession of collectors and museums. Like the Native Americans who want their ancestral bones and artifacts returned to them, the Māori are attempting to get their heads back.

Remember the Molucca Island giants in the *Mesoamerican* chapter? Some Molucca tribes, such the Ambonese, were fierce headhunters. They were not giants, but they may have preyed on giants in their headhunting excursions. Not all headhunters shrunk their heads. Most tribes preserved the head without shrinking it. Sometimes headhunters were cannibals; sometimes the heads were taken for ritualistic purposes; and sometimes they were taken to enslave the soul of the deceased, even in Europe.

According to ancient Greeks and Romans, the Celts nailed the heads of their enemies to walls, or dangled them from chariots or the necks of horses. If the enemy was a man of distinction, his head was embalmed in cedar oil and carefully preserved so that it could be displayed with pride. The Scythians were another race who revered the heads of their enemies, first by scalping them, and then by drinking wine from the skulls.

Every corner of the world has its horror story of severed heads, scalps, skulls, and war trophies made of the bones of enemies. It's a wonder that there's an old bone left for us to find.

Ground into Flour and Baked into Bread

Where else might these giant bones have gone? Well, maybe somebody ate them in a loaf of bread. The *Superstition* chapter highlighted Brazilian tribes grinding up bones for bread and wedding feasts. *The Quarterly Review, Volume XXI*, published in 1819 London, expanded on this.

> "The Tapuyas reduced the bones to powder, and mingled them as an act of piety with their food. Some of the Moxo tribes had a similar custom: they made their powder into cakes with a mixture of maize, and considered it the surest pledge of friendship to offer and partake of this family bread."

It's easy to point a finger at a remote jungle tribe, but a similar fate happened to bones in Europe. In June of 1590, during the siege of Paris, France, the city was running out of food. In desperation, the bones of the dead were ground into flour, and baked into a bread which became known as "Madame de Montpensier's bread" — for the madame's delight in the suggestion, though she herself did not partake.

Poor folks had resorted to eating horses, asses, dogs, cats, rats, and even balls of clay, when someone came up with the idea of baking bone bread. The bones were dug up from the cemetery of the Innocents, according to *A History of France, Volume II* by G. W. Kitchin in 1896. This is the same overcrowded cemetery that was featured in the *Make Room for Daddy* chapter. Unfortunately, the bone flour bread turned into a dismal failure, because everyone who ate the bread, died.

Corpse Medicine

The siege of 1590 was not the only incident of this nature — human remains used as corpse medicine was all the rage in 16th century Europe, and it had been going on for hundreds of years. It was common for medical remedies to include human bones, human blood, and human fat tissue. Grave robbers had a field day digging up the old bones.

An 1848 *Lexicon Medicum, Or, Medical Dictionary* by Robert Hooper, M.D. and Klein Grant, M.D. listed the *Cranium*

Humanum, or human skull, as a medical ingredient in oils, tinctures, and other preparations. Among the pharmaceuticals and ingredients which employed human body parts:

> **Unguentum Armarium:** Composed of human skull, human fat, mummy, human blood, linseed oil, turpentine, Armenian bole. The Emperor Maximilian deemed this prescription a great treasure.
>
> **Biolychnium:** A mysterious lamp prepared by a secret process from human blood, to indicate the health of the person to whom the blood belonged, according to whether the lamp burned brightly, dimly, or was extinguished.
>
> **Mummy:** Previously a very prominent article of the Materia Medica. Highly esteemed for its medicinal virtues by Arabian physicians, which led to an avid desire for mummies in Europe. "The great demand for mummies, and the high price they bore, induced [people] to prepare all the dead bodies they could get, in such a manner as to resemble the ancient mummies..." which were then sold. This mummy trafficking was exposed at the end of the 16th century, after which mummy medicine went out of fashion.

A History of the Materia Medica by John Hill, M.D. in 1751, gave a gruesome description of the use of mummies in medicine, which are differentiated by mummies embalmed in myrrh and spices, versus the liquor running from such mummies.

The first type comes in "large pieces, of a lax and friable texture, light and spongy, of a blackish-brown color, and often damp and clammy on the surface" with a strong, disagreeable smell. The second type is a shiny black solid substance; or a thick, opaque, viscous black fluid, which gives off an aromatic scent when burning.

Mummy pharmaceuticals were sold by druggists, and often passed off as Egyptian mummies when they were actually the flesh of executed criminals, or any other body that could be acquired. Corpse medicine left a dent in graveyards all across Europe and Egypt, where mummies were taken from Egyptian tombs, or bodies dug up from European graveyards to be turned into medicine.

However, you didn't have to be a mummy for your body to become corpse medicine. Bones, hair, nails, and teeth were prized by sorcerers and alewives. To treat a toothache, you'd take a tooth out of a skull and wear it. To render ale more intoxicating, just mix in ashes from burnt human bones. Is it any wonder that giant bones survived this assault on human remains?

Unknown Mexico, Volume 1, by Carl Lumholtz in 1902, demonstrated that giant's bones were used as a strengthening medicine, whether from giant mammoths or giant people, as long as the bones were thought to be from giants.

Bone China

Where else might the giant bones have gone? Maybe... just maybe... they wound up being made into bone china. While bone china is a porcelain that commonly consists of bone ash from animals, mixed with kaolin, and stone that is rich in feldspar, it exposes the darker side of humanity in the gruesome tales of using human bones instead of animal bones.

Cattle bones from slaughter houses are one of the commonly used bones, but throughout history, wherever animal bones have been used, somebody, somewhere, substituted human bones. You can even have your own bones turned into *Spone* — or human bone china — for your loved ones to remember you by.

In the 1700s, bone china was manufactured by Josiah Spode II, who added powdered cow bone ash to a secret clay mixture used by his deceased father, Josiah Spode. This new bone china had a translucency that was unsurpassed by other chinaware.

In 1999, Charles Krafft of Seattle, Washington, expanded on the concept to add human bone ash to create personalized bone china mementos, which he trademarked as *Spone*. Krafft may have been the first to trademark the concept of human bones in ceramics, but he was not the first to utilize it.

WHERE ARE THE BONES?

The 1970 publication of *Relics, Volume 3, Issues 5-6,* made mention of human bone chinaware being produced in China, Hungary, and Austria. Several other texts made reference to an old expression — "that human bones are an ingredient in china ware" — as meaning the amount of labor that goes into the making of bone china, rather than bones themselves, so one can only guess whether human bones were actually used.

Grave Robbers

Sometimes bones are dug up, not for the bones themselves, but for the treasure buried with them. Native American burial mounds frequently suffered this fate, especially by those who committed genocide against them.

In the United States, giants predated Native Americans, and their bones are often buried in mounds that were later misidentified as Native American burial mounds, especially in mounds where both types of bones were found. Mounds have been systematically dug up for the artifacts, which were then sold, often leaving the bones behind to deteriorate from exposure.

Archeological sites are also damaged by erosion, flooding, forest fires, earthquakes, landslides, volcanoes, exposure, weathering, and other actions of nature. Animals lay claim to these sites, causing further damage. Big business comes along, and may not even be aware of what lies underneath the ground, so we plow, mine, quarry, drill for oil and gas, cut down trees for lumber, plough through with highways, airports, shopping malls, housing developments, and factories.

Whatever old bones survive all of this become the target of looters and pothunters — those denizens of archeology whose goal is to collect artifacts for profit or personal use, rather than historical preservation. We may venerate our own ancestors and attempt to protect their graves, but the ancestors of others are fair game. Gold, silver, jewelry, gems, and valuable historical artifacts were big temptations for the grave robbers of old.

A 1990 report from the Society for American Archeology's Conference on Preventing Archeological Looting and Vandalism gave a grim view of how we treat the old bones. Vandals and looters have:

- attacked 90% of the known sites on federal lands in the Four Corners area of the American Southwest.
- assaulted nearly all of the Classic Mimbres sites in southwestern New Mexico.
- overran Revolutionary and Civil War battlefields for coins, guns, and bottles.

Today these artifacts are sold, displayed for profit, and hoarded away in personal collections. As we've seen from glimpses into our gruesome past, we once used human bones in food, medicine, or destroyed them out of fear. We've enacted a myriad of conflicting laws where you have issues of private property which cannot be taken by the government without compensation, and how you put a price on that property. If the owner wanted to build a high-dollar casino, but the government only wanted to pay for undeveloped land, an extended legal battle might ensue. As a casino, the government collects more taxes, and this might be taken into account as well.

Vandals and thieves destroy what they don't steal. A May 27, 1985 article in *The Spokesman-Review* entitled, "Hells Canyon Archeological Site Vandalized, Ruined" painted a grim picture. Prehistoric rock art is vandalized with graffiti. Artifacts are stolen by thieves who sell them to collectors. A single item can bring upwards of $1,000, which doesn't offer much protection for the relics. Even tourists leave their mark by "picking up" souvenirs.

Few do more damage than professional thieves such as Earl K. Shumway of Moab, Utah, who was convicted after a federal sting caught him trafficking ancient artifacts. He bragged about ransacking thousands of sites, and was quoted as saying, "Around here, it's not a crime — it's a way of life." For Shumway, it was a family business, handed down by his father and grandfather.

WHERE ARE THE BONES?

He was tried in *United States v. Shumway*, case numbers 95-4201 and 96-4000. Among his crimes was the destruction of the human remains of an infant, originally wrapped in a burial blanket. He dug up the infant and left the bones exposed. When investigators later assessed damage to the site, all that was left was the skull — the rest of the bones had long since disappeared. Part of the trial revolved around whether the skeleton was a "vulnerable victim" and thus protected by law, and the legal status of prehistoric human skeletal remains in general.

In recent decades we've passed laws to protect archeological discoveries, but these laws came long after the damage done in earlier centuries. Nor do the laws stop thieves like Shumway, who was quoted in a legal treatise about his case as saying, "If the government can come down here and say we don't have the right to dig in a place where we've lived all our lives, I'd just as soon go to prison. I'm not gonna bring my kid into a world where you can't go out and dig up an old ruin." He even appeared in a videotaped documentary about looting archeological sites. Grave robbing is not limited to thieves-for-profit, however.

American Medicine, Volume 5, published by the American-Medicine Publishing Company in 1903, discussed grave robbing laws. It referred to "indictments against physicians said to be implicated in the late grave robbing scandal…" Even physicians were not immune to the allure of digging up a grave, though usually for the purpose of studying the human body.

The publication *Proceedings of the Thirty-Ninth Annual Meeting of the State Historical Society of Wisconsin, Held December 10, 1891*, highlighted the acts of grave robbers. The museum added 254 specimens of prehistoric pottery to its inventory, which had been found in Arkansas and Missouri graves. Apparently grave robbing was such a problem that "in transatlantic cemeteries, similar vessels, when buried with the dead, were often purposely broken, either as a token of grief or to make them valueless in the eyes of grave-robbers."

A memoir entitled, *Two Women in the Klondike*, by Mary E. Hitchcock in 1899, mentioned grave robbing. A man admitted that he and several others intended to "open the grave of an Indian chief and take out a lot of curios," though they never followed through. Throughout history, however, grave robbing has been a plague on the bones of every civilization that has passed into memory.

The New Universal Traveller: Containing a Full and Distinct Account of All the Empires, Kingdoms, and States, in the Known World, by Jonathan Carver in 1779, described the funeral rituals in Siam. The body was burned, and then buried, and a pyramid was erected over the grave, but because of the acts of grave robbers, they stopped burying treasure with the bodies, and instead buried painted papers and other trifles.

What happens to bones once the grave has been opened? When bones are exposed to the elements, their surface deteriorates at the same time that organic contents are lost. Weathering bones develop fissures, and then cracks, as the surface deteriorates. Sometimes, bones are found which appear to be intact, but fall into dust when touched. *The Edinburgh Encyclopaedia, Volume 5*, published in 1832, relates one such incident:

> "Another tomb was opened, wherein a skeleton, turned towards the east, was seen. The hands were crossed on the breast, and but few teeth were in the jaws: it seemed to be that of an old man. When my guide stretched one arm to the head, and the other to the feet, designing to raise the skeleton, it immediately fell into a whitish humid dust. Nothing except the substance of the teeth, which were eleven in number, remained: the whole skeleton had vanished from view."

John Strang in his 1831 book, *Necropolis Glasguensis; With Observations On Ancient and Modern Tombs and Sepulture*, described a similar incident of bones disintegrating, which was quoted from an earlier source:

WHERE ARE THE BONES?

"In one of the receptacles I found two bodies, the head of the one touched the feet of the other. I could only distinguish, as to form, some vestiges of the principal bones. The extremities were nothing more than an almost insensible dust; what was left of the bones turned, when touched, into a moist yellow paste of a reddish hue. It would be difficult to form an exact idea of the remains of a human body, reduced to a condition so near to absolute annihilation… The two bodies that I saw had been buried for fourteen or fifteen centuries."

Thus is the fate of bones exposed by grave robbers, but not all bodies were originally preserved for posterity. Some were exposed intentionally at the time of death.

Pirate Treasure

Sea Island, Georgia, was the site of "bundle" burials of giant bones, where dead bodies were exposed in trees or temples until they decomposed, and the decomposed bones were then bundled together in mass graves with existing bones.

These coastal islands and their grave sites became the hunting ground of treasure hunters looking for buried treasure. The pirate Jean LaFitte was reputed to have buried his gold on Sea Island, and all of the coastal islands of Georgia were searched for buried treasure, "centuries after the disappearance of a strange tribe of giant American aboriginals," according to an August 2, 1936 article entitled, "Georgia's Sand-Dunes Yield Startling Proof of a Prehistoric Race of Giants" in *The Portsmouth Times* of Ohio. The chapter *Mound Builders of Georgia* goes into more detail about the giants found on Sea Island, and the archeologists who studied the site.

Anyone whose interest was gold would not be calling in archeologists to study the bones, and give up their treasure hole to science. They would summarily discard the bones, probably into the ocean to be carried off to sea, lest the bones tip off others to horn in on the treasure hunter's discovery.

Pirates and treasure hunters weren't the only destroyers of already dead bodies… other forms of destruction include fire, which if done properly, doesn't leave much behind for us to study, and sometimes, it was already dead bodies that were dug up and destroyed, all in the name of hatred or fear.

Witches, Giants, and the Fires of Fear

An author identified only as "A Watchman" wrote a book in 1834 entitled *A History of Popery*. The introduction was written by Samuel Miller, D.D., so his name often appears as the author. Among its topics: Heresy.

Heretics, which included everyone who didn't embrace the *accepted* forms of worship, in addition to anyone who even dared to question the Church, were often put to death lest they spread their mischievous thoughts and corrupt others. Nobody would speak in their defense for fear of being similarly accused. "No lawyer dared to plead even for his own brother" because "the malice of the papists went even beyond the grave. They often dug up the bones of those accused of heresy, and burnt them to ashes, and strewed them in the river."

This goes all the way back to the *Old Testament*, as shown in the chapter *Destruction of Bones in the Bible*, where the worshippers of Baal — i.e. the giants — were destroyed right down to their bones.

Witchcraft was a form of heresy, just like the worship of Baal, and both often led to the total annihilation of bones. Witchcraft, sorcery, and the magic arts were the nemesis of the Church. You couldn't engage in the practices of Satan without being a heretic, and Satan was just another name for Baal — the god of the giants — who'd plagued mankind for a millennia.

Even heretical books were burned, according to *A History of the Inquisition of the Middle Ages, Volume 1*, by Henry Charles Lea in 1888, including books by the esteemed Aristotle. The Jewish *Talmud* was another target of mass burning by the wagonloads. Undesirable versions of the *Bible* were also burned:

WHERE ARE THE BONES?

"Allusion has already been made to the burning of Romance versions of the Scriptures by Jayme I of Aragon, and to the commands of the Council of Narbonne, in 1229, against the possession of any portion of Holy Writ by laymen..."

Jayme I of Aragon was a Roman-Catholic king who lived from 1208 to 1276. His was an era of conflicting interpretations of the *Bible*, with Christians and Jews constantly bickering, according to the *Cyclopaedia of Biblical, Theological and Ecclesiastical Literature, Volume 6* in 1891. Translations of the *Bible* came under attack. *The Church of England, A True Branch of the Holy Catholic Church*, by Reverend Leicester Darwall in 1853, reported on a 1234 edict issued by the Council of Tarragona that:

"...no one shall have the books of the Old or New Testament in the Romance, or vernacular dialect. And if any one had such, and neglected to bring them within eight days after the publication of the order to the Bishop to be burnt, he should be regarded, whether clergyman or layman, as suspected of heresy."

This is echoed in *The History of the Inquisition of Spain*, by D. Juan Antonio Llorente in 1843, which connects King James (Jaymes) I of Aragon to the Tarragona edict. The edict was intended to oppose the progress of heresy by any means within their power. Romance languages included Spanish, Portuguese, French, Italian, and Romanian, as derived from a Roman version of Latin — hence the name "Romance." These translations were deemed heretical, and subsequently burned.

King James of Aragon was not the king who authorized the *King James Bible* that we have today. The latter King James was born in 1566 to Mary, Queen of Scots. Over three hundred years after James of Aragon went after bibles that he deemed unworthy, the battle of biblical translations was still going strong, along with the debate on which books should be included. King

James I of England hired 47 scholars to issue a new *Bible* that would satisfy the Puritans. This was the religious climate of the many Inquisitions, all of which went after heresy with a vengeance for a period lasting hundreds of years.

Witches were among the heretics of the Middle Ages; Giants and humans who worshipped Baal were heretics in the age of the *Old Testament*; and the best way to eliminate all vestiges of heresy was to burn it until there was nothing left to contaminate the rest of the world.

The bodies of heretics who hadn't already died by fire were dug up, and "their bones and stinking corpses" dragged through the streets in a grand procession which ended with burning their bones. We even left accounting records as to the cost of this exhumation and ultimate destruction, which Henry Lea put into the most descriptive words:

> "There is something grotesquely horrible in the contrast between this crowning exhibition of human perversity, and the cool business calculation of the cost of thus sending a human soul through flame to its Creator."

We associate death by burning with witches and heretics, but they weren't the only people to suffer such a fate. To be burned alive was a form of capital punishment in several ancient cultures including Babylon, Egypt, Assyria, and Rome. The Celts sacrificed humans to their gods in ritual burnings. Europeans roasted Native Americans in the fires of North America. Slaves were put to death by fire. The Greeks burned Turks; the Ottomans burned Christians; the Hindus burned widows; everybody burned somebody.

There've been so many different Inquisitions: the Spanish Inquisition, Medieval Inquisition, Episcopal Inquisition, Papal Inquisition, Roman Inquisition, Portuguese Inquisition, Goa Inquisition… and the list goes on. They all had one thing in common: If your religious beliefs were in any way different, and sometimes even if you'd converted to the acceptable religion, then you were destroyed, and fire was a favored form of elimination. What could be more different or frightening than a race of cannibalistic giants who worshipped Baal?

In the chapter *Mesoamerican Giants*, the Quiname giants committed sodomy, most likely forced on the Olmec men. The Olmecs were in Central America, far-removed from the Incas in South America, and yet the Incas were particularly horrified by the act of sodomy. If you committed sodomy, not only would you be burned alive, your house would be burned to the ground, your inheritances destroyed, your trees uprooted, and even your wife and children put to death. Every molecule of your life and memory would be completely erased. Why?

Were the Incas plagued by sodomizing Quiname giants? Or had they simply heard the tales of the long-dead Quinames, and reacted out of fear that the giants might somehow rise again?

Cremation

In addition to all of the people who've been incinerated out of superstition and fear, or just plain hatred, there is also the practice of cremation in general. Not all dead people are buried, which means that not all dead people leave bones behind. Some are cremated, a practice that goes back at least 20,000 years.

Every culture has its death ceremonies, and the popularity of cremation has waxed and waned through the centuries. It was common in Ancient Greece, Ancient Rome, Phoenicia, Ancient Persia, and among the early Germanic people. It was once the ceremony of choice for Hindus and Jains.

Even today, cremation rates are high in several countries, with Japan leading the way at 99.85% in 2008. China sported a 48.5% cremation rate in 2008, while India cremates 85% of the populace. In the UK, cremations in 2008 accounted for 72.44% of the bodies, while Denmark is at 76%, and Sweden is at 70%. Canada cremated 68.4% of their dead in 2009, while the United

States incinerated 40.62% of the bodies in 2010. Australia recorded 65% in 2008, while New Zealand recorded 70% in 2008. That's a lot of bones turned into ashes.

Cremations, even in a crematorium, do not incinerate bones into fine ash, and crematoriums must post-process the remains to finish grinding any surviving bones into fine sand. Even so, if bone fragments survived the funeral pyres of the Ancient World, it is unlikely that we'd find the shards today and equate them with giants, or that fragments would survive for thousands of years.

Most of the original giants were wiped out in the Great Deluge — a world-changing event with over 600 different versions across a multitude of cultures and countries. This flood sank entire continents, such as the lost continent of Atlantis. Virtually everything that existed before the worldwide flood was destroyed, carried far out into the ocean, or is now buried under hundreds of feet of silt and sand.

If pre-flood bones of giants exist, they may be buried deeper than a normal dig would unearth. *The Otago Witness* posted an article entitled, "Human Fossils in California" on April 2, 1864, relating some of the discoveries made by gold miners.

Indian arrowheads have been found buried at depths of 50 feet. Either a fluke accident caused them to get buried that deep, or their human owners lived before the great earth changes took place. In 1855, a mortar was found not less than 100 feet below ground. According to *The Universalist Quarterly and General Review* published in 1872, a great deluge might very well have eliminated the bones:

> "The Dutch government in 1853, drained off the Haarlem Lake, on which there had been many shipwrecks and naval fights, and where thousands had found a watery grave. The canals and trenches, dug to a considerable depth through the rescued land, must have had an aggregate length of thousands of miles, and yet not a single human bone was exhumed from first to last. Some weapons and a few coins, and one or two wrecked vessels, alone rewarded the

antiquaries, who watched the operations with the hope of a rich harvest. Here, as in cavern deposits and river gravels generally, works of art alone furnished evidence of the existence of man, even though no part of the deposit could be more than three hundred years old, as the lake was formed by an inundation toward the end of the sixteenth century."

Even the Smithsonian had something to say about the absence of bones in the Province of Chiriqui, in Panama. From the *Sixth Annual Report of the Bureau of American Ethnology*:

"The almost total absence of human remains has frequently been remarked, and the theory is advanced that cremation must have been practiced. We have no evidence, however, of such a custom among the historic tribes of this region, and, besides, such elaborate tombs would hardly be constructed for the deposition of ashes."

Battle of the Bones

Several reports stated that the Smithsonian Institution collected the bones of the giants. The Smithsonian was founded in 1846 when British scientist James Smithson bequeathed his estate to the United States, specifically to build "at Washington, under the name of the Smithsonian Institution, an establishment for the increase and diffusion of knowledge."

Smithson died in 1829, and in 1836 the U. S. Congress accepted the legacy. After several years of heated debate, the Smithsonian Institution was founded by President James Polk. It is governed by a Board of Regents, which consists of the Chief Justice of the United States, the Vice President of the United States, three members of the Senate, three members of the House of Representatives, and nine citizens.

In other words, the Smithsonian is intricately connected to the United States government, who many believe are responsible for the cover-up of evidence relating to extraterrestrials, UFOs, and other controversial issues. If there was an ancient race of giants as evidenced by the multitude of legends, bones, artifacts, and historical accounts, this could fall into the realm of extraterrestrial evidence, if the first-generation giants were indeed extraterrestrial as the *Book of Enoch*, *Book of Giants*, and the Sumerian tablets suggest.

Even if they were not extraterrestrial, but simply another race of humanoids who lived on Earth alongside humans, the evidence might still be kept under wraps. History as we know it would be completely discredited. It would have to be revised from man's first day on Earth, and this would have a domino effect. The government may not want to undertake the daunting task of rewriting history at this time.

The impact on religion would tilt the axis of the world, figuratively speaking. Darwinism versus Creationism versus Ancient Aliens on Earth — can there be a hotter topic in history?

If that isn't a big enough dilemma, the United States government is embroiled in a battle of the bones with Native Americans who are appalled that their ancestors and burial grounds are being dug up and decimated. They want all of the bones and artifacts returned, and the burial grounds protected.

Think of how you'd react if the graveyard of your great-great-grandparents was being excavated and the contents whisked away, put on display, dissected and studied — notwithstanding the fact that all over the world, ancient cemeteries eventually do get repurposed and their "contents" discarded, as we've seen.

Native American remains are all mixed up with the remains of the giants, and the mounds built by one sometimes became burial grounds for the other. This is a current, ongoing, legal battle which has resulted in several laws, including the Native American Graves Protection and Repatriation Act (NAGPRA) which was passed in 1990.

Museums and federal agencies are required to catalog their inventories and identify those which are Native American. Once the artifacts and bones are identified, a claim can be made, which is basically a demand for the items to be returned to their rightful owners, even if nobody knows who the rightful owners are. This includes human remains.

On the opposite end of the battle of the bones are the archeologists and scientists who want to keep the bones, in order to study human history such as the ancient races that once populated North America. Without the bones and artifacts, there is no evidence left to help us learn about the prehistoric eras of history. Our most ancient ancestors left no written records — all they left were bones, and pieces of their daily life for us to study.

When most of the bones were collected, we didn't have radio-carbon dating or DNA tests. Only by keeping the bones were we able to later run tests as those tests came into being. We can't even guess at what technology will gift us in the future, what tests we'll be able to run, or what knowledge we could gain.

Laws exist that protect archeological ownership of the bones if the outcome of studying the bones would be of major benefit to the United States, or the entire world. To get a glimpse inside one such legal battle of the bones, just do a search on the Kennewick Man.

Conspiracy theories aren't always about extraterrestrials. Some believe that the institutions in possession of the bones are withholding information, or denying that they have bones, so that they won't be forced to give them up. If the bones are reburied, they will be destroyed forever. Our chance to learn from them will evaporate.

It's also possible that the bones were destroyed long ago, for racial or religious reasons. In our ugly history, Native Americans were considered inferior to the invading Europeans. They were called "savages" and yet, according to Native American legends, a noble race of giants predated them, and some of their own royal lines were descended from these giants. Sometimes the giants were described as "white men." European invaders did not want evidence that might elevate the legal status of Native Americans, and this alone could account for the utter destruction of evidence — at least in the United States.

Then there is the distinct possibility that the bones simply disintegrated on their own. The Smithsonian reports often mentioned the fragility of the bones. They might indeed have been sent to the Smithsonian, only to crumble later. In those early days, especially before the institution got its funding, they were short-staffed, and often it was unpaid volunteers who did the work. There were no computers, just handwritten notes and typewriters. Hundreds of thousands of bones, and millions of other artifacts were sent there to be catalogued and studied, and then labeled and stored.

Can you even imagine trying to keep track of it all, without computers? Where each item might have an index card, like an old-fashioned library, with millions of cards? This is speculation of course, but having personally witnessed how offices worked before the computer age, how records were kept even by the most diligent person, nobody could have kept that many artifacts and bones organized to the point of being able to find a single one on request, within a reasonable length of time. It would be easier to simply say: "We have no record of that." Even bringing it all into the computer age would take decades of work, if not centuries.

Governments around the world have a lot on their plates — far beyond paying homage to the bones of a dead man, or admitting the existence of giants or extraterrestrials. Studying ancient history may help us to understand extraterrestrial races that visited us in the past, and who may do so again in the future. Look at the bigger picture… if giants were extraterrestrial, you can bet that sooner or later, they'll be back. Our own legends predict their return.

We do not have the technology to prevent an extraterrestrial race from coming to Earth. We don't have starships. We don't have interstellar colonies. We don't understand their wormholes.

But we do have history. We have legends left behind by our distant ancestors who battled the giants, and prevailed. That, alone, makes every piece of ancient history critically important.

To protect our future, we may need to better understand our past. The Battle of the Bones may end up being an issue of national security, or world security.

In the meantime, let's hope that if the giants return, they are benevolent giants such as Hiawatha, and so many others who lifted us out of savagery. We should hope for the best, but prepare for the worst, and to that end, let the government keep their secrets if it's for the greater good. We cannot begin to know what they might be working behind the scenes.

In the closing chapter, take a look at a tribe that might illustrate what we were before the giants came. In every legend where giants became our mentors, mankind did not possess the level of humanity that we're familiar with today. If this represents our ancestors, then the giants must have been saints.

19th Century Stone Age Giants

The word "lithic" pertains to stone, and the lithic ages were subdivisions of the Stone Age. The Paleolithic, Mesolithic and Neolithic eras all had some semblance of early humans. The Grigori came down near the end of the Stone Age, an age that lasted for millions of years, and their arrival coincides with mankind moving into the Bronze Age — the age of giants — and an age of advancements. We moved away from being nomadic hunter-gatherers, into an agrarian society where we started planting crops and keeping livestock, teachings which are credited to our giant benefactors. Their arrival lifted us up out of the dirt, and moved us into an era of civilization in an epoch known as the Neolithic Revolution.

Human-like species of the genus *Homo* had already been living for millions of years in a primitive state when the Grigori arrived. Some branches had already died out — among them, *Australopithecus* and *Paranthropus*. Humans today are *Homo sapiens*, but when the Grigori arrived, other *Homo* species may have existed such as *Homo heidelbergensis*, *Homo floresiensis*, *Homo neanderthalensis*, and *Homo erectus*.

Homo habilis was already extinct, according to the Smithsonian Institution's interactive timeline for human evolution. *Homo erectus* was the longest-lived species in our family tree, existing nine times longer than modern humans. The others were either fading out, or lived alongside us for awhile.

Homo floresiensis allegedly went extinct thousands of years ago, and yet there've been sightings of a species that matches the description of this diminutive humanoid, just as there've been sightings of Bigfoot throughout the ages, and we have no idea if these are remnants of a *Homo* genus thought long extinct.

This brings us to a modern day Stone Age species of giant known as the Seri, which terrorized their human neighbors right up into the 19th century. If the Seri carried the star seed genes of the Grigori giants, they did not also acquire the advanced knowledge, because the Nephilim and their descendants were highly civilized in comparison. Even if the hybrid Nephilim giants balked at the notion of growing their own food or livestock, or refused to put their muscles to work building, they had the wherewithal to have others do it for them. They lived in walled cities much to the surprise of Moses, and assembled armies of soldiers with shields and swords and spears. They traveled in large ships with oars and sails — big enough to carry raiding parties and pirate crews.

This is in stark contrast to the lifestyle of the Seri, who even when civilization knocked directly on their door and offered them entrance, they refused it. They wouldn't accept so much as a glass bead, or a metal knife, preferring smooth stones as both tools and weapons. Once a stone adopted a sharp edge, they discarded it. Neither did their arrows have stone points, being just an untipped shaft of wood. Horses weren't for riding — they were for *eating* — and so were humans. This was the way of the Seri, whose mode of living barely made it into the Stone Age.

A lengthy tract in the *Seventeenth Annual Report of the Bureau of American Ethnology*, published by the Smithsonian Institution in 1898, referred to them as *prelithic* and *protolithic* — which means they weren't even advanced enough to be called Stone Age or Paleolithic, and yet the Seri people were alive and well from 1540 into the 1900s. How could that be? This was not a tribe that no one could prove existed, like Bigfoot. This was a tribe that lived adjacent to Sonora, Mexico, and we have detailed reports of encounters with them. We even have photographs of their primitive huts, made of sticks and giant turtle shells.

HOUSE COVERING, TIBURON ISLAND

The Seri were not like their neighbors, and they were the bane of everyone who crossed their warpath. Their guttural language did not resemble any known tongue, and was made of less than 700 words that were almost impossible for others to mimic. They howled more like a wild animal than a human, and if a stranger approached, they growled and snarled instinctively as a dog might. This comes straight from first-hand encounters.

Attempting to approach Seri territory was generally suicide, and at the time of the Smithsonian report we'd only managed to acquire a single skeleton. That was in 1894, toward the end of their singular reign, and it may not have been a full-blooded Seri.

We started documenting Seri encounters in 1540, when explorer Don Rodrigo Maldonado brought back "an Indian so large and tall that the best man in the army reached only to his chest," with reports of still taller Indians along the coast. He referred to them as giants, and their main island was thus labeled *Isle de Gigante* on maps. Also in 1540, Spanish explorer Melchior Diaz encountered the same giants.

Maps of 1690 and 1720 were still calling the island *Gigante*, although historians today equate the name with a mountain rather than the gigantic stature of the Seri, which is now in dispute in spite of historical and genetic evidence.

The Seri were one of the most savage races ever documented in the history of mankind, and anyone unlucky enough to set foot on their island, rarely made it back out alive. The name of the island on a 1759 map was *Island of Get-Out-If-Can* or "get out if you can." This warning related to getting stranded by wicked currents, as ships often got stuck in the adjacent channel and subsequently attacked by vicious Seri cannibals.

The Seri skeleton represented a 'young, immature female' estimated to be in her early 20s. According to McGee and Hrdlicka, the two anthropologists that studied the Seri, this was a race that was slow to mature. McGee was quoted as saying that "the Seri never stop growing until death" and that they were "men and women, gigantic in stature." This quote came from *The Florida Star* on July 27, 1900, in an article entitled "The Tiburón Islanders." Saying it once wasn't enough, and McGee repeated that the Seri "seem to keep on growing all their lives."

This may not be as preposterous as it sounds. The bones of Charles Byrne, known as the Irish Giant of Derry, are at rest in the Hunterian Museum of the Royal College of Surgeons in London. His height is given variously as 7 feet 7 inches or 8 feet 4 inches. According to the *Catalogue of the Hunterian Collection in the Museum of the Royal College of Surgeons in London, Volumes 1-3*, published in 1830, he measured 8 feet 4 inches at death, and the shorter stature was given in *Acromegalic Gigantism, Physicians and Body Snatching. Past or Present?* by Wouter Herder.

19TH CENTURY STONE AGE GIANTS

The body snatching article detailed Byrne's obsession with NOT being handed over to science when he died, and the lengths that he took to prevent it. As soon as he took his last breath, however, the dirty deed occurred. Allegedly money changed hands and his final fate was the one he'd desperately tried to avoid. Not only does the article confirm the many accounts of grave robbing and body snatching, it also confirms McGee's odd statement about the Seri growth pattern.

Byrne was 22 years old when he died, but scientists determined that his "bone age" was only 17, and that he was still growing. His abnormal growth rate was attributed to a mutated gene, which was identified in four other Irish families who were believed to share a common ancestor with Byrnes, approximately 57-66 generations earlier. Some of the afflicted had abnormally large hands and feet, which was a trait also peculiar to the Seri tribe. This is detailed in "AIP Mutation in Pituitary Adenomas in the 18th Century and Today" in the *New England Journal of Medicine*, published in 2011.

If one generation is estimated at 20 years, that puts the ancestor between 1140 and 1320 years earlier, or between 691 and 871 A.D., a time span that coincides with the Viking invasion that followed the Fomorian's grip on Ireland. The Fomorians were themselves giants, and the gods of the Vikings were giants who lived physically on Earth. Is this a coincidence?

In Byrne the perpetual growth was abnormal, but for the Stone Age Seri it was typical. Could these genetic mutations prove the existence of a race of giants in ancient history?

McGee's belief that the Seri were giants was echoed in his attempt to secure a Seri family for the 1904 World's Fair in St. Louis. He was in charge of organizing a live exhibition of "all the world's peoples, ranging from the smallest pygmies to the most gigantic peoples" which would feature the Seri and Patagonians as primitive giants. This is documented in *The World's Work, Volume VIII, Number 4*, published in 1904, and *Overlord of the Savage*

World by John William Troutman in 1997. McGee was unable, however, to procure a family of Seri for the exhibit, and the Tehuelche Patagonians that he exhibited weren't as tall as legends had portrayed.

The Seri skeleton presented with extraordinary findings. It was examined by Dr. Ales Hrdlicka, who described the unusually shaped skull as "heavy" and "massive." The interior of the skull showed few traces of brain impressions, and from an evolutionary standpoint, the skull was inferior. The tibia, or shinbone of the leg, had platycnemic characteristics which Hrdlicka referred to as "simian." This is commonly associated with Neolithic, or New Stone Age skeletons.

The Neolithic Era started in 10200 B.C. and ended with the Neolithic Revolution into the Bronze Age, which varied from country to country. Generally, however, the Neolithic Era ended sometime between 4500 and 2000 B.C.

The Journal of the Ethnological Society of London, Volume 2, published in 1870 by Trübner & Co. of London, had a tract on platycnemic skeletons that were discovered in Denbighshire, England in 1869, and their comparison to platycnemic skeletons found in several other locations including Genista Cave in Gibraltar, a Cro-Magnon cave in France, and Perthi-Chwaren in Wales. This anomaly is associated specifically with skeletons dated to the Neolithic Age. Charles Darwin studied the bones.

The Seri skeleton, with its "exceptionally large stature," was comparable to bones from the Polished Stone Age, and yet the living Seri had not yet adopted the technology of that age. Hrdlicka compared the Seri skeleton to the bones of the Eyzies.

Eyzies refers to Cro-Magnon remains found in Les-Eyzies-de-Tayac, France, from the Late Stone Age/Upper Paleolithic period. Dr. Ales Hrdlicka was an anthropologist who studied human bones for a living, and his report stated that the Seri skeleton was *different* from a modern human, like something out of the Stone Age.

19TH CENTURY STONE AGE GIANTS

What a perfect opportunity to get a glimpse of how our remote ancestors may have lived, if you could get close enough to the Seri without getting killed. Were they related to the humans that the Grigori coveted? As crazy as it sounds to desire someone who'd rather eat you for dinner than say hello, the Seri were physically splendid. Even European women who caught a glimpse of Seri women, envied their physique. It takes a lot for a woman to envy another woman — especially if one is tribal.

Seri men had broad, deep chests, athletic builds, and slender but sinewy limbs that were beautifully proportioned. Their hands and feet were enormous, but their heads were the size of a normal man's head, which appeared small on their big bodies. This is an interesting observation — a giant in height with an ordinary-sized skull. Coincidentally, they had big teeth.

They did not have a lot of body hair, but the straight, black hair on their heads was long and luxuriant. Bright, black eyes gazed out from bronze skin.

This was the description of Seri at their best. At their worst, you'd think they were a different race altogether, with shaggy hair that was never washed or combed, and stuck out in a tangle in all directions like spines on a hedgehog. A cord dangled from the pierced septum in their nose, with colored stones that swung in front of their mouth at the end of the cords. Men and women painted their faces in bold lines and patterns, renewing the paint daily so that it resembled a tattoo. These patterns differentiated Seri clans, although by the time we got close enough to document the clans, we'd already been exterminating them for centuries.

Barefoot and naked from the waist up, their primary attire was a kilt made of pelican skins, which they wore with the feathers facing in. Belts were simple strips of deerskin, rabbit skin, snakeskin, or twisted human or horsehair tied in a knot. Necklaces were strings of seeds or shells, with pendants of nuts or snake rattles. Alternately, they wore necklaces made of human hair or a snakeskin, knotted to form a circle.

They did not bathe, ever, and their personal stench was so overwhelming that they reeked like a rotten, eight-day-old corpse.

Their huts were crude shelters built of sticks, covered in sponges, brush, or turtle shells, with no items of comfort and no decorations of any type. The huts did not keep out the rain or the cold, and offered scant protection from the wind and sun.

Natural stones worn smooth by the sea were their primary tools, and these stones were used for crushing bones, severing tendons, grinding seeds, and warfare. If a stone developed a sharp edge, it was discarded. Natural seashells were another tool, along with fish spines, plant thorns, bird mandibles, and the horns and teeth of animals. When given a chance to use a knife, they refused. The Seri were conspicuously unskilled with tools in general, though they were proficient with their big hands and teeth — frighteningly proficient.

Meals consisted of whatever fruits or vegetables they found growing in the wild, along with cactus, and sea foods including turtles, crabs, and fish. Animals were a staple, always eaten raw as the Seri did not possess the art of building a fire. Dinner included deer, swine, sheep, jaguars, pumas, pelicans, and even horses.

Their mode of fishing was unusual. They did not use nets, fishing poles, hooks or lines of any type. They did, however, tie a string to a pelican's leg, break one of its wings, and allow the live pelican to catch fish for them.

The Seri did not keep livestock — all food was captured wild and eaten raw. The only exception was half-breed coyote dogs, which were allowed to hang around as long as they fed themselves.

While the Seri did hunt with bows and arrows, they were adept runners and preferred to run down an animal on foot. The Seri could run down a wild horse, and catch it with nothing more than their hands and teeth, leaping like a jaguar onto its withers. With one hand on its jaw and another on its mane, they could bring it to the ground while breaking its neck. Big animals might be clubbed to death, though killing with bare hands was preferred.

Even their manner of eating was primitive, and tools were rarely used. First they sucked the blood of the animal, and then they ate the meat. Raw meat was torn off with their teeth, in a manner compared to coyotes, using a twisting or backward jerk of the head. The meat was then gnawed, sucked, and swallowed. They didn't limit themselves to fresh meat, either — carrion was also on the menu, and they seemed to prefer decayed meat.

Neither did they accumulate food for later. All food was caught or gathered in the moment, with no food stores. Even offal was considered edible, as were humans. They didn't kill humans just for food, they reveled in the act of killing and had an insatiable blood lust. Blood and entrails were the most prized portions of a dead human.

Even the Aztecs weren't as feared as the Seri, who hunted down humans as we hunt for deer. Humans might be eaten raw, or slightly cooked, though the manner of cooking isn't described unless by roasting in the sun. The Seri did not possess fire.

Those who crossed paths and lived to tell the tale referred to the Seri as "inhuman." Were they offshoots of the Quiname giants of Mesoamerica? Or were they a race unto themselves, a branch of ancient hominids thought long extinct?

Whatever their origin, the Seri were continuously at war, and everyone outside the tribe, including outcast tribal members, were "aliens" to be eliminated. Killing an alien was the height of glory, while mating with an alien was the most heinous of crimes and would get you evicted from the tribe.

Men had to pass a matrimonial test, and those who failed were evicted from the tribe and became targets for their brethren, just like any other alien. This created offshoot tribes, often of impure blood, who warred with one another. It also explains why the various groups labeled "Seri" were not all the same. The Seri who were eventually assimilated into our society were likely of the offshoot tribes — those who'd mingled beyond their bloodline. In the rare event that the Seri captured a woman and kept her as a slave, she was not allowed to reproduce and create mixed children. This was taboo.

Once missionaries and soldiers moved into the region and became targets for Seri attacks, it sparked a series of wars. Colonel Diego Ortiz Parrilla, the Governor of Sonora, Mexico, made several attempts to exterminate the Seri, and believed that he'd succeeded in 1749 when he boasted of annihilating all but a few captives. Five hundred soldiers went in, and two months later they returned with 28 captives — all women and children — and attempts were made to convert them to Christianity, and civility. An entire mission was set up for this purpose called *Conquest of the Seri* at Hermosillo. The bulk of the fierce Seri warriors, however, remained at large.

Between 1757 and 1763, the Seri managed to steal 4,000 mules and horses from the soldiers and missionaries, which they ate. Another troop was sent in to exterminate them, and was later found half-eaten. The year 1760 sported another failed attempt, and in 1761, soldiers managed to kill 49 Seri and capture 69 more, but the indomitable Seri were taking their toll on the invaders.

By 1763 the army, with its advanced weapons, was worn down by these Stone Age giants. In 1767, the Jesuits were expelled because they could not convert the Seri, nor could the army subdue them. Here was a race of humans, using nothing more than their hands, stones, bows and arrows, holding their own against armies of soldiers sent in to exterminate them.

In 1772 the Franciscans went in to convert the Seri, and Father Bernabe was found stoned to death. It "seemed impossible to crush this hydra-headed race" and at least 50 more attempts to exterminate them followed.

A German writer named Clemens Pajeken stated that "the Seris appear not to grasp the idea that they are human. Like beasts of prey of the wilderness, they go out to slay men and animals. They slay to satisfy a lust for slaughter." In 1824 their numbers were estimated between 1,000 and 4,000.

19TH CENTURY STONE AGE GIANTS

In 1844, Captain Victor Araiza got fed up with their raids, and attacked them. He killed 11, including women and children, and took 4 captives from infants to 11 years old.

The Mexican army and navy teamed up in 1844, complete with two 12 ton schooners and cannons. Over 100 troops invaded Tiburón, and were not attacked. They searched the island until they found a handful of women and children, and a couple of men, and captured them. When the soldiers found the main body of Seri, the natives prepared to attack, but on seeing the sheer numbers and power of the invaders, they instead sued for peace.

A total of 510 men, women, and children were taken captive. That left 37 Seri on Tiburón, by the soldiers' count. The 510 included 18 oldsters, 1 blind person, 1 idiotic boy, 6 cripples, 180 women, 160 children, and 144 men. There were differing counts according to which report is referenced.

They were marched overland to Hermosillo, where "for the first time in a thousand years" it was safe to land on the island of Tiburón — previously known as the Isle of Giants.

Seri children were distributed to Mexican families, and the adults were placed in the Pueblo Seri jail. The adults were later let out and put to work, and within two months they had gathered up their children and gone back to Tiburón, murdering everyone they met along the way.

At this point, the fiercest of the Seri on Tiburón were still living as they always had, barefooted, wearing pelican skins, painting their faces with prominent black lines, and piercing their septum and adorning it with dangling greenstone.

Hostilities ended after the 1844 raid, because for the next five years there was not a single Seri attack on Sonora. Pueblo Seri had less than a dozen aged Seri, and their extinction was predicted due to their singular nature of refusing to assimilate into society. When the aged Seri died, no more took their place, though Seri still lived freely on Tiburón Island, and along the coast of the mainland.

At the same time, a Mexican pioneer named Pascual Encinas believed that he could build a ranch on the Seri border, put the Seri to work on the ranch, and become a buffer between the tribal Seri and the rest of civilization. Instead of capturing them and forcing them into labor, he lured them with kindness and respect.

The venture was successful, except for integrating the Seri. While some did move onto his ranch, and others visited, they spurned the religious teaching, and seemed averse to work. Instead of caring for the livestock, they used it as a food source. A band of Seri women who were living on the ranch, broke the neck of a horse, sucked its blood, gorged its intestines, and buried other parts so that it could "ripen" for a feast. This was not the first, or last, theft of a horse.

It was too much for their benefactor, who'd done everything in his power to help them, and integrate them into society. Pascual declared war on them in 1860, vowing to kill a Seri for every horse he'd lost. He killed 70 of these "demons of Seri" and his onslaught convinced them to make peace, but as always, the peace did not last.

When cartographers attempted to map the region in 1873, they encountered hostile natives. An 1894 estimate numbered the free Seri at 300, with most of those being women and children, although the reclusive Seri were difficult to keep track of as they did not live in permanent settlements. McGee referred to them as "hopeless wanderers, roving from place to place and sleeping wherever exhaustion overtakes them, carrying their entire stock of personal belongings with them."

The Seri were alive and well in 1905, still cannibalizing, and still terrorizing their neighbors, when gold prospector Thomas Grindell made an expedition into Seri territory with three other men, a tale which is highlighted in Volume 19 of *The Wide World Magazine* published by George Newnes, Ltd. of London in 1907.

Four men set out for the island of Tiburón, the main island of the Seri that had once been called Get-Out-If-You-Can. They were David Ingram, Olan Ralls, Jack Hoffman, and Tom Grindell. They were stocked with two hundred rounds of ammunition, a rifle, revolver, and shotgun. When several months passed and the men failed to return, Tom's brother Edward set out to find them.

When Edward Grindell reached the town of Caborca on the mainland, local hunters described a grisly scene where Americans had been killed and eaten by the Seri. Nothing was left but men's hands tied to a plank, along with a tin camp-stove and broken cameras. Edward refused to equate the dead hands with his brother, and he organized a search party.

He found the guide who'd led his brother's party to the edge of Tiburón — Dolores Valenzuela — who was in fear of his own life over an unwritten law in Mexico that made it a serious offense to go out as a guide, and not bring the party back safely.

Dolores assured Edward that the Grindell party had come across the gruesome scene with the hands, so there was still hope of finding Thomas alive. But then Dolores disappeared among accusations that he was a "bad Indian" and a liar, not to be trusted. Try as he might, Edward could not find Dolores, and everyone believed that Dolores had simply told Edward what he wanted to hear — that his brother might still be alive. Without Dolores to help him retrace the Grindell expedition, Edward went back to Arizona.

Dolores turned up in Tucson, Arizona, where he'd gone to find Edward after fleeing Caborca. The Mexicans were planning to hang him over the missing Grindell party, and he wanted to help Edward find them in order to exonerate himself. They went back to Mexico to search for the missing men.

They traveled to the abandoned Seri camp, where human hands were still tied to planks. They were part of a macabre dance ritual, with two dance rings one inside the other. The outer ring was 40 feet in diameter and well-used. Near the edge was a fourteen foot long plank, firmly planted in the ground, which appeared to have washed in as driftwood.

A four foot long blood-stained branch was attached crosswise to the plank. At each end of the branch was a human hand, fastened with leather straps from a camera case. Printed pages from a book on navigation were also attached to the plank. Nearby was a small tin stove, a remnant of the victim's belongings.

The Seri had tied the wretched victim to this crude cross, and danced around the circle chanting. As they passed the victim, each Seri dancer would hack off a piece of flesh until the victim was dead. The remains were believed to represent two Arizona miners who went missing in 1905 named Miller and Olander.

Edward and Dolores kept searching, armed to the teeth and on the alert, when they started finding evidence. They found a dead pack-mule, canteens, and a rifle, identified as belonging to the Grindell party. Edward searched for an entire month, and finally had to go back to civilization for rest, fresh horses and supplies. Even after a fresh start, they failed to find the missing men, except for evidence that the missing men had wandered aimlessly, zigzagging back and forth as if lost.

Edward gave up, and was planning to head back to Arizona when Jack Hoffman, a member of the Grindell party, showed up nearly dead from starvation. His naked body was covered in wounds, his skin was burned black from exposure, and all of his fingernails were missing. His shoes were tied to his feet with rags. He was crazed, and it was several days before he could even speak coherently.

The Grindell party had split up when they ran out of water after wandering lost, with Ralls going in one direction, Grindell in another, and Hoffman and Ingram in a third. Hoffman heard gunshots not long after Grindell left, but they never saw him again or learned his fate.

Hoffman and Ingram were out of water, with their swollen tongues hanging out of parched throats, and Ingram fell down and wouldn't get back up. Hoffman went on alone under the broiling sun, and finally came to the sea. He survived only by the grace of a pipe that distilled sea water. Eventually he wandered into a two-man camp of fishermen who were not Seri, and they escorted him to safety. The other three men were never seen again, though Thomas' bones were eventually found as evidence that he'd died of thirst. The Grindell party did not become victims of the Seri, as Miller and Olander had. It seemed as if centuries of extermination and capture had finally taken its toll.

The Seri who were captured and taken to missions were always the weakest members of the tribe — the aged, feeble, women and children. The Seri usually disposed of their weaker members, so this was on par. By 1950, there were only 200 known Seri left alive on Tiburón. The rest were either dead, or scattered across the continent, assimilated into civilized society.

The Seri of the 1500s were so tall that an ordinary man stood only chest-high against them. By the time the exterminations ended, the Seri measured just over 6 feet tall. This estimate comes from an 1894 comparison of 40 adult Seri in Rancho de San Francisco de Costa Rica, and these are likely representatives from the assimilated tribes. The vast difference in height was attributed to the exaggeration of early explorers. There is another explanation, however.

In the earliest days of exploration, identifying tribes was mostly guesswork, and the Seri were so reclusive that we could not get a firm grip on whether they were related to neighboring tribes. Thus we often got it wrong. Eventually several Seri tribes were identified, who shared variants of the same language and customs, but were in other ways distinct.

> Seri — on Tiburón Island and the mainland across from it
> Tepoca — an expelled tribe, timid even in 1536, extinct except as mixed blood
> Guayma — an expelled tribe, mild enough to provide guides in 1701, extinct except as mixed blood, possibly with the neighboring Pimas whom they allied with during wars
> Upanguayma — expelled, extinct except as mixed blood

There were other possible variants, but only the Seri of Tiburón are likely to have maintained the purest original bloodline, who would die before giving up their freedom or their Pre-Stone Age way of life. Yet even they may have succumbed.

The Seri expelled warriors who failed the matrimonial test, plus anyone who wanted to mate outside the tribe. These outcasts formed their own tribes, if they managed to survive being enemies of their brethren. Yet all were referred to as Seri by outsiders, even with the variances in height and temperament.

Anthropologist William McGee traveled to Seri territory to study them, and the Guayma were at war with the Seri. The Guayma and Upanguayma were either labeled extinct, or said to survive only by mixed blood. The timid Tepoca and vicious Seri were thought to still exist with pure blood in 1898 — the Seri on Tiburón Island, and the Tepoca along the mainland coast. Jesuit missionaries and Franciscan friars had spent 200 years attempting to scatter and divide the Seri, and to assimilate them, and they'd finally succeeded to some degree.

McGee did not believe that the romantic rumors of a white slave girl becoming the ancestor of a Seri clan were true. He was deeply invested in the purity of the Seri bloodline, because he wanted to showcase them at an anthropological exhibition that would feature not only a Stone Age tribe, but "pygmies and giants" which would include both Seri and Patagonian tribes.

According to McGee, "not a single known fact" gave even a hint of possibility of the mixing "of the Seri blood with that of other varieties of the genus *Homo*." With that statement, he differentiated the Seri from *Homo sapiens* — us — just as Hrdlicka had differentiated them after studying a skeleton.

And yet, as the Seri were being systematically executed, they were teaming up with neighboring tribes in their battles against the Europeans. In 1780, The Seri of Tiburón and Tepoca formed an alliance with the unrelated Pimas in the Cimarrones-Migneletes war. These Seri who shunned outside contact had been decimated to near-extinction several times, and were forced to let outsiders into their inner circle, at least in battle.

By 1896, a Seri named Mudo was described as 7 feet tall by most accounts, though he's also described as 6 feet 3 inches based on a photograph. His tribal affiliation isn't mentioned. Seri children who'd been taken during the wars were being brought up in Mexican homes, which may be where the description of Seri at their best arises. They would undoubtedly end up with non-Seri spouses, and mixed-Seri children. As there is such a discrepancy in height from the 1500s to the 1900s, the Seri divisions are important.

A 1799 description of the Seri by Don José Cortez divided them into three tribes: Tiburón, Tepoca, and Seri. He considered the Tiburón and Tepoca as "worthy of greater consideration than the Seri" though their bloodthirsty traits were the same. The worthy tribes far outnumbered the unworthy Seri.

By 1815, the Pueblo mission of Seri had been Mexicanized. In 1826, Lieutenant Hardy gave a first-hand description of the Seri on Tiburón. They were "very stout, tall, and well-built fellows, exceedingly like the Twelchii tribe of Indians in Patagonia…" The men were using stone arrowheads on their arrows, which was unprecedented for the Seri, and they seemed mild-mannered. Hardy also differentiated the Seri from the Tepoca, with one being inferior "both in courage and stature." The two tribes were at war.

The comparison to the Twelchii is an indication of size. Patagonia in South America had a tribe of Tehuelche Indians, aka Twelchii, which were reputed to be of "extraordinary size" according to Magellan and Captain Byron. They were "giants of enormous stature." Later descriptions said that they topped out at 6 feet 4 inches tall.

In 1774, Thomas Falkner gave first-hand descriptions after spending 40 years in Patagonia. The "Puelches" were a large race, reaching up to 7 feet 6 inches tall.

In 1853, Captain Bourne wrote *The Giants of Patagonia* with his own first-hand accounts:

> "In person they are large; on first sight, they appear absolutely gigantic. They are taller than any other race I have ever seen… the only standard of measurement I have is my own height, which is about 5 feet 10 inches. I could stand very easily under the arms of many of them, and all the men were at least a head taller than myself. Their average height, I should think, is 6 feet 6 inches… to a little less than 7 feet high."

Coincidentally, a genetic mutation known as C16301T has since been identified among some Tehuelche Patagonians and Seri. This is not a height gene, but it could link these two groups of alleged giants. Some Seri also share a genetic mutation at position 16311 with the Hopewell Mound Builders of Ohio.

As of 1903, the Tehuelche were intermixing with Europeans, and only then were they having many children. When two full-blooded Tehuelche mated, there were few children born.

Scientists have proven the existence of a "height gene" that's passed down genetically, identified as HMGA2. The single gene only has a small impact, but when added to the hundreds more that are believed to exist, the difference could be dramatic.

Like the Seri, the Tehuelche had well-developed chests, muscular frames, and were finely proportioned with big hands and feet. Their deep, heavy voices spoke in a guttural tone — the worst Bourne had ever heard. They were excessively filthy, and never washed. Their hands and faces were so encrusted with dirt that only a couple of places allowed their skin to show through. They painted their faces in broad stripes. They were far more advanced than the Seri, however, as they rode horses, and used knives and swords. They were also cannibals.

In 1520, an Italian on Magellan's crew described Patagonians so tall that the sailors only reached their waist, and Magellan intended to take some back to the emperor as specimens, but failed. They were too big to overpower, so Magellan tricked two of them into putting on shackles, as if they were jewelry. Once snared, they screamed with rage and their brethren came running. An intense battle ensued and the emperor did not get his "gift." At least two were 9 feet tall.

Anthony Knivet encountered the dead bodies of two giant Patagonians in 1601 at Port Desire near the Strait of Magellan. They were 10.5 feet tall.

The name *Patagonian* became a synonym for "giant" in every European language.

A Chronological History of the Voyages and Discoveries in the South Sea, Volume V, published in 1817, brings up an interesting point in the concept of determining height. A French officer measured "the shortest man of six" at Boucault Bay in the Strait of Magellan. The man was 5 feet 7 inches tall in "French measure, which is equal to 5 feet 11 inches and a quarter" in English measure. Rarely do you see this distinction in the old texts, and it would explain some of the discrepancies.

Also, two ships landing in a port at different times will encounter different people onshore. The giants were nomadic, and moved from place to place rather than living in villages. Thus one ship might encounter a tribe of wandering giants, while another might encounter ordinary villagers.

By whatever measurement, the Seri ranged from 6 feet tall to gigantic, where an ordinary man stood only as high as their chest. The comparison to Patagonians puts their height at up to 10.5 feet tall. Add to that their viciousness in hunting down humans, and you can see why so many campaigns were sent to exterminate them.

No people in history were more dreaded than the Seri, and survivors were more afraid of their "throttling hands and rending teeth" than their clubs, or poison arrows. Attacks on humans were up close and personal, and once caught you were savagely attacked with their teeth, or pummeled with stones the size of a fist. The Seri did not throw stones, or use them as projectiles in any manner. They were handheld weapons to pummel you with.

They usually attacked en masse, overwhelming the victim with sheer numbers, "despite the individual advantages growing out of gigantic stature, immense strength, and superior swiftness." They might discharge a cloud of arrows, or rush the victim and bash out his brains with stones, or break his neck, or crush his chest by jumping on it. These were their methods of attack and once disabled, human victims were "rent and consumed like beasts." This is a far cry from the timid Tepoca, who were also labeled as Seri, or the Guayma Seri, who were civil enough in 1701 to provide Indian guides outside the tribe.

Few dared to encroach their borders because Seri arrows were so poisonous that you were dead within days, even from a superficial wound. There was no cure for the poison, and they used a poison unlike any other. Neighboring tribes used plants and other natural poisons, but the Seri concocted a special brew.

It started with the decomposing lung or liver of a cow or human, mixed with unmentionable filth and allowed to putrefy. They kept a store of rotting bodies and feces as ingredients for this purpose. Once the organ became septic, it was put in a hole and covered with venomous snakes, scorpions, spiders, and centipedes. The creatures were agitated into a fury, until they attacked the organ and injected their venom. Then they were killed, and their poison parts added to the death-brew.

The disgusting mixture was allowed to simmer in the desert sun, to fester and rot until its putrid potency took on the fetid odor of death. The poison brew was laden with morbific germs, and the effects were painfully brutal.

One victim suffered a small nick on his wrist, and it stripped the flesh from his entire arm, though he survived. That was the power of the poison. First, the injury itself would swell, and then the skin would rot and fall off leaving the bones and sinews bare. You'd break out in a pestilential stink. More often than not, your entire body would swell until the flesh burst open and fell to pieces, and death was a gift of peace from the agony.

Another description comes from the fate of Pascual's horse, Pascual being the rancher who tried to help the Seri. His horse received only a minor arrow wound. The next morning, the wound was swollen and inflamed, and the horse was too stiff to be ridden. By afternoon, the glands were swollen under the horse's jaw, and there was a purulent discharge from its eyes and nostrils.

On the second morning, the horse could barely move. Its head was enormous from the swelling, as were its legs and abdomen, and there were fetid ulcers around the throat and jaw.

By the third morning, the ulcers on its body were suppurating, leaving tendrils of putrefied flesh and pus hanging from its head and neck. On that day, the horse died, emitting a stench so unpalatable that even the coyotes and buzzards did not approach. This was the power of Seri arrow poison, and these were the giants who terrorized the people of Sonora, Mexico.

Seri territory is within the Sonora province, and the *Superstition* chapter told us about mummies in Sonora, Mexico, that represented an advanced race of giants that were 8 feet tall. However, archeologists who attempted to retrieve the bones were attacked by Sonorans. The attack was not made to protect sacred bones, but to destroy the bones out of superstitious fear. The mummies could not have been Seri, as the Seri were too primitive to preserve their dead in such a manner, but any giant skeleton would have been an object of fear to the Sonorans, who'd spent hundreds of years battling giant Seri cannibals.

Also adjacent to Sonora is Chihuahua, Mexico — where 34 giant skeletons were discovered in Barranco de Cobre, or Copper Canyon. The skeletons, which ranged from 7 feet 6 inches, to 8 feet tall, were found in a cave, each wrapped up like a silkworm in its own basket, and some of them were mummified.

These canyons were home to the Tarahumara people, whose legends included a race of giants. The giants taught them agriculture, but they also ate Tarahumara children. The Tarahumara, who'd been tasked with providing the giants with food, got fed up and poisoned them to death. All of these tribes were accessible to one another.

Even the giant cannibals who taught the Tarahumara were more civilized than the Seri, as they at least had knowledge of planting corn and building a fire, which suggests that one was not an offshoot of the other.

Three thousand miles south of Sonora, at the northern edge of South America, there were tribes who believed that the dead could rise up out of their graves and live again. Among these tribes were the Quimbayas and Chibchas, who'd burn a body to ashes to prevent its resurrection. Did the people of Mexico have similar fears? Is that why the Sonorans were so intent on destroying the giant bones?

The Quimbayas are linked to extraterrestrial visitors by way of golden artifacts:

ONE OF MANY QUIMBAYA ARTEFACTS THAT RESEMBLE AIRPLANES

Their reign spanned from around 100 B.C. to 900 A.D., and they lived in the Andes Mountains where South America meets Central America. Their language shared no commonality with neighboring tongues. They were ceremonial cannibals, meaning they only ate human flesh on special occasions.

A neighboring tribe, the Chibchas, had legends of a hero named Bochica. Prior to the arrival of Bochica, the Chibchas were savages, and Bochica taught them how to cultivate corn and potatoes, spin yarn and make garments, and how to live in an organized community. Neither Bochica nor his wife are called giants, but a third party in their affairs was a giant tasked with holding up Earth, much as the Greek giant Atlas whose image shows him carrying the world on his great shoulders. This legend comes from *The World's History, Volume I, Pre-history of America and the Pacific Ocean* edited by Dr. H. F. Helmolt in 1901.

The Modern Traveler — Colombia, printed for James Duncan in 1825, gives us a more in-depth look at the Chibchas and Bochica:

> "...the inhabitants of the plain of Bogotá lived like barbarians, naked, without agriculture, without any form of laws or worship. Suddenly there appeared among them an old man... who appeared to be of a race unlike that of the natives, having a long and bushy beard. He was known by three distinct appellations: Bochica, Nemquetheba, and Zuhé. This old man, like Manco-Capac, instructed men how to clothe themselves, build huts, till the ground, and form themselves into communities."

Bochica's wife did not want mankind to possess knowledge of agriculture, laws, and so forth, so she sent a deluge which killed most of the Chibchas. A few found refuge on top of the mountains. Bochica banished his wife up into the heavens, and he built new towns for the people.

American Archaeological Research, No. I, The Serpent Symbol by E.G. Squier in 1851, states that Nemquetheba was known as "Envoy of God" and that among his other attributes, Bochica was a law-giver, who founded a new manner of worship, and regulated the calendar.

Manco-Capac was a god who came down to the people of Peru at a time when they lived half-naked in holes and caves, subsisting on whatever came their way, even eating human flesh. They were without law, government, or religion, like so many brute beasts. Manco-Capac and his brethren lifted them out of brutality and taught them the arts of life including agriculture, spinning and weaving, trades, and building roads, cities, and aqueducts. These tribes were once like the Seri — except that the Seri were not lifted up by a god who came down to teach them, and the Seri shunned human teachers.

The Quarterly Journal of Science, Literature and Art, Volume 25, published in 1828 by Henry Colburn, claims that south of the line (meaning the Mexican/American border) no annals existed prior to the mysterious appearance of Manco-Capac in 1283 A.D. His era coincides with the artefact that almost perfectly represents an airplane.

The American Anthropologist, Volume 8, published for The American Anthropological Association in 1906, adds that Bochica arrived on a rainbow with a golden rod in his hand. This gives us no less than four mythologies of rainbow-wormholes, comparing the Anáye legends of North America, the Mairu legends of Europe, Norse mythology of Scandinavia, and now the Chibchas.

Norse mythology has a rainbow-bridge that both gods and giants traveled on from their worlds to Earth, and would return on at the end of the world causing destruction to humans. The Anáye rainbow-wormhole led straight up into the sky, allowing you to look down upon Earth, with the mountains and lakes appearing tiny from overhead. When Bochica's rainbow appears again, many will die, just like in the Norse legends.

This brings us back to the spectacular Quimbaya golden artifacts that look like modern airplanes — created hundreds of years before we ever invented airplanes. They fashioned dozens of these miniature airplanes, each with a slightly different design, but all of them clearly representing aircraft, except they weren't referred to as such. Were they vehicles of the benevolent gods, who lifted mankind out of savagery?

Did the Seri personify what these other tribes were before the space-faring gods, with the power of flight, came down and brought civilization? Were they — *us* — in our original form?

They would have been tall enough to solve the issue of physical mating and birthing, as would the Tehuelche Patagonians that some Seri are genetically linked to. The Seri lifestyle was so frighteningly barbaric, even into the 1800s, it explains how their offspring, without civilized supervision, could have wrought havoc on everyone else.

The Stone Age lasted for millions of years, with our lifestyle virtually unchanged until the arrival of an advanced race from the stars. That's what our legends tell us. That's what the artifacts tell us. That's what the bones tell us.

Several branches of humanoids came and went, and eventually died out when humans in our present form — *Homo sapiens* — went forth and multiplied, and took over.

William McGee, one of the leading anthropologists of the Smithsonian Institution, stated that "there is not a single known fact indicating [mixing] of the Seri blood with that of other varieties of the genus *Homo*." Dr. Ales Hrdlicka, another prominent anthropologist at the Smithsonian, differentiated the Seri skeleton, likening it to Stone Age skeletons. The testimony of two anthropologists suggests that the Seri were representative of humans in the Stone Age, both physically, and in lifestyle.

Maybe somewhere in the history of the Seri, we would find answers to the greatest mysteries of humankind, if we'd been able to study Seri skeletons from the 1500s and earlier, back when Maldonado described "an Indian so large and tall that the best man in the army reached only to his chest," with reports of even taller Indians along the coast.

Where would they fit in the evolutionary tree, if the skeleton that Hrdlicka studied was not like us, as he intimated? In all likelihood, it wasn't even a full-blooded Seri, and yet still, Hrdlicka compared it to skeletons from the Stone Age.

What is their relationship to the humans that the Grigori mated with, and the resulting Nephilim generations? Do the Seri represent the original humans? Or do they represent the human-giant hybrids in the earliest generations? Or were they among the races that we thought were extinct? How do you reconcile a tribe that is stubbornly attached to a pre-Stone Age way of life that we can't even fathom? They wouldn't embrace so much as a glass bead, or a knife. Is that why our earliest ancestors lived in the same way for millions of years? We refused to change until someone forced us to? Is that the big secret?

EPILOGUE

Giants come in two parts: the legends, and the bones. Legends are easily dismissed, especially the farther away you get in time from the original sightings. It's hard to wrap our minds around something that our ancestors witnessed hundreds or thousands of years ago, even sightings that spanned the entire world, by civilizations who had no contact with one another. They described exactly what they saw, often giving us an actual size such as Goliath in the *Bible*.

Somewhere along the way, it was decided that we should put an end to our belief in giants, and the entire subject became one of ridicule. Was this done for the same reason as today's campaign against UFOs? To distance us in every way possible from the extraterrestrial entities who once visited Earth?

The second part of both equations is physical evidence. It's no secret that the government shows up wherever UFOs are seen, and if there's a shred of physical evidence, it gets carted off. As you can see by the multitude of news reports, the same thing happens to the bones of giants. Agencies such as the Smithsonian Institute, which is under government supervision, come and collect the bones and we never hear about them again. In some cases, when pressed for information, we're told that the evidence "disappeared" or that they never had it.

ANCIENT ALIENS AND THE AGE OF GIANTS

With the many cases of bones crumbling to dust as soon as they are exposed to air, or disintegrating when attempts are made to retrieve them, it's possible that the bones really did disappear, literally. Still, with the volume of evidence that we do have, you would expect to hear official confirmation that a race of giants once existed, both as our benefactors, and our enemies. I suspect that the same citizens who believe in UFOs will see an identical pattern unfolding with the giants:

- Giants existed.
- Giants were extraterrestrial.
- Giants came to Earth.
- Giants mated with humans and produced offspring.
- Those offspring were targeted in an obliteration campaign, probably to protect our species.
- All surviving evidence that it ever happened disappeared into some government facility.

Why would such a cover-up be necessary? Humans can get just as ugly as the giants that we resemble. That same ugliness is inherent in our very nature, and one of the few institutions that keeps it in check is religion — our belief in an afterlife, angels, demons, all-powerful deities, reincarnation, and so forth.

Life after death probably does exist for the human soul, but the attempt to extricate the historical thread from the spiritual thread is a challenge that must be handled carefully, and to give credit, small steps are being taken in that direction.

Even the Vatican has come forward with statements that allow for extraterrestrials to exist within the Christian faith. Father José Gabriel Funes of the Vatican Observatory gave an interview in 2008 which became known as *The Extraterrestrial Is My Brother* interview. He stated that it's possible to believe in God, and in extraterrestrials. He explained how we did not have today's level of scientific knowledge at the time the *Bible* was written, so the *Bible* is not a science book, but rather a letter from God to his people.

EPILOGUE

Regarding extraterrestrials, he stated that God could have created other intelligent beings, and then he quoted St. Francis: "If we consider Earthly creatures as brother and sister, why cannot we also speak of an extraterrestrial brother?"

He fueled the hypothesis that beings could exist who are similar to us, or more evolved than us, though he did not offer any indication or acknowledgement of past contact, stating that "until now, we have had no proof."

Moving forward is a series of baby steps, and logically so. An interesting point came up at the 2013 Citizen Hearing on Disclosure, where six former Congressmen were interviewed for a documentary regarding UFOs. Among the issues discussed:

> What if the President appeared on national television and admitted to the existence of UFOs flying our skies? How would we handle an identified alien presence? With a Congressional hearing? A United Nations commission? Would we send a special emissary on behalf of the Children of Earth? We'd have to yield some sovereignty to the United Nations, as this would be a worldwide issue and not a countrywide issue, and that opens up a major can of worms. Are we ready to think in terms of a united world government in order to address the alien issue on a global level?

Valid points indeed. It's easy to get hung up on wanting to know what happened yesterday, without giving thought to how that knowledge might affect tomorrow. If giants visited us in the past, they may come again, and how would we react? How SHOULD we react? Do we even know?

Stand in the middle of your living room, and spend three minutes visualizing a giant that is two, or even three times taller than you are. Where would his head be? Touching your ceiling? So tall that he'd need a hole in your ceiling to stand up straight?

Imagine how living alongside this giant would affect your daily life. How would he treat you? As an equal? Or would he brush you off as an annoyance to kick out of his way? How would his arrival affect the food supply? The water supply? Or even your commute to work?

He'd need a gigantic vehicle to drive down the road. How would that impact YOU, with a vehicle half the size? Our minivans and SUVs would be like golf carts competing on a superhighway of race cars. Who do you think would win that race?

Humans once co-existed with a species of small humanoids who were three to four feet tall, and we wiped them out. We're finding their bones today, and there've been sightings of a remnant few in recent centuries. This is detailed in the book *Ancient Aliens and the Lost Islands* by Lars Bergen and Sharon Delarose.

They were smaller, so they became a target, and now they are gone. Would the same happen to us against a race of giants? We treated the dwarf races abominably, as if they were animals — less than human — who did not rate the same respect as our fellow humans.

The whole concept of "do unto others" jumps into the spotlight when those *others* aren't the same. If we don't respect other humanoid species on Earth, then how can we expect extraterrestrial humanoids to respect us?

We don't even respect our own species. Look at the wars and conflicts around the world. Humans target humans for differences in race, religion, nationality, sexual orientation, political beliefs, and it doesn't stop there. We don't respect our neighbors, and if we are a reflection of the giants, what future could we hope for if they return to Earth?

Extraterrestrials are up there, right now, flying the skies. Several species are watching us, and have been for millennia. You can bet that they are judging our actions against our own kind, and imagine if they treated us the same way we treat others.

Think about that the next time you're on the verge of doing or saying something that would impact somebody else in a bad way. The very ripples that you send out into the world travel far beyond what you perceive, right out into the cosmos, where they can be seen and judged by space-faring beings. These beings have the power to rescue our sorry asses in the event of a global disaster, and they have the choice to simply let us perish.

Our own flood myths include that very scenario according to ancient astronaut theorists. The gods did not *send* the Great Flood, but they did have to decide whether to allow humans to continue, or allow us to perish as a race. A few of them chose to help us, much to the disagreement of their brethren. Most of them wanted us *gone*.

If there is even a grain of truth in the legends that were etched in stone long before all of the other mythologies and religions that we hold dear — then think long and hard. We do not have the technology to evacuate Earth if a global disaster strikes. Would any of them choose to help us right now?

Our fate may very well be in YOUR hands — each and every human being on the planet, and your actions collectively. Don't be that one straw that sinks us all.

Book Excerpt: Ancient Aliens and the Lost Islands

Our ancestors left us with rich descriptions of earthly paradise, which was more often than not on an island. They told stories about the supernatural beings that lived in paradise, or who lived on earth among us. Once you start looking at the details, the descriptions sound suspiciously extraterrestrial.

Today, we have ancient astronaut theorists who've set out to prove that extraterrestrials visited us in the distant past, and overtly interacted with humans, unlike the aliens today who operate in secrecy. These ancient astronaut theorists look for truth hidden in the mysteries of the Nazca lines, Sumerian texts about the Anunnaki deities, petroglyphs and hieroglyphs that appear to depict alien astronauts and their spaceships, and structures built thousands of years ago that couldn't possibly have been built with human technology alone.

However, the island paradise where the extraterrestrials lived is shrouded mostly in myths and legends, lacking even the physical evidence that ancient astronaut theorists can point to. All we have are fragments of stories, many of which were undoubtedly tall tales, and a handful of odd clues hidden in the extraordinary tales.

BOOK EXCERPT: ANCIENT ALIENS AND THE LOST ISLANDS

Paradise went by many names, including Ogygia, Atlantis, Avalon, Otherworld, Yma, Elysium, Land of the Living, Island of the Living, Island of Life, Country of Youth, Land of Youth, Delightful Plain, Land of Virtues, Land of Promise, Earthly Paradise, Terrestrial Paradise, and dozens of others in a multitude of languages. We can't even agree as to whether they pointed to a single location, or multiple locations.

Atlantis would have been wiped out during the great flood by most accounts, the flood being an event told not only in the *Bible*, but also in the legends of the Greeks, East Indians, Native Americans, Mesopotamians, and the Iranian sacred books of Zoroastrianism. Yet this *Otherworld* paradise, as I've chosen to call it from among its various names, survived the flood because those who traveled to the Otherworld and came back to tell the tale lived long after the great flood.

Most descriptions of the Otherworld referred to an island, and through the centuries, maps pinpointed the location of this island in so many different places that the notion of an island that nobody could find became a legend in itself. However, if the island were accessible only through a portal, and portals exist in multiple locations, that could explain how one or more hidden islands could exist in different locations. Even today we have theories about portals in places like the Bermuda Triangle.

By whatever name or location, however, the descriptions were the same. The healing waters rejuvenated you, and as long as you remained there, you never grew old. All of your favorite foods and beverages seemed to be at your beck and call, as if provided by a *Star Trek* food replicator. The sun shined day and night over a land that never got cold, where flowers bloomed year round, and where fruit trees were perpetually laden with fruit. There was no rain, clouds, snow, or hail.

This is the description that most legends agree on, but a few of the legends add details such as a peculiarly bright atmosphere that was amber in color, palaces that floated in midair, revolving castles, nicely trimmed grass, speedboats, computers, cloaking technology, bizarre animals, traveling through a strange mist to get there, and "dark clouds" inside which an entire race of supernatural beings moved to a new location.

One such paradise was the kingdom of Prester John, also known as Presbyter Johannes, whose kingdom bordered Earthly Paradise. Prester John's lost Christian realm was the object of countless expeditions for hundreds of years, with a description straight out of a fairytale book.

Prester John's kingdom boasted streams whose bottoms and banks glistened with precious gemstones so plentiful that John's scepter was made of pure emeralds, and even platters and cups were made of precious gems. Gold was also abundant, and the ants dug it up while tunneling, creating mountains of gold. These little gold diggers actually existed, as exposed in the *Legendary Creatures* chapter.

Prester John's kingdom was the highest place on earth, higher than Noah's flood which saved it from being inundated, so high that it nearly touched the moon. It was surrounded by a moss-covered wall with a single entry which was "closed with burning fire so that no mortal man dared to enter."

Residents lived for hundreds of years by drinking from a rejuvenating spring which reset their bodies back to an age of thirty. Nudiosi pebbles allowed the blind to see again, as well as made the wearer invisible.

John himself was described as having "supernatural longevity" and his kingdom was considered to be both celestial and immortal. Now we have our first clue, as *celestial* can pertain to the sky, the universe beyond earth's atmosphere, celestial bodies such as stars and planets, or an invisible heaven, though even the word *heaven* includes non-spiritual references. Various translations of the word *heaven* include "heights, elevation, sky, clouds," and "whirlwind." Therefore, a celestial kingdom could refer to an orbiting kingdom or one that exists on another planet.

BOOK EXCERPT: ANCIENT ALIENS AND THE LOST ISLANDS

Prester John was a priest as well as a king, and he was allegedly descended from one of the Three Magi who traveled from the east to worship the newborn Jesus. Apparently he wasn't originally a priest, as his story began when he got lost in a forest while hunting. There he met a "celestial being" who promised to guide him back to the road if he embraced the doctrine of Christ. Who was this *celestial* being? And is this linked to his kingdom being described as *celestial*?

"Celestial Empire" was a name given to China, and a Chinaman was sometimes called a *celestial* back when the Prester John legends were prevalent. However, a celestial from China would not likely have had Christian roots. That leaves either a traveler from a distant planet, which would be an *extraterrestrial*, or it could have been an *angel*, which can have extraterrestrial roots according to ancient astronaut theories.

Another clue comes from bizarre creatures in Prester John's kingdom such as Centaurs, Satyrs, Fauns, Cyclops, Gryphons, Phoenix birds, horned men, giants, white lions and white bears. On the surface, this sounds totally far-fetched. Few believe that any of these creatures ever existed. However, in every legend you'll find a grain of truth and for most of these creatures, there exists some basis in fact which I've demonstrated in the *Legendary Creatures* chapter. There you'll find evidence for the existence of Satyrs, Gryphons, Phoenix birds, giants, and gold digging ants.

White lions and white bears are directly linked to extraterrestrial visitation, according to an old African legend that involved an aging, dying queen who was rejuvenated after meeting the occupants of an extraterrestrial craft. Being a story of extraterrestrial visitation, and human rejuvenation, as opposed to an island paradise, this story is told the chapter *Touched By Celestial Beings*. Could Prester John's white lions and bears have been caused by an extraterrestrial visitor as well?

Next to Prester John's kingdom was Earthly Paradise, which was neither in heaven, nor on Earth, in spite of its name. What does that mean, exactly? If it wasn't on Earth, why was it called Earthly Paradise? Was it a spirit realm, another dimension, a city or ship orbiting in space, or another planet? Its location was described in conjunction with the biblical flood.

Noah's flood was forty fathoms high, engulfing the tallest mountains on Earth, and Earthly Paradise was forty fathoms higher than that, "hanging" in between heaven and Earth. *Hanging* or *hangeth* was the word used in the old texts.

This location is given in the 1844 book *St. Patrick's Purgatory; an essay on the legends of purgatory, hell, and paradise* by Thomas Wright. The same description is also given in the 1869 book *Curious Myths of the Middle Ages* by S. Baring-Gould, and both books are quoting from the same source, which is an "unnamed manuscript" in the British Museum.

Earthly Paradise, which is an unfitting name for a place which is obviously not on or of Earth, is described as being perfectly level with no hills or hollows, no frost, snow, hail, rain, heat or hunger. Night never falls, and the sun shines *seven times brighter than Earth's sun*. The Well of Life is found there, along with the Phoenix bird. If the sun shines seven times brighter than Earth's sun, this could indicate a planet orbiting a sun in another galaxy. It could also be describing a climate-controlled city orbiting Earth with very bright, artificial lighting, or sunlight seemingly brighter for its orbiting location.

Prester John's *celestial* kingdom, which was so high that it nearly touched the moon, bordered Earthly Paradise, which "hangs" somewhere between heaven and Earth. It's no wonder that your average explorer couldn't find them!

Not all paradises had Christian connections. Another paradise was Elysium, which in Celtic depictions was a land of the gods, accessible only to mortals who were related to the gods or invited by the gods. This was not an afterlife, but a place for the living that later got redefined as an afterlife. Humans tend to redefine history to match our current beliefs. An entire discourse was written about Elysium in the *Encyclopedia of Religion and Ethics, Volume II* published in 1910, from different points of view, along with a mention of the Tuatha dé Danann (peoples of the goddess Dana.) The Tuatha were a significant race of supernatural beings who lived among us for hundreds of years, and whose technology far surpassed our own, as subsequent chapters will demonstrate. The encyclopedic entry connected all of the physical paradises together, as if they pointed to a single place with different names, depending on who was giving the description.

Some believed this Otherworld to be an island, while others thought it was underground, or even under the water. In some descriptions, it was a "mysterious land revealing itself suddenly on Earth's surface, and entered through a mist" or where you became enveloped in a mist while journeying into or out of it. Sometimes a supernatural being appeared out of a "magic mist," or the mist hid a "supernatural dwelling."

Ireland was the home of the very real people known as the Tuatha dé Danann, who controlled some of these supernatural mists. In the story of Cormac mac Airt, the king of Ireland in the 3rd century who disappeared for seven months in 248 A.D., Cormac encountered a man from the Land of Promise who described it as a place where nobody had a care in the world. There was no envy, jealousy, sorrow, sin, and nobody grew old.

The mysterious man offered Cormac a glittering silver branch from which dangled several golden apples, that when jangled together produced strange music that made you forget all of your troubles. In exchange for this branch (or wand) with its musical apple chimes, the man wanted his choice of anything in Cormac's kingdom. Cormac accepted the offer not knowing what he'd be trading, and unfortunately what the stranger wanted was Cormac's wife and children, which were whisked away to this Otherworld.

When news spread that the queen and her children were gone, the people raised such an uproar that Cormac jangled the wand that made you forget your troubles, and his people were no longer concerned. Even for Cormac, the wand couldn't permanently replace the loss of his family, and after a year he set out to find his wife and children in the Otherworld.

He set out in the direction that he'd seen the man from the Land of Promise go, and soon a "dark magical mist" surrounded Cormac. When the mist cleared, he was in the Land of Promise. He traveled across flatlands where he saw "strange, foreign-looking" people performing unusual tasks, and eventually he came across a stately palace — one of the homes of Manannán mac Lir, and the very place where his family had been taken. Manannán and his wife appeared to Cormac as a very tall couple wearing clothes of many colors.

Manannán was one of the leaders of the Tuatha dé Danann, and he'd set up this whole trade to lure Cormac to his home so that he could teach Cormac valuable lessons, and so that the two could bond in friendship. That night, Cormac and his family were permanently reunited at Manannán's dinner table, and Manannán reverted to his "true form" though this true form was not described.

Cormac and his family slept at Manannán's house that night, and when they woke the next morning, they were back in their own home, in possession of three magical gifts from their divine host: a goblet that indicated when someone was lying, a tablecloth that produced any food their heart desired, and the wand he'd originally traded for. Cormac was allowed to keep these magical items until the day he died, at which point they'd be taken away, probably back to the Otherworld.

As the wisdom that Manannán shared with Cormac includes incredible links between some of the most sacred sites in the world, I've expanded on the details in a chapter devoted to the teachings and wisdom of these ancient visitors.

Cormac's story has been retold in many old texts including *The Mythology of All Races*, edited by Louis Herbert Gray, Ph.D. in

1918, and *Transactions of the Ossianic Society for the year 1855, Volume III* in 1857, and *The voyage of Bran, son of Febal, to the land of the living: Volume 1* by Alfred Trübner Nutt in 1895. Cormac was lucky, because not all who visit the Otherworld come back into their own time.

Another Irishman named Bran visited an Otherworld after receiving a silver branch, though his had white apple blossoms instead of golden apples. Bran searched for this Otherworld somewhere across the ocean, and on the way he encountered Manannán in a boat, though apparently it was not Manannán's island that they visited. Instead, they traveled to the Island of Joy, and then to the Island of Women, where they lingered. As they ate, the food on their plates seemed to replenish itself, and the food was always what their heart most desired to eat. They stayed for a year, and then attempted to go back home for a visit. They were warned not to disembark from the boat during the visit. They could zip around the ocean on their otherworldly boat, and even talk to people on shore, as long as they remained in the boat.

There's always a rebel who doesn't listen, so of course one man climbed out of the boat and immediately turned into a heap of ashes. Apparently, several hundred years had passed during their absence. Bran stayed in the boat, related his tale of the Otherworld to the people on shore, and then sailed off, presumably to return to the island he'd been living on.

This Otherworld has a time differential where a day passes there, but a year passes on Earth. Those who were able to tell the tale, such as in the Voyage of Bran, did so from a vessel that could travel in between worlds, and as long as they did not leave the vessel, they could communicate with their earthly brethren.

Sometimes the Otherworld is described as being many islands. The Island of Joy, the Island of Women, and Manannán's island are three different islands in the Otherworld. It may be that they visited, literally, some ocean on another world which has many continents and islands, just as we do.

BOOK EXCERPT: ANCIENT ALIENS AND THE LOST ISLANDS

Another reference to paradise which hints at an off-world location falls under the name Terrestrial Paradise. Volumes have been written, including a 750 page treatise by Carlo Giangolino in 1649. Imagine — 750 pages devoted to unlocking the secrets of Terrestrial Paradise. There are as many opinions on its nature and location as there are people pursuing the mystery.

A discussion took place in 1691 that Bishop Pierre Daniel Huet of Avranches, France, summarized as follows: There is no consensus about the location of this paradise as some place it in the 3rd heaven, or the 4th heaven, or the lunar heaven, or on the moon itself, or on a mountain near the lunar heaven, or in the middle region of the air, above the earth, under the earth, in any number of earthly locations, or in a place where men simply cannot reach. They don't even agree on whether this Terrestrial Paradise has animals in it, but some believe that wherever it is, at least three humans are living there as immortals, at least until the end of the world: Enoch, Elias, and St. John the Evangelist.

So the Otherworld of the Tuatha dé Danann may be a series of islands, and the Christian Terrestrial Paradise is a place whose location could be virtually anywhere on the Earth, moon, some level of heaven, or anywhere in between.

There is a concept known as *seven heavens* which are presumed to be spiritual realms where we go after we die, though some interpretations involve alternate universes or even planets. Several religions have this concept including Islam, Judaism, Hinduism, Hermeticism, and Gnosticism. There are also beliefs in seven levels of an underworld, or seven upper worlds. Even the Ancient Egyptians had a version of seven heavens, and Norse mythology spoke of nine worlds, one of which was a location that they called heaven or Asgard, where a physical race of beings lived that traveled to and from Earth across a "bridge" between our worlds.

The word *heaven* itself means different things including the atmosphere in which birds fly, and the space that holds the sun, moon, and stars. It's also the realm where angels travel, and where God resides. Sometimes it's a place of paradise; other times it's a place of hell, as the various "levels" of heaven are not all paradises. If there's a Christian Rapture, both the living and the dead will be taken where there's a "new" heaven and Earth. So will the living have to die and become spirits? Or will the dead be brought back to life in physical bodies? We're not given a definitive description of this world except that we are "changed" in order to live there.

The Apostle Paul wrote about a man who went to the 3rd heaven, and Paul did not know whether the man went in his physical body or not. In the biblical *2 Corinthians 12:2-4*, the Apostle Paul wrote:

> "I knew a man in Christ above fourteen years ago, (whether in the body, I cannot tell; or whether out of the body, I cannot tell: God knoweth;) such a one caught up to the third heaven. And I knew such a man, (whether in the body, or out of the body, I cannot tell: God knoweth;) How that he was caught up into paradise, and heard unspeakable words, which it is not lawful for a man to utter."

So we've got a variety of opinions on the nature and location of Terrestrial Paradise, as well as the various levels of heaven including their nature. In other words, *it is possible* that Terrestrial Paradise exists on a planetary body, or floating up in the air like a great spaceship city, or hidden somewhere on Earth.

According to the 1855 *Encyclopedia Metropolitana or System of Universal Knowledge*, which reprinted Bishop Huet's summary on the location of Terrestrial Paradise, another aspect was its size, which was sixty times bigger than Earth in its dimensions according to "certain Talmudists" (Huet's quotes, not mine.)

Sixty times bigger than Earth definitely moves it off of Earth, and could indicate another planet if this place were indeed physical as some believe. If this is the same paradise with an amber atmosphere where its sun shines brighter than Earth's sun, and most travelers pass through some sort of strange mist to get there, and then find buildings floating in the air, could the mist be a form of star gate or wormhole across the galaxy?

Some paradise legends have connections beyond the typical description, such as a strange form of wordplay. One involves King Yima in Zoroastrianism, which is an ancient Iranian religion where Yima's kingdom is paradise. Another is about a Christian monk who went in search of, *and found*, the physical paradise island of Yma. Incidentally, the Celts also believed in Yma, a place where the spirits of the departed lived in a happy land called Yma, aka Hy-ma, Flathinnis, Noble Island, Isle of the Just, or Isle of the Good. The Norse gods include the creator god Ymir. So we have both physical and spiritual paradises in the Yima connection.

That's a mighty big coincidence for Zoroastrianism, Nordic and Celtic beliefs, and Christianity to share such similar words, with three of them connected to a land of paradise, and the paradise legends don't end with the Yima connection. They continue with palaces that float in the air, this time, on the island of Ogygia, which some believe was the mythical Atlantis.

Controversy surrounds Ogygia, which is both a place, and a person, and few agree on the details of either one. The person Ogyges or Ogygia was either an aborigine, or the son of a god, or a Titan (giant), or a prince. One historian puts his lifetime at the same time as the biblical *Exodus*, when Moses led the Israelites out of Egypt, while other historians send him much further back in time.

His realm was either a portion of Greece, Ireland, Iceland, America, or the island of Atlantis, or Ogygia. You see how this gets convoluted, with so many different versions floating around, mixing legends with facts, and not all depictions painted a glorified vision of the place known as Ogygia.

Among the paradise legends, however, Ogygia is an island of enchanting beauty, where youths and maidens dance on dewy grass, everything exists in abundance, and a spring flows with waters that bless you with the gift of life. Imagine that… another paradise with a Fountain of Youth.

In the center of the island, *floating in the air*, is a palace of glass with transparent walls, where the souls of the blessed live. The Merddin Emrys visited this house of glass, and here the island intersects with tales of the Merddin Emrys, also known as the legendary wizard Merlin who was gifted with supernatural powers.

The next paradise is the island of Avalon, also called the Vale of Apples, which also boasts a *glass palace where time passes differently*, which is ruled by the Lady of the Lake, or in some accounts, the fairy Morgana, who is linked to both Merlin, as well as the Tuatha dé Danann.

A curious phrase comes to us from the Avalon tales, which suggests that Avalon is *not of this Earth* but either exists in another dimension or on another planet. This reference comes from the 1869 book *Curious Myths of the Middle Ages* by S. Baring-Gould in which a man visited paradise and met Morgana.

Ogier the Dane traveled on horseback to a valley where he rested by a sparkling fountain surrounded by fragrant shrubs. There he encountered a beautiful maiden who gave him a golden crown wreathed in blossoms. The minute he put the crown on, he completely forgot his past, his battles, and everything that had ever happened in his life. All of his memories were replaced with desire for this beautiful maiden — Morgana.

One day the crown fell off and he remembered his old life, and grew homesick for his family and friends. He begged Morgana to permit him to "return to Earth" and she consented. He'd spent no more than a few hours in Avalon, but back "on Earth" a full two hundred years had passed. Everyone and everything he knew was gone, so he went back to Avalon and remained there with Morgana.

This legend differs from stories where the traveler turns to dust as soon as they set foot on their home turf. Ogier simply

BOOK EXCERPT: ANCIENT ALIENS AND THE LOST ISLANDS

traveled through time, found the world changed, and then went back to Avalon. The key phrase is that he asked permission *to return to Earth*. So where was he, if not on Earth? And what sort of place would have such a time differential?

Morgana was also known as Morgan le Fay, or Morgan the Fairy, who was a powerful sorceress connected to Merlin and the Arthurian legends, as well as Avalon, which was also known as the Isle of Apples.

A description of Avalon was echoed almost word for word in a description of Ogygia, both being islands of enchanting beauty where youths and maidens danced in dewy grass among green trees laden with apples. In Avalon, everything existed in abundance, and a *glass palace with transparent walls floated in the air*, visited by the Merddin Emrys! Here we have one island, with many names, where each story provides another clue, and all of the clues point to a place of extraterrestrial origin or construct, accessible to Earth, *but not existing on Earth*.

Avalon is a legendary island, and is also known as one of the Fortunate Isles, which is another name for Yma — the name of the island(s) that the monks were searching for *and found* in the year 512 A.D. This island was seen as recently as 1958.

Avalon produced such an abundance of food that no one needed to plough or work for food. Apple trees, grain, and grapes grew naturally, and the green grass was always clipped close. Keep that little factoid in mind about the trimmed grass, as it becomes important in the *Legendary Creatures* chapter.

Avalon had no thieves, no robbers, no enemies, no violence, no sickness, no death, no sorrow, no old age, no winter, and no summer, which mirrors all of the other paradises. It was forever springtime, and the apple trees produced both fruit and flowers on the same branch.

This legend differs by telling us who was in charge — nine sisters (including Morgana) who ruled over Avalon with a pleasing set of laws. Morgana was a fairy, and Merlin was a shape shifter, which brings us to the legends surrounding the Isle of Man which is a real island situated off the coast of Ireland.

Dating events in ancient history is difficult, because we aren't always given a clear set of dates for events, but so much revolves around Manannán mac Lir that we can at least attempt to narrow it down. The first king of the Tuatha dé Danann was Nuada, who ruled Ireland sometime around 1500 B.C. according to mainstream scholars, which gives us a starting date.

We have two people whose lives intersect with Manannán — Cormac mac Airt, and Manannán's run in with none other than the legendary St. Patrick. Cormac existed somewhere between the 2nd and 4th centuries A.D., and St. Patrick's time would have been in the 5th century, which situates Manannán somewhere between 100 A.D. and 500 A.D., or even spanning that entire range considering the Tuatha dé Danann lifespan. So the next reference to *ancient times*, and the later references to motor boats and revolving castles, should put the timeline into perspective as far as what you'd expect to find technologically.

In ancient times, the Isle of Man was ruled by Manannán mac Lir, who gave the island his name, and whose nickname was *king of the mists*. He was a sea god who "drew his misty cloak around the island" to hide it from invaders. The Isle of Man was home to several shape shifters, including a giant, a hairy ogre known as a Buggane, and a hairy water goblin or horse called a Glashtyn. With all the shape shifting going on, I'm not sure how they knew that the beings were different. You can't help but wonder with shape shifters — what is their true form? It's interesting that the Buggane was actually intelligent enough to talk to humans, and he was magical.

Fairies also inhabited the island, though they weren't called fairies, they were called *the little folk* or *themselves*, and wouldn't you know it? Fairies were also shape shifters. Coincidentally, so were the Tuatha dé Danann. About the only creature on the Isle of Man who was NOT a shape shifter was the Fenodyree — a busy little being who was stuck with his small, hairy form. Along with magical creatures, this island had a revolving castle, a magic cauldron, and a speedboat called Wave Sweeper, all of which were hidden behind Manannán's otherworldly mist.

Today's Isle of Man is not a hidden land of supernatural beings who live in revolving castles. There are several possible explanations. Ancient history was interlaced with highly imaginative fiction; or the advanced visitors simply up and moved elsewhere taking all of their extraordinary paraphernalia with them; or Manannán's island was through a portal *near* the Isle of Man; or the island itself had a portal to their world — a portal which is now closed.

Consider our concept of space travel. We don't envision ourselves moving into the housing of the locals, nor do we envision ourselves building houses like the ones we live in on Earth. We envision our space travelers landing on a planet in their ship, and *living in* that ship, until such time that we decide to fire up the engines and fly away. The television series *Stargate Atlantis* was based on this premise, which could explain not only rotating castles, but "islands" which were surrounded by a shining mirrored wall.

As for evidence, which they surely would have left behind — what happens to evidence today? The government *immediately* surrounds the area, gathers up every last shred of evidence, and hides it away. For example, in Texas a segment of roadway was replaced *twice* after the Cash-Landrum UFO incident. Once wasn't good enough to remove the evidence — they dug it up and hauled it away *twice*. Governments gather up the pieces like hamsters hoarding away food, and they don't show the rest of us what they've gathered. So is there physical evidence beyond the descriptions? Probably, but until the government throws open the doors of information, we'll never see it.

So who were these Tuatha dé Danann? They were depicted as tall humans with blond hair, and blue or grey eyes, created of flesh and bone which could be injured, just like us. They had a succession of high kings that ruled Ireland including one named Eochaidh Ollathair who carried a special title of *Dagda Mór* or *the Dagda*, which meant either "shining divinity" or "the good god" while *ollathair* meant "all father." The Dagda was not the father of the Tuatha race, but he was one of the most important among them as evidenced by his titles.

The Dagda was immortal, and forever young, which were traits shared by all of the Tuatha dé Danann. At one point, the Tuatha lived in some undefined "northern islands" of the world, but later moved "in dark clouds" to Ireland, drawing an invisible wall around them which hid them from the eyes of men, and which was impassable, which is a reference to Manannán mac Lir's cloaking technology.

This is further expanded in *The Book of the Taking of Ireland* which is also known as *The Book of Invasions* — a controversial early history of Ireland from which many of the Tuatha dé Danann legends come. Trouble arises because an accurate, unbiased, pre-Christian history simply doesn't exist. Early writers did everything in their power to erase all vestiges of blasphemous worship, and this was sometimes done by burning the existing texts and then rewriting history in a way that was more favorable to a new set of beliefs.

The arrival of the Tuatha dé Danann to Ireland brought darkness over the sun for three days and three nights, and "the truth was not known beneath the sky of stars, *whether they were of heaven or of Earth*." Almost 4,000 years have passed since these extraterrestrials made Irish history, and humans still haven't duplicated some of the technologies they possessed such as the cloaking device, though it isn't for lack of trying.

Scientists yearn to create cloaking technology that renders our ships invisible, and if there's any truth to the *Philadelphia Experiment* stories, we've actually made progress though at great cost. This cloaking experiment caused us to "move through time" as well as to a different location. Fact or fiction? I don't know, but you can bet they're working hard on turning it into fact.

The Tuatha dé Danann often retreated to a hidden island which went by many names including Land of the Young, Land of Promise, Earthly Paradise, Land of the Ever Living, Mag Mell, and even within a single story you might see this island given three different names. That's what makes the whole concept of an island paradise confusing — all of the different names — so we don't know if they were talking about one island, or ten islands.

Another clue that their hidey hole was not located on Earth was the amber-colored, "peculiarly bright atmosphere." Sometimes glittering city domes and pinnacles make up the skyline, and other times you see fortresses which appear to be built of gold, silver or white marble. If these cities or fortresses existed on Earth, even the government couldn't have erased all traces of them. Time flowed differently there and one hundred years was as a single day, or several hundred years passed in the span of one of our years.

Other names for this place included Theirna-na-Oge, Tír-na-m Beo, Oilean-na-m Beo, Tír-nam Buadha, Hy-na-Beatha, Tír-na-nóg, and Tír-Tairngire. All of these translate into variations of "land" or "island" of the living, of life, of the young, of promise, of virtues, or delightful plain. Sometimes it's described as an island, and other times it's an underwater city.

Sometimes the island appeared as if out of nowhere, and when you attempted to travel to it, with your eyes looking straight at it, the island suddenly disappeared right in front of you (which sounds suspiciously like a cloaking device.)

Something else that figures in not only the Tuatha dé Danann legends, but also the Norse and Native American legends, are the self-propelled boats made of crystal, glass, stone, or copper. These boats are identical to motorboats, and they figure into many of the legends, along with a magical mist that descends on a man and seemingly transports him to an unusual place. In other words, this mist doesn't always stay in one place to hide an island — it can move around, envelope a person wherever they are standing, and suddenly that person is somewhere else.

Were all of these legends flat out myths created in the imaginations of ancient man? Or was it simply a case of misinterpretation of advanced extraterrestrial technology?

If you plucked an ordinary man from a thousand years ago and brought him into our world today, he'd probably be bowing at our feet, kissing the ground and calling us gods. A thousand years ago they were dying by the millions from plagues, while we're reattaching severed limbs and replacing worn out hearts.

Our ancestors fought battles hand-to-hand with swords, or at a distance with crossbows. Imagine their reaction to witnessing a bomb dropped from an airplane, or shots fired from a war plane which could take out an entire troop with a single blow.

How would they interpret the simple act of putting dirty dishes into a box, pushing a button, and later opening the box to find clean dishes? We put dirty clothes in a machine, and magically the clothes come out clean, and then dry. We hit a button and our homes are heated, with no visible source of fire anywhere. Hot air without a fire? Cold air in the middle of summer? This would surely have been called magic.

We see incredible visions on a screen in our living room, which can be beautiful, magical, or terrifying. We carry telephones which show us the living image of our friends and family who are thousands of miles away. We send messages which they receive instantly, a feat that in centuries past would have taken *months* via letter carried on horseback. What would our ancestors have called us, if they could see us now? Wizards? Genies? Witches? Gods?

How many ancient stories referred to voices of the gods coming out of nowhere? Would a cell phone or radio projecting a voice be interpreted the same way? We travel in an enclosed vehicle on wheels with temperature control, music, lights, electric windows, electric seats, heated seats, and a gas pedal which propels us forward at "magic speeds." Even the power of electricity, prior to its invention, would have been called magic. When the camera was first invented, some people believed it would steal your very soul to have a photo taken.

We fly through the air in planes. Food is at our fingertips in grocery stores. We dine in revolving restaurants at the top of tall towers. Wouldn't all of this be described as some mystical, magical, godlike paradise to someone who lived four thousand years ago? If a simple camera had a terrifying effect, how would they have perceived our current technology?

What technologies have we not yet mastered, that an extraterrestrial civilization might bring? Human transporters that would beam you from here to there? Such a transporter would seemingly make a person "disappear" like a genie. Would they have brought cloaking devices to hide humans, vehicles, or entire cities, as in islands "hidden in the mists" that appeared and disappeared? What about flying cities that could move from one location to another, float on the water, or hover in the air? Aren't we now building space stations that people can live on?

If you believe that we will master these technologies, then you have to consider the possibility that an extraterrestrial race already mastered it, and visited us in the distant past, leaving behind legends so fantastic that we don't believe them today, but our ancestors believed them enough to chase after these earthly paradises that seemingly just vanished from the maps.

One of the oldest paradise legends comes from a text dated approximately 3000 B.C., which Sumerian clay tablets referred to as *Dilmun* or *Telmun*. Unlike paradise where everyone seems to be permanently at leisure, Dilmun had an active trade route with surrounding regions. Dilmun was also known as the Land of the Living, as well as being the place where Ziusudra — the hero of

BOOK EXCERPT: ANCIENT ALIENS AND THE LOST ISLANDS

the Sumerian flood epic — was taken by the gods to live forever. His very name means "found long life" or "life of long days."

Dilmun is described as a faraway place, an island by some accounts, where there is no sickness, death, or strife, and where the wolf doesn't snatch the lamb, and neither do any of the other animals kill one another. It was a pure, clean, bright, prosperous land, dotted with "great dwellings." Archeologists are still trying to locate Dilmun.

http://www.sharondelarose.com/books/alien-ufo-otherworlds/ancient-aliens-and-the-lost-islands-through-the-wormhole/

BOOK EXCERPT: ALIEN NIGHTMARES

They can make you see things, override your memory, do whatever they want to you, and there's not a damn thing you can do about it. They can make you believe that their presence is just a bad dream, one that doesn't match what really happened. All you are left with are false memories and nightmares. For this reason, few abductees ever realize that they were even abducted. Could your dreams be more significant than you realize.

When I discovered that a dream I had at 34 years old was actually a resurfacing memory from when I was 2 years old, and I was able to corroborate the events with both a witness to the original event and to a newspaper clipping, I finally grasped the reality behind the dreams which I had so meticulously logged. If this dream was a genuine memory, how many of the other dreams were also memories of real events?

UFOs and extraterrestrials flew in and out of my dreams for decades, starting in early childhood. I lived in an extraordinary world full of terrifying creatures, whirlwinds, bizarre tasks and puzzles, and night visitors who took me against my will and then left me feeling drugged. There was no such thing as a safe place to hide and I knew it. Even on vacation, they found me.

I do not possess a single "waking memory" of an alien abduction. What I remember are incredibly vivid UFO dreams and the terror that those "dreams" left me with. While I refer to them as dreams, it may be more appropriate to call them screen memories of repeated UFO abductions, which is what I now believe them to be.

Screen memories are false memories that overwrite actual events which, if remembered, would be highly traumatic. Some UFO researchers refer to screen memories as "merciful amnesia."

Screen memories make it possible to have a lifetime of alien abduction experiences and not be aware that you were ever abducted. All you are left with is a jumble of bizarre memories, vivid dreams, and seemingly irrational fears. You may remember seeing or dreaming about bright lights, UFOs, monsters, floating in the air, or being paralyzed. My dreams took me far beyond that into another world which was sometimes beautiful and other times terrifying.

Many alien abductions occur at night, which allows the truth to be hidden under the guise of a dream. Such dreams are incredibly vivid and you wake up knowing that somehow, this dream was not like the others. Even without being aware that you were abducted you wake up feeling sheer, utter terror which can haunt you for a lifetime.

Such is the curse of post traumatic stress disorder which plagues those who've experienced a major traumatic event or series of events. Battle-worn soldiers, rape victims, accident victims, prisoners of war, and even children who've been bullied may be haunted by flashbacks and nightmares, reliving their experiences over and over. The nightmares are often a combination of actual memories interspersed with ordinary dreams, making it difficult to separate dreams from reality.

So what manner of nightmares haunt alien abductees? What sort of flashbacks do you relive if you've been repeatedly abducted by aliens in UFOs?

For me it started with a whirlwind dream which was totally nonsensical and yet became one of my smoking guns - it linked my dreams to reality in a very physical way. I do not remember feeling terror on those nights when the whirlwind dream came, but every other night was full of terror, especially when the dreams included monsters such as a frightening creature which I nicknamed the Skeleton Monster. This entity bore a striking resemblance to the alien Greys and it came to me several times prior to my 10th birthday.

I attributed the dreams to being a child with a vivid imagination, believing that I was simply plagued with nightmares of nonsense. When the alien Greys became household images decades later, I remembered my childhood Skeleton Monster and began to put the pieces together. I had already discovered that one dream was a resurfacing memory, could the alien monster dreams also be memories?

Another piece fell into place when I realized that waking from bizarre dreams feeling drugged wasn't normal, especially when it had been happening since early childhood. I began to see the pattern left behind by the alien visitors. What you are about to read are the clues I've put together, the remnants of what I do remember, and the vivid imagery which led me to the conclusion that extraterrestrials had come calling.

Flying Saucer in My Back Yard

This particular dream was extremely vivid and it came when I was 35 years old, but the house involved was my childhood home. I lived in that house from age 6 through age 13 in the 1960s.

The dream referred to the craft as being a "flying saucer" instead of a UFO. "Flying saucer" was the expression used throughout the 1950s and 1960s. For me to use the 1960s terminology in the dream itself, and dream about the house I lived in during the 1960s, makes me suspect a resurfacing memory, especially once I'd discovered that other dreams were resurfacing memories. Even the slang in the dream denotes the 60s using "neat" instead of "cool" along with the mention of a black light.

Flying saucer in my back yard: I looked out my 2nd floor bedroom window and saw a flying saucer hovering at window level. Neat! I want to go outside!

There was a whirring sound and the flying saucer landed in my back yard. It was a silver-white color — a milky silver — and it was shaped like two inverted saucers. The flying saucer lent an unearthly feel to everything surrounding it.

I started to go outside but stopped. I wasn't ready to go yet. If I went to the flying saucer, it would take me away and there was something I needed to do first. I went back inside to do it, and to tell my mom I was leaving. I don't remember her reaction but it may have been matter-of-fact.

In the back yard where the saucer had landed, there was a grapevine growing along the entire fence that separated us from our neighbor's house, and it must have been fall because the grapes were ripe and full.

In the flash of an eye the flying saucer was gone. I could see it in the distance over a city off to the right. The flying saucer put on quite a show in the sky which consisted of geometrical patterns similar to crop circles hanging over the horizon. The patterns moved around and I wondered what was going on.

In my back yard, the flying saucer had left behind a glowing set of concentric circles near the weeping willow tree. I wanted to go out and see the glowing circles. I very much wanted to touch them but I was afraid. The whole back yard had an otherworldly feel and the very air was different.

The air itself seemed to glow, kind of like what you experience with a black light in a room full of black light posters, only in a milky-silver-white color instead of purple. It was as if the air itself were a milky-silver color. It was spooky.

I knew that alien beings were in the flying saucer but I wasn't sure what type of beings and that spooked me, too. I expected the mushroom-skinned aliens such as my Skeleton Monster.

BOOK EXCERPT: ALIEN NIGHTMARES

> I'd been very excited to go into the saucer until it came, and I realized that if I went away with it I'd never come back. It was scary not knowing where I'd be going, and it was scary leaving my mom.

It took a long time to "wake up" from this dream and it felt vividly real. The details were incredible with the air itself having been changed and the crop circles in the back yard. The milky-silver color of both the UFO and the air around it was important. I do not know why, but I do know that it was somehow important.

I felt no fear initially and had been eager to go to the UFO, unlike many later dreams where I'd not wanted to go. That I'd described the grapes as being ripe is another detail that lends credence to this being a memory rather than a dream. My childhood back yard did indeed have a weeping willow tree and my bedroom was at the back of the house on the 2nd floor, putting the dream in perfect harmony with my childhood home.

The odd reference to extraterrestrials who were NOT the same as my mushroom-skinned Skeleton Monster stands out, though I'm not sure what to make of it. Apparently I was not afraid of the mushroom-skinned aliens, but I was afraid of some other type of alien.

Having a matter-of-fact discussion with my mom was a bit of a stretch, however. I do NOT remember my mother as ever believing in anything out of the ordinary. She shunned anything that did not fit in with her concept of a solid, middle class life.

While it isn't possible to pinpoint a date for the original event if this was indeed a resurfacing memory, it would have occurred between 1963 and 1970 in Rochester, New York. The reference to ripe grapes narrows it down to August, September or October. As the hottest known UFO activity in the area occurred from 1965-1967, these are the most likely years for a UFO "visit" putting me between 8 and 10 years old. The dream is pretty specific in that it was not my first encounter.

BOOK EXCERPT: ALIEN NIGHTMARES

The year 1965 coincides with a major UFO event in New York State. While the event occurred in November long after the grape season had ended, if UFOs were indeed involved as many suspected, it would suggest that UFOs could have been active in the area during the fall of that year as well.

On November 9, 1965, a massive power blackout known as the Big Blackout occurred for several hours which encompassed the entire states of New York, Vermont, Massachusetts, Maine, New Hampshire, Connecticut, and portions of Canada.

Just before the power went dead there were numerous UFO sightings including one directly over the Sir Adam Beck power plant in Ontario, Canada, and another over the Niagara Falls power station in New York. Sightings were reported by hundreds of people including airline pilots as well as the Deputy Aviation Commissioner of Syracuse. Newspapers across the northeast were flooded with calls reporting UFOs. The Syracuse Herald-Journal alone received over a hundred reports. Even after the blackout, witnesses were spellbound by the UFO activity in the skies.

Allegedly, the U.S. military was aware of the UFO presence 45 minutes prior to the blackout. Two commercial airline pilots saw military jets chasing disc-shaped objects over Pennsylvania. As expected, the "official" statement came down offering a scientific explanation for the blackout which discredited the UFO connection in spite of the many witnesses.

1965 was also the year of the Kecksburg, Pennsylvania UFO incident a month later on December 9, 1965. Thousands of witnesses across the northeast saw a giant fireball streak across the sky. Residents of several states including Ohio, New York, Pennsylvania, and Michigan, in addition to Ontario, Canada saw the fireball which was initially reported as a meteorite, though many believed they were seeing a plane going down in flames.

Kecksburg, Pennsylvania was the reputed location where the object went down and crashed, signaling its location with a beacon of blue smoke rising from the crash site — an event which was seen by several residents. Shortly after the crash, a second UFO hovered over the crash site. Those who saw the final descent described an object that appeared to be guiding itself around ridges and attempting to gain altitude.

Searchers found an object the size of a small car in the shape of an acorn, with hieroglyphic writing around its lower edge. The military came and secured the area, later stating that nothing was found there. The "nothing" that they "didn't find" was hauled away under a tarp on a flatbed truck and explained away in typical official manner.

John Murphy, a local reporter who'd been on the scene before the military arrived, had taken photos and interviewed witnesses. The photos were summarily seized but Murphy was unwilling to let the incident die peacefully. He scheduled a radio documentary featuring the interviews but before it could air, two men-in-black paid him a visit and he postponed the show, later airing a very different version than originally planned.

Murphy gave up his investigation into the case doing a complete about-face, and walked away from what had been his obsession. He became despondent and refused all discussion of the event until three years later, when he was killed by a hit-and-run driver while crossing the road.

In June 1966 which was 6 months after the Kecksburg crash, a former RCAF pilot spotted a UFO over Lake Ontario, which is 20 miles from Rochester, New York. The pilot and a friend were boating when they saw lights on the water and went to investigate. When they got within a mile, the lights rose up making both a humming and swishing sound. It was a disc encircled with bright yellow lights on the upper portion, blue-green lights around the lower portion, and it had a dome on top. The UFO hovered briefly, then took off at high speed and disappeared. A month later an FCC engineer spotted a UFO over Canandaigua Lake just 31 miles away.

August/September 1967 brought a barrage of Rochester area UFO sightings in Henrietta, Churchville, and Pultneyville which are 7, 14, and 23 miles away from Rochester respectively. These would coincide with grapes ripening on the vine.

Across Lake Ontario in Toronto, Canada, 5 policemen spotted a UFO in September 1967 which moved at low altitude over the highway in front of a pursuing police car. The object stopped suddenly, veered, and accelerated away according to the Toronto Telegram, a daily newspaper which was considered conservative. This was not a tabloid-type newspaper.

Nearby cities also had sightings including Barrie, Ontario and both Rochester and Syracuse, New York. In addition, on September 14/15 there was a sighting in "western New York" which was reported by a member of the military. The next most significant event was in Ithaca, New York where over a thousand UFO sightings occurred in 1967-1968 and included actual alien encounters. Ithaca was a mere 75 miles away from Rochester.

UFO enthusiasts categorize a large number of sightings concentrated in one place as a "flap." The rash of sightings around Ithaca became known as the "Great Ithaca Flap."

Here I was living in the house where I "dreamed" of a UFO landing in the back yard. I was a child experiencing the Skeleton Monster and Whirlwind dreams right in the middle of the hottest UFO activity imaginable: The Big Blackout of 1965, the Kecksburg crash of 1965, the scattering of local UFO reports in 1966 from credible witnesses, and the Great Ithaca Flap of New York in 1967-1968 all of which perfectly coincided with my bizarre childhood "dreams."

http://www.sharondelarose.com/books/alien-ufo-otherworlds/alien-nightmares/

GLOSSARY OF BIBLICAL GIANTS

Multiple versions of the *Bible* have been quoted, as not all bibles carry the same wording in their texts. These versions are identified as follows:

ASV: American Standard Version — 1901 revision of the King James Bible, which originally came out in 1611.
CEV: Contemporary English Version — 1995.
DARBY: Darby Translation — first published in 1890 by John Nelson Darby, an Anglo-Irish Bible teacher who was also fluent in French and German.
KJ21: 21st Century King James Version — 1994 revision of the King James Bible which replaces obsolete words.
KJV: King James Version — 1987 version.
NLT: New Living Translation — 2007 version.
NLV: New Life Version — 1969 version.
WYC: Wycliffe Bible — The first English translation of the Bible was from John Wycliffe and John Purvey in 1382. This is called the Early Version. A more readable version came out in 1390 and is called the Late Version. It was republished in 2001 by Terence P. Noble, after revisions to make it more readable, and this is the version referenced. As with other bibles, several hundred "obsolete" words have been replaced, but the original passages from the 1382 version are shown in brackets, alongside the 1390 passages.

ANCIENT ALIENS AND THE AGE OF GIANTS

Some of the biblical passages that identify giants are as follows, which demonstrates changes in the wording:

The Nephilim as giants from Genesis 6:4

> KJ21: "There were giants on the earth in those days; and also after that, when the sons of God came in unto the daughters of men and they bore children to them..."

> ASV: "The Nephilim were in the earth in those days, and also after that, when the sons of God came unto the daughters of men, and they bare children to them..."

Linking the Rephaims, Zuzims, Emims, Ashtaroth, and Sodom and Gomorrah from Genesis 14:5-9

> WYC: "Therefore Chedorlaomer came in the fourteenth year, and [the] kings that were with him, and they smited Rephaims in Ashteroth Karnaim, and Zuzims with them (and the Zuzims in Ham), and Emims in Shaveh Kiriathaim, and Horites in the hills of Seir (and the Horites in the hill country of Seir), till to the field places of Elparan, which is in (the) wilderness. And they turned again, and came till to the well of Mishpat; that is Kadesh (And then they returned, and came unto Enmishpat; that is Kadesh). And they smited all the country of (the) men of Amalek, and (also the) Amorites, that dwelled in Hazazontamar. And the king of Sodom, and the king of Gomorrah, and the king of Admah, and the king of Zeboiim, also and the king of Bela, which is (now called) Zoar, went out, and [they] dressed (the) battle array against them in the valley of wood (and they directed the battle array against them in the Siddim Valley), that is, against Chedorlaomer, king of Elamites, and Tidal, king of folks (king of Goiim), and Amraphel, king of Shinar, and Arioch, king of Ellasar; four kings against five."

GLOSSARY OF BIBLICAL GIANTS

Identifying the Emims and Anakims as giants from Deuteronomy 2:10-11

WYC: "Emim were the first dwellers thereof, a great people, and strong, and so high, (The Emims were the first inhabitants there, a great and strong people, and so tall,) that they were believed to be as giants, of the generation of Anakim, and they were like the sons of Anakim; forsooth Moabites call them Emim (but the Moabites call them the Emims)."

The Zamzummims as giants from Deuteronomy 2:20

WYC: "It is reckoned the land of giants, and giants inhabited therein sometime, which giants Ammonites call Zamzummims; (It is reckoned the land of giants, and giants lived there some time ago, whom the Ammonites called the Zamzummims;)..."

KJV: "(That also was accounted a land of giants: giants dwelt therein in old time; and the Ammonites call them Zamzummims;..."

King Og and the Rephaim as giants, along with Mount Hermon and Ashtaroth, from Joshua 12:4-5

WYC: "The term of Og, king of Bashan, of the relics of Rephaim, that is, giants, that dwelled in Ashtaroth and in Edrei, (And there was Og, the king of Bashan, of the remnant of the Rephaim, that is, of the giants, who lived in Ashtaroth and in Edrei,) and he was lord in the hill of Hermon, and in Salcah, and in all Bashan, till to the terms of Geshurites and Maachathites, and of the half part of Gilead, and to the term of Sihon, king of Heshbon. (and he ruled Mount Hermon, and Salcah, and all of Bashan, unto the borders of the Geshurites and the Maachathites, and also ruled half of Gilead, unto the border of Sihon, the king of Heshbon.)"

Connecting Canaan and his descendants the Hittites, with some of the known giants, and Sodom and Gomorrah, from Genesis 10:15-19

> WYC: "Forsooth Canaan engendered Sidon, his first engendered son, (and) Heth, (And Canaan begat Sidon, his first-born son, and the Hittites,) and Jebusites, and Amorites, Girgashites, (and) Hivites, and Arkites, (and) Sinites, and Arvadites, (and) Zemarites, and Hamathites; and [the] peoples of (the) Canaanites were sown abroad by these men. And the terms of Canaan were made to men coming from Sidon to Gerar, till to Gaza (And Canaan's borders went from Sidon to Gerar, and unto Gaza), (and then) till thou enter into Sodom, and Gomorrah…"

Linking King Og, the Rephaim, and Ashtaroth to giants, as doing battle with Moses, from Joshua 13:12

> WYC: "…all the realm of Og in Bashan, that reigned in Ashtaroth, and in Edrei; he was of the relics of Rephaim, that is, of giants; and Moses smote them, and did away them. (and all the kingdom of Og in Bashan, who reigned in Ashtaroth, and in Edrei; he was of the remnant of the Rephaim, that is, of the giants; and Moses struck them down, and did them away.)"

> ASV: "…all the kingdom of Og in Bashan, who reigned in Ashtaroth and in Edrei (the same was left of the remnant of the Rephaim); for these did Moses smite, and drove them out."

In the various translations, the giants were not completely eliminated — they were driven out, expelled, and dispossessed of their lands. Thus they migrated to other parts of the world.

GLOSSARY OF BIBLICAL GIANTS

The Amorites as giants from Amos 2:9

> WYC: "Forsooth I destroyed Amorite from the face of them, whose highness was the highness of cedars, and he was strong as an oak; and I all-brake the fruit of him above, and the roots of him beneath. (And I destroyed the Amorites before them, who were as tall as cedars, and were as strong as oaks; and I altogether broke their fruit above, and their roots below.)"

"Giants" are listed in the 1906 *Jewish Encyclopedia* as the progeny of the Bene Elohim (sons of God/sons of Elohim in various bibles) with the daughters of men. *Elohim* can refer to God in the singular, or "gods" in the plural, and entire tracts have been written on the translation and meaning of this single word.

Their descendants are the Nefilim (Nephilim), Gibborim, Refa'im (Rephaim), Zuzim aka Zamzummim, Emim, Anakim, Eliud/Elyo, Amalekite, and possibly the Amorites, Canaanites, Hittites, Philistines, Horim, Kenites, and the Avim. Named giants include Og, Sihon, and Goliath. The famed Jericho was "the city of giants" just as Canaan was "the land of giants."

The giants are described as extraordinary in stature, of immense height, mighty men, powerful and numerous and tall.

Elsewhere, the Canaanites are listed with their own religion which includes a multitude of deities including variations of Baal and Molech, the latter being the national god of the Ammonites.

* * *

The *Book of Enoch* has multiple versions and a few bibles include it in their canon. The Ethiopian Orthodox Tewahedo Church, and the Eritrean Orthodox Tewahedo Church, both do.

In the early days, books were written by hand — copied from other handwritten versions of the book. Most of the fragments that we have of the *Book of Enoch* predate Jesus by 200-300 years, but the book itself claims to have been written by Enoch prior to the Great Flood. The *New Testament* quotes from it, early Church Fathers embraced it as scripture, and it was found with the Dead Sea scrolls, but due to its controversial nature regarding the Grigori and the giants, it was not included in most bibles.

The reason that we have so many *different* religious sects within Christianity, Judaism, etc. is the issue of translation and interpretation. Each sect has a slightly different interpretation of the *Bible*, and that's why bibles were summarily burned — to erase translations that a particular king or religious leader found undesirable. We've demonstrated that even today, different bibles offer different wording for the same passage. That's all it took — one man, or a small group of men, to mold the *Bible* and its teachings to their view — just burn every *Bible* whose translation you did not like so that it could not be copied.

Consider this: The *Old Testament* covers a period all the way back to the Great Flood, and earlier. That's thousands of years before the time of Christ, and yet, our earliest biblical manuscripts are only a couple hundred years older than Christ, and most came after. Surely there were manuscripts written when the events occurred, and yet, we don't have them. Why? Were they burned for heresy?

When the Dead Sea scrolls were unearthed, they became some of the earliest biblical texts, and extra-biblical texts, that we have. They predated the *Bible* burnings of later ages, being hidden away in caves. Among them: the *Book of Enoch* and the *Book of Giants*. Yet even they are young, dating thousands of years after the events that they portray.

As the Ethiopian Orthodox Church is one of the few who include the *Book of Enoch* in their official *Bible*, theirs is the translation most often used here. Over 100 chapters make up the *Book of Enoch*, including chapters on Noah and the Grigori.

The *Book of Giants* also predates Jesus, and contains Sumerian mythology which is considered "pagan" such as the Epic of Gilgamesh. Some biblical scholars, including Józef T. Milik, believe that the *Book of Giants* was once part of the *Book of*

GLOSSARY OF BIBLICAL GIANTS

Enoch. Milik studied at the Pontifical Biblical Institute in Rome. He was fluent in several languages including Sumerian, Egyptian, Arabic, and Hittite, and devoted himself to deciphering and translating hundreds of texts in the Dead Sea scrolls.

One set of texts that predates all of the biblical manuscripts, are the Sumerian tablets engraved in stone. These tablets give us an alternate version of biblical stories such as Adam and Eve, and Noah's flood. There were thousands of fragments dating back to 1750 B.C., which is much older than the *Bible*.

These tablets became one of the smoking guns for ancient alien theory, and ancient astronauts visiting Earth. They support the Enoch stories where visitors came and mingled with humans, but it went awry.

No conspiracy theory could be more ripe than the disappearance of these tablets from the Iraqi Museum as detailed in the chapter *Casualties of War*. Who took them, and why? Were they taken to protect them from being destroyed by war? Or were they taken in a modern-day *Bible* burning frenzy, to eliminate a version of history that some find distasteful?

Yes, we may have photographs that preserve them, hopefully all over the world in the hands of scholars. But a photograph can't be used to definitively prove an ancient date, and photographs can be manipulated. The truest evidence of our most ancient history is gone, just like the hundreds, or thousands, of ancient bibles that were burned.

Coincidentally, this isn't the first time that Sumerian tablets have been stolen. *Records of the Past, Volumes XII*, published in 1913 by Records of Past Exploration Society in Washington, D.C., mention an earlier theft. Tablets were stolen from the French expedition at Telloh, and later resurfaced for sale. They were purchased in 1890 by the Berlin Museum. Another set was believed stolen from the Expedition of the University of Pennsylvania, later resurfaced for sale, and was subsequently purchased by the British Museum.

ANCIENT ALIENS AND THE AGE OF GIANTS

The Contemporary Review, Volume 71, published in 1897 by Isbister and Company Limited of London, also mentioned thefts. There were upwards of 33,000 clay tablets, and they were about 5,000 years old. Most were in Constantinople, where Assyrian scholars were translating them. Some were at the Louvre Museum in France, having been gifted by the Turkish government, but "a very large number [had] been stolen by the Arabs, and [were] at present being offered for sale in England." Hopefully, as with previous thefts, the tablets will resurface in a museum far away from war zones.

The 1897 book mentioned 33,000 tablets. The theft from the Iraqi museum mentioned 15,000 artifacts, which included tablets. Is there even an accounting of how many Sumerian tablets actually exist, and where they are? Have any gone missing and never turned up? Would we even know?

As distressing as the thefts are, however, of greater interest is that not all Sumerian fragments had been published or translated at the time those thefts took place. In other words, we cannot be certain that every missing fragment exists in translated or printed form, or that it has even been photographed. That leaves us with the biblical texts as they currently exist, and the Dead Sea scrolls, most of which are on fragile parchment and papyrus, which brings us back around to the Grigori in the *Book of Enoch*.

***

The Grigori, Egregori, or Watchers as they are variously called, are described in the *Book of Enoch*. The Grigori are listed in *The Expositor's Greek Testament, Volume V*, edited by William Robertson Nicoll and published in 1910, in its segment on the fallen angels, taken from the *Book of Enoch*.

> "These are the Grigori, who with their prince Satanail rejected the holy Lord…"

GLOSSARY OF BIBLICAL GIANTS

The *Apocrypha and Pseudepigrapha of the Old Testament in English, Volume 2*, published in 1913, as edited by R. H. Charles and other scholars, also uses Grigori in *The Book of the Secrets of Enoch* 18:1:

"The men took me to the fifth heaven and placed me, and there I saw many and countless soldiers, called Grigori, of human appearance, and their size was greater than that of great giants."

In the *Bible*, which doesn't go into detail about the Grigori, it's been glossed over as "watchers" or "angels who keep watch."

ASV: Daniel 4:13: "I saw in the visions of my head upon my bed, and, behold, a watcher and a holy one came down from heaven."

NLV: Daniel 4:13: "In the dreams I had as I lay on my bed, I looked and saw an angel who kept watch. He was a holy one who came down from heaven."

ASV: Daniel 4:17: "The sentence is by the decree of the watchers…"

NLV: Daniel 4:17: "This penalty is by the law of the angels who keep watch."

WYC: Numbers 23:14: "And when he had led Balaam into a high place, on the top of the hill of Pisgah, he builded there seven altars to Balaam, and when calves and rams were put above them, (And so when he had led Balaam to the Field of Zophim, that is, to the Field of the Watchers, on top of Mount Pisgah, he built seven altars for Balaam, and when a calf and a ram were offered on each altar,)"

DARBY: Numbers 23:14: "And he took him to the watchmen's field, to the top of Pisgah, and built seven altars, and offered up a bullock and a ram on [each] altar."

Printed in Dunstable, United Kingdom